Tin Cans & Greyhounds

TIN CANS & GREYHOUNDS

THE DESTROYERS THAT WON TWO WORLD WARS

CLINT JOHNSON

REGNERY
HISTORY

Regnery® is a registered trademark of Salem Communications Holding Corporation
Cataloging-in-Publication data on file with the Library of Congress

ISBN 978-1-62157-647-1
ebook ISBN 978-1-62157-767-6

Published in the United States by
Regnery History
An Imprint of Regnery Publishing
A Division of Salem Media Group
300 New Jersey Ave NW
Washington, DC 20001
www.Regnery.com

Manufactured in the United States of America

10 9 8 7 6 5 4 3 2 1

Books are available in quantity for promotional or premium use. For information on discounts and terms, please visit our website: www.Regnery.com.

To all Destroyer Men who served in the Tin Can Navy while aboard these Greyhounds of the Sea.

"When at grips with the enemy on the sea, under the sea, or in the air, no taskforce commander ever had enough destroyers. They were indispensible in every operation, a lance to thrust forward, a shield."

–ADMIRAL WALDEN L. AINSWORTH
Commander of Destroyer Forces in the Pacific, 1942

CONTENTS

Preface   ix

Chapter 1
The Early Years: *"Weather today fine, but high waves."*   1

Chapter 2
World War I in Europe: *"Do as much damage as possible."*   17

Chapter 3
U.S. Enters the War: *"We are ready now, sir!"*   27

Chapter 4
The 1920s: *"We have no destroyers today!"*   45

Chapter 5
The 1930s: *"A destroyer is not a likely target."*   57

Chapter 6
Atlantic Theater 1939-1941: *"Keep on engaging the enemy."*   71

Chapter 7
Pacific Theater 1941: *"Suddenly and deliberately attacked."*   93

Chapter 8
Atlantic Theater 1942:
"American beacons and searchlights visible at night."   105

Chapter 9
Pacific Theater 1942:
"Courageous abandon against fearful odds."   123

Chapter 10
Atlantic Theater 1943:
*"Wiped out every exposed member of the sub's
crew topside."*   151

Chapter 11
Pacific Theater 1943:
"Our losses for this single battle were fantastic."   165

Chapter 12
Atlantic Theater 1944:
"Man on deck of sub attempting to man gun disintegrates."   193

Chapter 13
Pacific Theater 1944:
*"A fight against overwhelming odds from
which survival can't be expected."*   207

Chapter 14
Atlantic Theater 1945:*"I think that is the end of the sub."*   229

Chapter 15
Pacific Theater 1945:*"The gates of hell awaited us."*   241

Appendix   263
Bibliography   265
Acknowledgments   279
Notes   283

Preface

I may deploy a bold argument in this book, but I'll guess tens of thousands of Destroyer Men would agree with me.

Destroyers played the major role in fighting both world wars.

Yes, soldiers of all nations fought each other face to face. Airmen were the most likely to die in combat, falling from the skies due to machine gun and cannon fire, ground anti-aircraft artillery, weather, and mechanical failures. Sailors braved the dark, unforgiving ocean from the single coxswain on a landing craft to the admiral on a battleship commanding tens of thousands of men in hundreds of ships.

But I think all of them depended on Destroyer Men.

It was destroyers that escorted the convoys which successfully supplied troops on battlefields in both world wars. It was destroyers that sank the submarines stalking the convoys. It was destroyers that rushed in to rescue men from sinking ships. And it was destroyers that scraped their keels on the ocean's sandy bottom to provide bombardment support for beach landings of the soldiers who would fight the land war.

This book started when I stumbled on the stories of the USS *Jacob Jones* (DD-61), the only U.S. warship lost in World War I, and the USS

Jacob Jones (DD-130), the only U.S. warship lost in American mainland waters in World War II. The coincidences in the stories of their sinking struck me as intriguing, but I soon realized that there was not enough there for an entire book.

Researching those two ships showed me there was no general history of the development of the destroyer classes that spanned both world wars. I wanted to learn more about the destroyers of the principal warring nations of the United States, Great Britain, Germany, and Japan.

I was surprised at some things I found.

Great Britain essentially invented the destroyer in the 1870s and thought it would rule the waves. But it was Japan that sobered the rest of the world just thirty years later when its British-built and home-built destroyers played a major role in sinking much of the supposedly superior Russian fleet.

Had America not sent dozens of destroyers to a tiny Irish coastal town in May 1917, Germany might have defeated Great Britain before the end of the year.

While Germany had the technological ability to build the V-1 and V-2 rockets, it invested little toward designing good destroyers.

Readers know the German Enigma machine codes were broken, but may not know that a handful of British Destroyer Men risked their lives, and some died, in capturing the machines and codebooks.

Japan's most historic destroyer did not win any battles for its own country, but it played the major role in the most important American naval victory of the war.

Had it not been for the dogged determination of United States Destroyer Men, Guadalcanal might have stayed in Japanese hands in 1942 and the U.S. invasion fleet off the Philippines in 1944 might have been destroyed.

After finishing this manuscript, I came away with a profound respect for the ships called the Greyhounds of the Sea and their crews who proudly call themselves Tin Can Sailors.

I only wish the governments in all four of these nations had saved the earliest and most important examples of their destroyers. What a marvel it would have been to walk the decks of the first destroyer in the U.S. Navy, the USS *Bainbridge* (DD-1), or the USS *Clemson* (DD-186), the lead ship of the post-World War I era class that proved so valuable through World War II.

The sole survivor of the deadly Japanese *Kagero*-destroyer class from World War II was the *Yukikaze,* which was scrapped in 1970. What was Great Britain thinking in 1967 when it scrapped the HMS *Petard,* arguably that nation's most famous World War II destroyer? The *Petard* captured Enigma machine codebooks and sank three different submarines in three different oceans, and it was still cut up. The United States unceremoniously sold the USS *O'Bannon* (DD-450) in 1970, and it was broken up two years later. The *O'Bannon* was a ship with seventeen battle stars, of which Admiral William Halsey said: "The history of the Pacific war can never be written without telling the story of the USS *O'Bannon.* Time after time, the *O'Bannon* and her gallant little sisters were called upon to turn back the enemy. They never disappointed me."

Regrettably, I could not continue this book through the Korean and Vietnam Wars—wars that saw the continued service of World War II era destroyers. There simply was not enough space. To those Destroyer Men who served during that time, I apologize.

While we have a few destroyers preserved as ship museums, the most famous are long gone. Soon we will also lose the last of World War II's Destroyer Men. If you meet an elderly Destroyer Man, talk to him. He may well have some World War II stories that he is waiting and willing to tell.

Clint Johnson, January 2019.

1

The Early Years

"Weather today fine, but high waves."

The graceful but deadly Greyhound of the Seas, the destroyer, was designed in response to a crude weapon originally controlled by a man holding ropes on the water's edge.

The idea for a shore-controlled weapon evolved from an attack during the American Civil War.

On the night of October 27, 1864, United States Navy Lieutenant William B. Cushing successfully sank the CSS *Albemarle,* a 158-foot-long Confederate ironclad, by lowering a wooden spar with a keg of gunpowder dangling from its end under the *Albemarle's* keel. Cushing's attacking craft was a simple 45-foot-long wooden launch powered by an exposed steam engine.

The concept of a small boat sinking a capital ship by something other than cannon fire was intriguing, but the practicality of reaching an alert enemy ship with a keg of explosives was doubtful. Cushing's successful attack was daring, but also lucky. The *Albemarle* was tied up at a wharf on the narrow Roanoke River in Plymouth, North Carolina, guarded by sleepy pickets who did not alert the *Albemarle's* crew that an unidentified launch was approaching.

Still, the *Albemarle's* sinking sparked imaginations.

Just two years after the *Albemarle's* sinking, the self-powered torpedo was introduced by British-born engineer Robert Whitehead. Whitehead's original prototype in 1866 was based on an Austrian naval officer's concept of a warhead-tipped cylinder powered by wound springs turning a propeller and guided by ropes held by handlers onshore.

Whitehead's torpedo improvements included making it self-guided and powered by compressed air. His earliest practical prototype had a speed of 7 knots carrying a warhead weighing up to sixty pounds, but its range was only 200 yards. That was point-blank range for defending cannon fire, so initially it was not very practical. Before naval customers would be interested, Whitehead had to increase the range of the torpedo to keep its launching craft out of the reach of enemy cannons. He also had to improve its ability to stay on target through wind and wave action.

By 1870, the Whitehead torpedo had a range of more than 700 yards.

The new weapon promised to change naval warfare. For centuries, ships had fired on each other with cannons to put holes in enemy hulls or to knock down rigging before boarding and settling the battle with cutlasses. The torpedo theoretically gave navies the new combat option of staying out of cannon range, and virtually eliminated the need for hand-to-hand combat.

As countries all over the world started buying or developing their own torpedoes, Navy planners began designing small boats to carry them. The chosen name for the new craft was simple—the torpedo boat.

In 1873, the British launched the HMS *Vesuvius*, a 90-foot-long boat capable of 9.7 knots armed with a single torpedo tube. She was followed by HMS *Lightning* four years later. Neither proved to be very seaworthy in the open ocean, so replacement designs were started almost immediately.

As the world's navies moved into the new decade of the 1880s—theoretically armed with weapons capable of killing ships with one strike and no longer needing to land multiple gun hits—naval strategists realized the torpedo's rapid technological advances had created a new problem.

All the navies now had small boats capable of delivering a potentially devastating torpedo attack against larger ships, and there was as yet no good defense against those same boats.

Within a decade of the development of the torpedo boat came designs for the torpedo boat destroyer, commonly called "TBDs."

The British remained the preeminent designers, launching the HMS *Rattlesnake*, now designated a torpedo gunboat, in 1886. She was among the first of the dual-purpose boats—one that could both attack torpedo boats and fire torpedoes herself. She carried a 4-inch gun, six 3-pounder cannons, and four 14-inch (in circumference) torpedoes. She could make nearly 20 knots. As deadly as she seemed to be on paper, within ten years, other designs had made her obsolete.

Speed to reach targets became the principal goal of the designers. Nations competed to see which country could design a TBD that could reach enemy fleets fastest with the most torpedoes. But attaining such speed came with a price: lightly built boats that did not perform well in the ocean.

In April 1892, the British Admiralty, fearing French-built torpedo boats crossing the English Channel, put out a bid notice asking shipbuilders to design "large sea-going torpedo boats."[1] The Admiralty specified boats around 200 tons with speeds of 27 knots. They were to be armed with a single twelve-pounder cannon, one six-pounder cannon, and an 18-inch bow torpedo tube. Built in 1893, the first two, HMS *Daring* and HMS *Decoy,* displaced 260 tons.

The United States started fifteen years behind every other country in designing torpedo boats. It spent nearly two years building the aptly-named USS *Cushing,* which was commissioned in 1890. The *Cushing* was a 116-ton, 138-foot long, steel-hulled boat armed with three six-pounder cannons and three 18-inch torpedo tubes. Designated TB-1, she could make 22 knots, at least 5 knots slower than the top capacity of the leading British torpedo boats.

The United States studied the *Cushing's* performance for over two years, then waited another two years before commissioning its second torpedo boat in 1894, the USS *Ericsson* (TB-2). The *Ericsson* was named after John Ericsson, the designer of the USS *Monitor,* the United States Navy's first ironclad. Curiously, instead of building her in any number of oceanside shipyards, the *Ericsson* was built in the nation's heartland, Dubuque, Iowa, a Mississippi River town. The *Ericsson* weighed 4 more tons than the *Cushing,* but its draft was similar at just under 5 feet. It was armed with four 1-pounder cannons compared to the *Cushing's* three 6-pounders, and two 18-inch torpedoes.

Just one year after launching the *Cushing,* the first warship sunk by a torpedo was recorded, not in a conflict between world naval powers, but during the Chilean Civil War of 1891. It had taken seventeen years for the theoretical deployment of torpedo boats to be practically applied.

On April 18, 1891, two British-built torpedo boats, the *Almirante Lynch* and the *Almirante Condell,* were delivered to the Chilean government to fight rebels. They each carried five torpedo tubes and three 3-inch guns. The government, eager to use its investment, did not spend much time training their crews. On April 23, the two boats attacked a rebel-crewed armored ship, the *Blanco Encalada.* She was a 3,500-ton frigate built in England in 1875, just four years after the British bought the rights to manufacture the Whitehead torpedo.

The first torpedo attack in the world was not dramatic.

The government torpedo boats launched five torpedoes from a range of less than one hundred yards, but only one found the *Blanco Encalada.* It sank within two minutes, taking 182 sailors with her. The other four torpedoes probably missed due to the crews' lack of training since one was launched from a range of just fifty yards at a ship more than 210 feet long—the naval equivalent of trying to hit the broad side of a barn.

Still, one small vessel had sunk a much larger ship using a single torpedo. The seventeen-year potential for a new type of naval warfare had finally been realized.

The Spanish-American War of 1898 gave the world's naval planners a chance to watch the performance of torpedo boats under real battle conditions with both sides firing at each other.

Just as had been seen in Chile, the value of the torpedo boat was still underwhelming.

The first significant action took place on May 11, 1898, when the USS *Winslow* (TB-5) entered the harbor of Cardenas, Cuba, to investigate a Spanish gunboat tied up at the docks. A third-generation torpedo boat, the *Winslow,* was 161 feet long, displaced 142 tons, and was armed with three 1-pounder cannons and three 18-inch torpedoes. She could make 25 knots.

USS *Winslow* (TB-5) was severely damaged in her first and only engagement in 1898. *Naval Historical Heritage Command (NHHC) photo.*

As the *Winslow* came within 1,500 yards of the Cuban gunboat, she came under accurate fire. One early shell disabled her steering gear. Now out of control, she swung broadside to the enemy ship. She was struck again and her port engine was knocked out. As the torpedo boat was being towed out of the action, yet another Spanish shell hit her, mortally wounding five men, including Ensign Worth Bagley. Bagley was the only naval officer to lose his life during the short war. Three enlisted men aboard the *Winslow* were awarded Medals of Honor for saving the boat from the heavy Spanish fire.

It was an inauspicious beginning to the U.S. Navy's torpedo boat war record. No torpedoes were launched at the enemy and no hits were recorded on the Spanish gunboat by the *Winslow*. She would be repaired and serve out the rest of her career as a training vessel before being sold for scrap in 1911.

Less than two months later came the more decisive Battle of Santiago de Cuba on July 3, 1898. This was primarily a battle between capital ships—American battleships against Spanish cruisers—but the British-built *Furor*, a 370-ton, 220-foot-long torpedo boat destroyer employed by the Spanish, gave the Americans pause. Built in 1896, she was armed with two 14-pounders, eight 6-pounders, two machine guns, and two 14-inch torpedo tubes. She could make 28 knots. The *Winslow*, the U.S. Navy's state-of-the-art torpedo boat, had just been destroyed by a puny gunboat tied up at a dock. In theory, if the American-designed *Winslow* had gone head-to-head with the British-designed *Furor*, it would have been no match.

During the battle, however, the U.S. Navy's battleships and cruisers hit the *Furor* several times while it was coming out of the harbor. The *Furor* was not able to utilize its weapons against any American ship and was finished off by an armed U.S. yacht, the USS *Gloucester*.

The Spanish squadron was completely destroyed as it tried to break the American blockade, with all of its ships sunk and only one American killed.

The only role an American torpedo boat played in the action was when the captain of the USS *Ericsson* (TB-2) swooped alongside the blazing Spanish cruiser, *Vizcaya*. At significant risk to his own boat, the captain towed lifeboats filled with one hundred Spanish officers and crew to safety as the cruiser's own ammunition exploded from the intense heat. It would mark the first time in American history that the forerunner of the destroyer would rescue men from sinking ships—an act that would be repeated time and again in two upcoming world wars.

The U.S. Navy must have been discouraged by the relatively poor performance of the *Winslow*. The *Furor*, although it had ultimately been sunk, was twice as large and had heavier guns than any torpedo boat in U.S. service. The *Furor* also had crossed the ocean to Cuba, something no one in the U.S. Navy would attempt in any of its torpedo boats.

Convinced they had been thinking too small, U.S. Navy designers started work on the nation's first true ocean-going destroyer, though the designation torpedo boat destroyer would remain.

Within a year after the Battle of Santiago, the USS *Bainbridge* (DD-1) was under construction by Neafie and Levy Ship and Engine Building Company in Philadelphia. She was 250 feet long—twice as long as the pioneering *Cushing*—with a beam of 23.7 feet and a draft of just over 9 feet when loaded. Weighing 420 tons, she was armed with two 3-inch guns, five 6-pounders, and two 18-inch torpedo tubes. Sixteen similar-sized destroyers would be authorized by Congress at the same time.

USS *Bainbridge* (DD-1), the United States' first designated destroyer, spent most of its career in the Philippines. *NHHC photo.*

Commissioned in 1902, the *Bainbridge* set out for China in December, where she showed the flag proving to observant Far Eastern powers that the U.S. now had the will and means to keep warships smaller than battleships and cruisers in waters far from the United States. The *Bainbridge* kept a close eye on both the Japanese and the Russians, patrolling the Philippine Islands to make sure neither nation ventured into territory the Americans had won during the Spanish-American War. For the next fourteen years, the *Bainbridge* remained in Far Eastern waters, out of the view of Americans.

The American taxpayers never laid eyes on their Navy's first destroyer, but it served as a constant reminder to the Japanese that the United States felt it belonged in Asian waters.

It would take more than thirty years after the invention of the powered torpedo and the fast boats to transport them before their value on the high seas would be proven. The successful torpedo attack against the *Blanco Encalada* in 1891 had been within a bay, proving nothing about the viability of the torpedo on the open ocean. The British, who had perfected torpedoes, torpedo boats, and torpedo boat destroyers, would not be the navy to demonstrate to the world how such weapons could devastate an enemy.

It would be the Japanese navy, albeit using British-built torpedo boats.

Japan had been a mysterious place to Americans and Europeans through the mid-nineteenth century. Once Japan allowed Western trade in 1853, the nation quickly expanded its sphere of influence in Asia, just as Europe was doing in Africa and India, and the United States was doing in the Philippines. In the 1880s and 1890s, Japan set its sights on China and Korea, countries Russia was also interested in because they offered warm water ports while Russian territorial ports froze over during the winter.

For a while, Russia and Japan negotiated with each other, with Japan offering to let Russia dominate Manchuria in exchange for allowing Japan to dominate Korea. Czar Nicholas II refused those terms, confident his vast Russian empire could easily crush Japan if it came to war.

War came on the night of February 8, 1904, when Japan made a surprise attack on Port Arthur, China, while its ministers were in St. Petersburg, Russia, negotiating a long-term peace treaty. Ten Japanese torpedo boats, either built in Great Britain or modeled after British boats, used the darkness to cruise into the harbor and launch sixteen Whitehead torpedoes at the tied-up Russian fleet. Fortunately for the forward-thinking Russians, the anti-torpedo net they had deployed caught most of the torpedoes. However, three did slip through, damaging two Russian battleships and a heavy cruiser.

The opinions of war planners were split on the effectiveness of the Japanese attack. Some pointed out how small boats had successfully damaged ships much larger without firing a single cannon to give themselves away in the darkness. Others pointed out that only three torpedoes had found their mark. The rest had been stopped by nothing more than wire mesh.

In response to the relatively minor attack, the angry Russians launched their Baltic Fleet on an 18,000-mile voyage around the world to confront the Japanese. The Russian commanders were confident its fleet of thirty-eight ships, including eight battleships, could handle the Japanese, whom they called "monkeys."

What the Old World Europeans did not realize was that the Japanese fleet they would face consisted of eighty-nine ships, including four battleships, twenty-seven cruisers, twenty-one destroyers, and thirty-seven torpedo boats.

As the Russian fleet neared Japanese-controlled waters off the coast of Korea, it adhered to international law by ordering its hospital ships to remain lighted at night to keep them from being mistaken for warships. Those ships were spotted by Japanese picket boats, which then used a new weapon of war, the wireless radio, to report the location of the oncoming Russian fleet.

As he left port to engage the Russians, the Japanese commander, Admiral Togo Heihachiro, wired the navy minister in Tokyo a message that would become famous in Japanese navy lore: "Weather today fine, but high waves."[2]

In fact, there was a heavy mist over the seas, but Togo later wrote that the wireless reports detailing the advancing Russian warships were: "as though they had been under our very eyes."[3]

On the afternoon of May 27, 1905, the Japanese caught the Russian fleet in the Tsushima Strait between Japan and Korea. The Russian crews were weary from the long voyage, and their ships' hulls were weighted down from fouling. The rested Japanese were crewing their newest ships and boats, eager for a fight the Russians did not expect.

At 2:00 p.m., Admiral Togo issued another famous order by signal flags: "The Empire's fate depends on the results of this battle. Let every man do his utmost duty."[4]

The Japanese fleet crossed the Russian's "T," meaning all Japanese ships crossed the line of the Russian ships with all their guns to bear from the beam while the Russians could only fire from their forward gun mounts. The battle ranged into the night with twenty Japanese destroyers and thirty-seven torpedo boats moving in around 8:00 p.m.

The battle was a disaster for the Russians. They lost more than twenty ships, including six of eight battleships. The Japanese lost only three torpedo boats. While the Port Arthur torpedo attacks had produced few hits because of the torpedo net, the Japanese, now on the open ocean, fired more than seventy torpedoes, scoring many hits on the battleships and cruisers.

The admirals of the supposed world naval powers were shocked at how easily the Japanese destroyed the Russian fleet. Two lessons were learned: bigger guns on bigger ships were better at long-range battles than ships equipped with a variety of smaller guns, and more importantly for the history of destroyers, the battle proved that small, fast torpedo boats could inflict damage on much larger ships.

Three Japanese-built destroyers of the *Harusame* class were at the battle, as were torpedo boats built in Great Britain. The *Harusames* weighed 375 tons and were 227 feet long. Each was armed with two 18-inch torpedo tubes and two twelve-pounder guns.

The Japanese were elated by their victory at Tsushima Strait, much of it achieved at night with the torpedo. They were particularly proud that some of the torpedoes used in the attack were built in Japan, even if the designs had been copied from the British. The Japanese congratulated themselves as the first Asian force to defeat a Western force. Victory had come barely sixty years after the Westerners had forced themselves on the Japanese empire in the 1850s.

Among the Japanese who fought the battle was a young officer named Isoroku Yamamoto. He would take to heart the evidence that devastating an enemy in one blow could be the key to future military successes.

With the way now open to take on weak China and Korea, the Japanese thought of themselves as invincible. That attitude worried the Western powers.

From 1907 to 1909, United States President Theodore Roosevelt sent the "Great White Fleet" of sixteen battleships around the world to demonstrate that the U.S. too was a world naval power. At the same time, he realized the potential enemies he hoped would be impressed would not be pushovers in any theoretical future conflict. With nine versions of the 420-ton *Bainbridge* class destroyer already in service, the president pushed Congress to approve more large destroyers.

While no American destroyers had the range to accompany the Great White Fleet, they proved themselves to be vital vessels in several locations around the world.

During the 1906 San Francisco earthquake, USS *Perry* (DD-11) and USS *Preble* (DD-12), both *Bainbridge* class, played vital roles in fighting the city's fires and keeping looters at bay. Their crews had been thrown out of their bunks in the predawn hours of April 18 by the heavy waves in the bay caused by the earthquake.

During the summer of 1907 in the Philippines, the U.S. nervously eyed the Japanese—the undisputed victors of the Russo-Japanese War of 1904-1905. The Great White Fleet would soon be on its way around the world, and Navy strategists wondered if it might be ambushed like the Russians had been just two years earlier. If the fleet's battleships were damaged or destroyed, the way would be open for the Japanese to attack the Philippines. There would not be much to oppose them other than a handful of ships that had been virtually neglected by the admirals back in the United States.

The next summer, a twenty-three-year-old ensign, just two years out of the U.S. Naval Academy, was commanding the USS *Decatur* (DD-5), the nation's fifth *Bainbridge*-class destroyer. With one order in 1907, the young officer had jumped from commanding a river gunboat and twenty-seven men to one of the nation's first destroyers and a crew of seventy-five.

The ensign wondered why a vice admiral that he did not know had given such a prestigious command to someone so young. When the ensign visited his new command for the first time, he understood. He later described his first destroyer command as "a beat-up old destroyer." In fact, the ship was only nine years old, but she was missing some equipment, provisions, drinking water, and fuel. Her previous commander had probably been relieved of command for letting the ship sink into such disrepair. The ensign learned just how bad of repair when he tried to back out of the harbor and discovered the engine telegraphs—a mechanical device signaling desired engine speeds to the engine room from the bridge—had been hooked up in reverse, and no officer had bothered to fix them.

The ensign got the *Decatur* back into shape, but the desire to head home for leave may have clouded his thinking while on duty. While entering Batangas Harbor, south of Manila Bay, on the evening of July 7, 1908, he just glanced around the familiar harbor rather than take bearings from landmarks. It was a careless error in judgment. Within a few minutes, the ship had run aground on a mudbank.

After unsuccessfully trying to back the destroyer off the mudbank, the ensign did something that shocked the bridge crew.

"The advice of my grandfather returned to me: 'Don't worry about things over which you have no control.' So, I set up a cot on deck and went to sleep."[5]

The next day, a small steamer pulled the *Decatur* free. The ensign dutifully reported the accident to his superiors. Acting on the report, his superiors charged him with "culpable inefficiency in the performance of duty."[6]

The court of inquiry was lenient, giving the ensign just a letter of reprimand in his record. Still, he was relieved of command of the *Decatur* and sent home, just as he had been wanting for months. The incident was soon forgotten and within eighteen months, the ensign was promoted to full lieutenant, skipping the grade of lieutenant junior grade.

Ensign Chester Nimitz (sitting fourth from the right) carelessly ran his destroyer, the USS *Decatur* (DD-5), aground in the Philippines, but his career did not suffer. *NHHC photo.*

The ensign's name was Chester Nimitz, who would one day hold the title of commander in chief of the United States Pacific Fleet. The young officer who had carelessly run his destroyer aground in 1908 would be the architect for the U.S. Navy defeating the Japanese during World War II.

Nimitz was not the only future famous admiral to cruise around the Philippines in a destroyer before World War I. In 1913, Lietuenant Raymond Spruance, twenty-six years old, was assigned to command the USS *Bainbridge* (DD-1). While taking command of the Navy's first destroyer might have sounded like an honor, the reality was different.

"Those destroyers had been the most completely ragtime, non-reg bunch of ships that you've ever seen in your life. The officers were dissolute, drunken, crooked, the darndest bunch of people you've ever seen, and demoralized completely by life in the Asiatic Station...The idea of sending Spruance there was to try to straighten out this bunch of tough eggs and get the destroyers back on their feet," wrote Charles J. Moore, Spruance's engineering officer.[7]

Spruance took the assignment in stride and spent his year on the *Bainbridge* putting her back into fighting trim by making friends with his crew. He surprised them by teaching them to swim.

By 1908, American destroyers being laid down had grown in weight to 700 tons and 293 feet long with a beam of 26 feet, and a top speed of 31 knots. The *Smith* class was the first class to use steam turbine propulsion and the last class to burn coal to produce the steam. Armament was five 3-inch guns and three single torpedo mounts.

The follow-up *Paulding* class, built from 1909 to 1911, made the switch to fuel oil, which burned at twice the temperature of coal and could be more easily obtained in far-flung ports. The *Pauldings* came in at 742 tons.

The *Smith* and the *Paulding* classes were apparently less than comfortable on the high seas as they soon acquired the nickname "flivvers," the same nickname given the Ford Model T car, which delivered bone-shaking jolts to its owners. Twenty-six flivvers would be built and delivered by 1912.

U.S. Navy designers, watching other nations launching bigger destroyers, finally broke the 1,000-ton weight class in 1913 with the USS *Cassin* (DD-43). She was just over 305 feet long with a beam of 31 feet and a draft of just over 9 feet. While the number of guns was decreased to just four, they were 4-inch, rapid-firing guns. She bristled with four twin torpedo mounts for 18-inch torpedoes.

Twenty-six 1,000-tonners in five similar classes would be built in four years, ending with the 1915 *Sampson* class, stretching out to 315 feet and with a complement of just over one hundred men. In fifteen years, from laying down the *Bainbridge* (DD-1) to the launch of the last of the 1,000-tonners, the USS *Shaw* (DD-68) destroyer length had grown just 70 feet to 315 feet, but the displacement had more than doubled from 420 tons to 1,110 tons. Yet, even with the heavier displacement, the destroyers' speed had increased one more knot to 29 knots. Designers were perfecting the steam turbines of the destroyers with each new class. While best known by the nickname "1,000-tonners," the ships also were known as "broken-deckers" for the raised forecastle or raised deck forward of the bridge, a naval design dating back centuries, and which most of the previous torpedo boat designs had also featured.

Despite regularly incorporating design advances of one class over the preceding class, by 1915, the United States was still thirty years behind other nations in terms of numbers of destroyers being laid down and attainable speeds of those ships. The world's leading destroyer designer, Great Britain, kept improving its designs.

It took four years for the U.S. to put twenty-six destroyers of four different classes of 1,000-tonners onto the ocean. Great Britain launched eighty-five *Admiralty* M-class destroyers in 1914 alone—the year World War I began. The British *M* class was 46 feet shorter than the American *Sampson* class, but the *M* class came in at the same 1,000 tons in displacement. The *M* class could make 34 knots, 5 knots faster than the *Sampson*. The difference was that the British turbines produced eight thousand more shaft horsepower than the American ships, a fact probably related to the thirty years of additional experience the British had in developing marine turbines. Both countries had settled on 4-inch guns as their main armament. Curiously, the British, who had invented the powered torpedo, carried only four tubes on the *M* class compared to twelve tubes mounted in triple tube configuration carried on American *Sampson*-class destroyers. Both nations were now using 21-inch circumference torpedoes.

During the early part of the twentieth century, the Germans ignored the development of heavier destroyers by other countries. Instead of joining the race to lay down larger ships, the Germans stayed with the original idea of designing torpedo boats to launch torpedoes against larger ships. The average weight for German torpedo boats was around 650 tons, compared to the British destroyers approaching 1,000 tons. The common German torpedo boat had only four torpedo tubes and two guns, compared to a British destroyer's four tubes and three guns.

In 1914, Japan had only two operational destroyers, but it soon launched a building campaign to construct ten *Kaba*-class destroyers with a length of 260 feet, displacing 655 tons that could make 30 knots.

As tensions mounted in 1914, Great Britain remained the world leader in destroyer design and in the number of ships deployed. While Germany ignored the rush to develop bigger, faster destroyers, it was putting its development money into boats operating under the surface of the ocean.

CHAPTER

2

World War I in Europe

"Do as much damage as possible."

When war broke out in Europe on July 28, 1914, the United States
looked on with detached interest.

If the European nations wanted to make good on entanglements in
each other's treaties, that was fine, but the U.S. had no such agreements
with any nation. President Woodrow Wilson issued a neutrality procla-
mation barely a week after the war started.

"The United States must be neutral in fact, as well as in name, during
these days that are to try men's souls," Wilson said in an address to
Congress.[1]

Within a few months, souls were tried indeed, as many lives were
lost to a new naval weapon: the submarine.

On September 22, 1914, three obsolete British armored cruisers were
sunk by the German *U-9* in the North Sea off the Netherlands, resulting
in the loss of more than 1,400 British sailors. The only defense the ships
could muster was trying to ram the submarine after the release of two
torpedoes caused it to break the ocean's surface and reveal its location.
The ramming attempt failed, and the cruiser was then sunk by the *U-9*.

The shocking attack flummoxed the British. Other than laying mines in areas where U-boats might sail, there was no defense against a vessel that could dive out of sight where traditional guns could not reach.

The first weapons designed to attack submarines were sinkable mines attached to lanyards attached to buoys dropped from patrol boats. When the mine reached its desired depth at the end of the lanyard, the charge detonated. The weapon worked, but the sinkable mines were inaccurate and took too long to deploy.

One inventor, Herbert Taylor, read about the cruiser attacks and designed a device that he called a "hydrostatic pistol": an explosive trigger that used water depth pressure to explode at preset depths. Within months, the mating of the hydrostatic pistol (or trigger) with the sinkable mine resulted in a brand-new naval weapon: the depth charge. A retired British naval officer, Alban L. Gwynne, contributed to the design by inventing a primer safety system to ensure the depth charges only exploded in the water and did not go off through rough handling or from the jarring of heavy seas.

Now there was an anti-submarine weapon, the depth charge, but it needed a ship from which to be deployed. Battleships and cruisers were too big and ungainly in the ocean. Depth charges would have to be dropped from small, fast ships that could change course on the surface to match what the submarine was doing below the surface.

On March 22, 1916, the first U-boat was sunk by a British Q-ship: a warship disguised as a merchantman which lured the submarine to the surface by appearing to surrender. Once fired upon, the submarine would submerge, but would then be sunk by depth charges.

Now proven in combat, depth charges were loaded onto many types of patrolling vessels. However, the added topside weight of a supply of depth charges, each weighing 300 pounds, had not been figured into destroyer designs. Just staying afloat with them was a formidable challenge for the crews.

"The whole ship's company was in a state of jitters. We were in a shocking state of instability and our metacentric height must have been halfway up to the funnels! We hung on a roll to a degree that was terrify-ing!" wrote the captain of the HMS *Cockatrice* after his ship had depth charge racks installed on its stern. His destroyer was a 267-foot-long, 930-ton *Acasta*-class destroyer laid down in 1912, three years before the invention of depth charges.[2]

While the British were experimenting with this viable method for sinking U-boats, the United States was still struggling to decide whether to enter the war. Nine months after Wilson made his neutrality speech, a German cruiser sank an American merchantman carrying grain to Great Britain. Several months later, the RMS *Lusitania*, a British ocean liner, was sunk by another U-boat, killing more than 1,198 people, including 128 Americans.

The loss of American lives was not enough to incite the U.S. govern-ment to declare war against Germany, but the sinking of the *Lusitania* did make the government take stock of its Navy. The nation's aging fleet of battleships and newer cruisers were useless against German subma-rines. As proven by the British, the best vessel for attacking German submarines was the ocean-going destroyer, but the U.S. Navy had only sixteen torpedo boats including the original destroyer, the USS *Bain-bridge*, at 420 tons. The destroyer fleet included twenty-six flivvers coming in from 700 to 740 tons, and eight of the relatively new 1,000-tonners. None of them had been designed to drop depth charges. Many were scattered around the Far East and the American Pacific coast while the Germans were in the Atlantic.

By contrast, the British had more than three hundred destroyers divided among eleven classes that had been constantly updated in design since the Japanese victory in the Russo-Japanese War of 1905. Germany had similar numbers of large torpedo boats with sizes reaching 260 feet and 1,051 tons. They carried mines but no depth charges.

It would take the largest naval battle of World War I, the Battle of Jutland, on May 31, 1916, off Denmark's North Sea coast, to convince the United States that it needed to upgrade its Navy. The massive battle involved more than 250 British and German ships, with most of the fighting done by battleships. After Jutland, the admirals of both sides were convinced that big ships, big guns, thicker armor, better armor-piercing rounds to penetrate that thick armor, and better trained gunners would decide naval engagements in future wars.

Neither side's destroyers—seventy-eight destroyers for the British and sixty-one torpedo boats for the Germans—played major roles. Still, the British lost eight destroyers while the Germans lost five torpedo boats.

President Wilson, who had preached against joining the European war just a year earlier, now gave a speech declaring he would create "incomparably the greatest Navy in the world."[3] He pushed through the Naval Act of 1916—commonly called the "Big Navy Act"—which called for spending five hundred million dollars on the construction of ten new battleships, six cruisers, thirty submarines, and fifty destroyers over three years. While naval strategists initially focused on the construction of big battleships, the authorization of those fifty new destroyers was the best move President Wilson could have made for the United States, as was proven twenty-five years later.

The first of these newly constructed destroyers broke with naval tradition with their new flush deck design, which eliminated the raised forecastle—the deck in front of the bridge—that had been standard on naval ships dating back centuries. U.S. naval designers now believed that by making the entire deck flush from bow to stern, it gave the destroyer greater structural integrity because it eliminated the potential weak point where the raised forecastle met the deck in front of the bridge, a focus of waves in heavy seas.

The new class was the *Caldwell*, consisting of just six ships, each with a length of around 315 feet, a beam of 31 feet, and draft of eight feet. Like their 1,000-tonner predecessors, the *Caldwell* class still displaced just over 1,120 tons and had a design speed of 32 knots. Its range was about 2,500 miles, the same as the 1,000-tonners. Each ship was designed to carry four 4-inch guns and twelve torpedo tubes mounted in four triple mounts firing 21-inch torpedoes. All of the *Caldwells* were commissioned in time to serve in the war.

Besides the nickname "flush deckers," this new destroyer class was also called "four stackers" or "four pipers," in reference to the four smokestacks connected to the two engine rooms. Still, not all flush deckers had four stacks. Three ships of the *Caldwell* class had three smokestacks as shipbuilders had leeway to improve performance, save weight, and advance design efficiencies.

The British had been upgrading their destroyer designs virtually every year for several years before the war started. The *Admiralty R*-class destroyers, sixty-two of which were ordered in 1915 and built over the next two years, were 975 tons and 276 feet long with a beam of nearly 27 feet and a draft of nearly 10 feet. Its rated speed was 36 knots—4 knots faster than the American *Caldwell* class was expected to make.

By the start of World War I, Japan had ended its practice of purchasing British destroyers and was now building its own, just ten years after its stunning victory in the Russo-Japan War of 1904-1905. The Japanese were designing destroyers smaller than those of the Americans and British. The *Kaba*-class destroyer, which saw escort service in the Mediterranean Sea on the side of the Allies, weighed 655 tons, was 260 feet long, and was armed with two torpedo tubes as well as five guns. The *Kaba* class was followed up by the *Momo* class, which came in at 835 tons. Just four copies were made. All of them also served with the British and were based in Malta.

Building just four copies of the *Momo* class may have been a harbinger of the future financial and industrial ability of Japan to build destroyers. What should have been a concern for the Japanese was that they were still behind the world in power plant design. The *Momo* was its first class to use only fuel oil while the rest of the world's navies had switched from coal to oil at least six years earlier.

What should have troubled Allied war planners was that the ten *Kaba* destroyers were built quickly in eight different shipyards with excellent quality control. All of the destroyers performed up to design specifications, though they had a limited range of 1,200 nautical miles compared to the British *Admiralty R* class, which had a range of 3,440 nautical miles. For armament, the Japanese installed one 4.7-inch quick-firing gun that was based on a tried and true British design: four 3-inch guns and four torpedo tubes.

Within just four years, the hulls of the *Enoki* class in 1918, which followed the *Momo* class, grew longer and wider. The *Enoki* class was 850 tons with a length of 275 feet. This class now carried six torpedo tubes compared to four on the *Kaba*. Each of the six ships of the *Enoki* class also carried three 4.7-inch guns—triple the gun armament of the *Kaba* class completed just three years earlier. The Japanese *Enoki* destroyers were so respected for their design that the French ordered a dozen barely ten years after the Japanese had been buying their destroyers from the British and French.

On October 7, 1916, the U.S. Navy got a firsthand look at what its British counterparts were facing in the same Atlantic Ocean some 3,300 miles to the east.

Without even so much as a wireless radio request to enter the harbor, the *SM U-53*, a German U-boat armed with seven torpedoes for its four tubes and two 3.5-inch deck guns, cruised into the harbor at Newport, Rhode Island. Home to the U.S. Second Naval District and the U.S. Naval War College, Newport was arguably one of the most important installations in the Navy. No challenges were issued to the submarine before it anchored near the base's flotilla of seventeen destroyers.

Within a few minutes, a startled U.S. Navy officer came on board to ask the *U-53's* captain, Hans Rose, if the crew wished to be interned. A surprised Rose laughed and replied no, but he would like to see the base commander.

Rose's secret mission to Newport, ordered in August 1916, was to determine whether the U-boat's range could be stretched from the 5,600 nautical miles it was designed for to 7,800 miles. He had done it, confirming that U-boats could cross the Atlantic and return to Germany. Since the U.S. was a neutral country, sailing into Newport's harbor was not against international law. Of course, Rose did not disclose to the Americans that he had a second part to his mission.

"After leaving Newport, you will take the opportunity to do as much damage as possible along the American coast among commercial ships. Always observe international law and keep well within its limits," his orders read.[4]

After meeting the base's commanders, Rose boarded the USS *Birmingham*, a light cruiser and flagship of the squadron. He enjoyed a few cigarettes with Captain Albert Gleaves, whom he described as "competent" compared to Admiral Austin Knight, whom Rose dismissed as one "not quite sure what he ought to do, and [who] feared to assume responsibility."[5]

Returning to his submarine, Rose found its deck swarming with U.S. naval officers, who were most interested in his boat's diesel engines. Soon, Gleaves, along with his wife and daughter, came aboard for a tour. With the party in full swing, Admiral Knight sent an officer with a note to Rose claiming that the harbor master had not given the *U-53* freedom of the port, and all communications with the land must cease. A sly Rose, recognizing the lie, replied that the admiral was mistaken; the harbor master was on board enjoying the port (wine) Rose was sharing with him.

The flustered officer insisted that all communications cease, and Rose surmised that the Navy Department in Washington had ordered Knight to end the visit. Within ten minutes, the guests had been shuffled off the deck and Rose pulled up anchor.

"To the accompaniment of cheers from the American torpedo boat fleet, and excited celebrations along the water front, we sped out of the harbor, waving our caps and cheering," Rose wrote in a 1926 article for the *Living Age* magazine.[6]

The next day, off Nantucket Island, Rose would complete the secret part of his mission.

At 5:35 a.m. on October 8, 1916, the *U-53* stopped an American steamer, but since she was not carrying war materials to Britain, was allowed to proceed. An hour and a half later, the *U-53* sank a British steamer after the crew had made their way into lifeboats. For the next twelve hours, the submarine stopped ships, assessed if they are British or carrying "contraband" for the war effort, and then sank them.

By 5:30 p.m., a full twelve hours after the U-boat began its attacks, the entire flotilla of seventeen American destroyers based at Newport reached the area. Rose remained on the surface, confident that the Americans would not interfere as he was in international waters and following the law by attacking only ships carrying war material to the enemies of Germany. With a passenger ship just 500 yards away and virtually surrounded by American destroyers, Rose ordered the crew and passengers to leave.

The American destroyers vainly attempted to stop his attacks peacefully with the USS *Winslow* (DD-53), identified by Rose's post-war memory of its hull number, coming so close that Rose had to throw the *U-53*'s engines in reverse to avoid a collision. When preparing to send a torpedo into one cargo ship, Rose politely asked over the wireless for the unidentified destroyer to "give way a little" so he could sink the ship. He at once complies with my request," Rose said.[7]

By 10:30 p.m., the last ship was sunk with the *U-53*'s last torpedo. Over the course of seventeen hours, Rose had stopped seven ships, released two, and sunk five, totaling more than 20,000 tons. He allowed two other passenger ships to sail past as he worried they were not equipped with enough lifeboats.

All the American destroyers could do was pick up the passengers from the ocean. Rose had not violated any international or American laws. He had not attacked any neutral American ships. All the sinking of the British, Dutch, and Norwegian ships had come in international waters.

Still, rash action by one of the destroyer captains could have created an international incident that might have led to the United States entering the war in 1916.

In his post-war account, Rose wrote: "My heart still beats faster when I think of the terrible risks that we ran..."[8]

Rose did not board any of the American destroyers while in Newport and recorded no impressions of them, though he implied in his post-war account that he knew the United States would soon go to war with Germany.

Five were *Paulding* class, the flivvers, weighing 740 tons and armed with five 3-inch guns and six torpedo tubes; double the number of tubes carried by the previous destroyer class, the *Smith*. The flivver class leader, USS *Paulding* (DD-22), was the oldest destroyer on scene. The other nine were 1,000-tonners armed with 4-inch guns. Present were three 1,000-tonner class leaders, the USS *Cassin* (DD-43), the USS *Alywin* (DD-47), and the USS *O'Brien* (DD-51). The newest destroyer present was the USS *Porter* (DD-59), a *Tucker* class measuring 315 feet long with a crew of 101. It mounted four 4-inch guns and eight 21-inch torpedo tubes. The flotilla represented a good cross-section of the American destroyer fleet.

In just five years, American destroyer designs had changed. The hull was lengthened by more than twenty-two feet, eleven crew were added, the guns were enlarged from 3-inchers to 4-inchers, and the torpedoes went from 18 inches to 21 inches. None of the destroyers were yet armed with depth charges, which were still being perfected by the British navy. Even Rose, who had sunk his first British cargo ship in July off Norway with the loss of thirty lives, had not yet encountered depth charges.

All seventeen of these destroyers would sail to Ireland in May 1917 to escort convoys operating between the bases in England and the warfront in France.

The official American government reaction to the U-boat attacks just off its coast was muted. President Wilson issued a mild official statement: "The government will, of course, first inform itself as to all the facts that there may be no mistake or doubt, so far as they are concerned, and the country may rest assured that the German government will be held to the complete fulfillment of its promises to the government of the United States. I have no right to question their willingness to fulfill them."[9]

A number of newspaper editorials took a stance stronger than the government's. The *Boston Herald* wrote: "The European War has been transferred to our own shores. Germany is, for practical purposes, block-ading the ports of the United States." The *Philadelphia Inquirer* wrote: "To bring submarine atrocities to our very door is a bold thing for the Berlin militarists to do—and a dangerous thing, unless they have made up their minds to defy the United States." The *New York Times* wrote: "One rash act, a single mistake on the part of the U-boat commander, causing the loss of even one American life, would provoke instant action by the American government."[10]

The British government, which earlier agreed to an American request to keep its cruisers away from American ports, was outraged that the U.S. destroyers had not taken offensive action. The British issued a thinly veiled threat: "…any place which provides a submarine warship far from its base with an opportunity for rest and replenishment of its supplies, thereby furnishes such addition to its powers that the place becomes, in fact, through the advantages which it gives, a base of naval operations… The allied governments take this opportunity to point out to the neutral powers the grave danger incurred by neutral submarines in the navigation of regions frequented by belligerent submarines."[11]

The British government just warned the American government that it might sink an American submarine in international waters.

Captain Rose commented on the strange encounter ten years later: "Had these Americans foreseen that a year later I would sink one of their destroyers, the *Jacob Jones,* perhaps their conduct would have been different."[12]The USS *Jacob Jones* (DD-61) was not based at Newport, but its future captain, Lieutenant David W. Bagley, was in command of the USS *Drayton* (DD-23), one of the seventeen destroyers shadowing *U-53* that day.

CHAPTER

3

U.S. Enters the War

"We are ready now, sir!"

The death of 128 U.S. passengers aboard the torpedoed RMS *Lusitania* on May 7, 1915, did not result in a declaration of war against Germany by the United States.

Nor did the sinking of five cargo vessels by the *U-53* within a few miles of Nantucket Island and in view of seventeen American destroyers on October 1916.

For two years of the war in Europe, the Germans had been cordial to the Americans on the other side of the Atlantic, confident that they could win the land war over the British and French. But by early January 1917, that land victory had proven elusive. The Germans then took a calculated risk: they would attempt to starve Great Britain of ocean-borne supplies before the slow-moving American republic could motivate itself to figure out which side it supported.

On January 31, 1917, Germany announced it would no longer honor any previous agreements not to attack passenger ships or allow cargo ships to disembark their crews before being torpedoed. Unrestricted submarine warfare had returned. Within a few hours, an American ship was torpedoed. Three more were sunk in March.

The Americans, who had ignored the deaths of its citizens being killed by Germans when traveling on other nations' ships, finally were pushed to act. President Wilson asked for a declaration of war and on April 6, 1917, it was approved by Congress.

Admiral William Sims was sent to Great Britain to command all U.S. Naval forces. *NHHC photo.*

In anticipation of a declaration of war against Germany, U.S. Admiral William Sowden Sims had been sent to London in March to assess the situation. Until Sims' visit, Wilson's dedication to neutrality had been so complete that he had little firsthand knowledge of how well the British were fighting the war; not much more than what he read in the newspapers.

Sims discovered that since the resumption of unrestricted submarine warfare just two months earlier, British shipping losses had doubled to more than a million tons per month. British Admiral John Jellicoe calmly told Sims that the Germans "will win unless we can stop these losses and stop them soon."[1]

Even the German torpedo boats, two-thirds the size of most British destroyers with smaller and fewer deck guns, had been giving the British problems. In the First Battle of Dover Strait on October 26-27, 1916, more than five months after the indecisive Battle of Jutland, twenty-three

German torpedo boats attacked the Dover Barrage, a defensive line of underwater mines, submarine nets, and armed trawlers further protected by British destroyers. A twenty-year-old destroyer, the HMS *Flirt,* stood little chance against the fast torpedo boats. A newer *Tribal*-class destroyer, the HMS *Nubian,* rushed to the action and was surprised with a torpedo to its bow. Six British ships were sunk in the debacle, while only one German torpedo boat was damaged.

In the early morning of April 20, 1917, the Dover Strait was attacked again. This time, the British destroyers were better acquitted. The HMS *Swift* had been intended to be the first of a new, larger class of destroyers at more than 353 feet long when she was constructed in 1907, but the Admiralty was disappointed in her performance and never ordered another one. The *Swift* and the HMS *Broke,* a two-year-old *Faulknor* class at 1,700 tons and 331 feet long, faced down six German torpedo boats. One German torpedo boat, the *G85* at 274 feet and 1,051 tons, was sunk by a *Swift* torpedo. The *G42*, a slightly larger torpedo boat, was rammed by the *Broke.* The *Broke's* crew then repelled German boarders using rifles with fixed bayonets, pistols, and cutlasses. Every German on the *G42's* deck became the target of small arms fire.

Apparently sobered by the fierce defense of the Dover Strait by the two British destroyers in the half hour battle, the remaining four German torpedo boats retreated to their base even though the two British ships were severely damaged.

The violent, close up battle and lopsided victory attracted the attention of British admirals. Twenty-four Distinguished Service Medals were awarded to Destroyer Men on the two ships.

The British did not want the Americans to help them fight more surface actions like this one. They wanted American destroyers to find and destroy U-boats. That request puzzled Admiral Sims. To that date, there had not been a proven technical means of finding submarines other than to look for a periscope breaking the surface of the ocean. Instead of trying to literally find a periscope-sized needle sticking up in an ocean-sized haystack, Sims suggested what the British really needed was a fleet of destroyers to escort convoys of merchant ships to their ports. Sims was proposing a defensive strategy of American destroyers protecting British shipping from U-boats instead of an aggressive strategy of finding U-boats.

To Sims' surprise, the British were not immediately sold on the American idea of safety in numbers by forming convoys. Even more surprising was the reaction of President Woodrow Wilson to the idea. The formerly pacifist president favored a major naval campaign to capture and destroy U-boat bases. That would take months to plan; time the British did not have as they were already being strangled by the loss of food, oil, and other war necessities. Sims also recognized that the Americans had no experience in organizing amphibious assaults on heavily defended coastal facilities.

Sims stood his ground. He offered destroyers to escort merchant ship convoys running war supplies from Great Britain to France. The British reluctantly agreed. He also convinced President Wilson that his idea was impossible.

On April 24, 1917, just eighteen days after the United States had declared war on Germany, the U.S. Navy's Destroyer Division 8 set sail for Queenstown (now Cobh), Ireland: a tiny coastal town. It was familiar to Americans as the last port of call for the RMS *Titanic* in 1912, and where the *Lusitania's* survivors and the dead were taken in 1915.

Commander Joseph Taussig commanded the first American destroyers to arrive in Great Britain in May of 1917. *NHHC photo*

Commanding the first six destroyers was Commander Joseph Kne-fler Taussig, a forty-year-old career Navy man born in Dresden, Germany, where his U.S. Navy admiral father was stationed. The destroyers, the first help given to the British in the war, arrived on May 4. Taussig commanded from his flagship, the USS *Wadsworth* (DD-60), and other destroyers, including the USS *Conyngham* (DD-58), USS *Davis* (DD-65), USS *McDougal* (DD-54), and USS *Wainwright* (DD-62). The sixth member of the division, the USS *Jacob Jones* (DD-61), would stay behind for now to act as a mail ship.

The division destroyers were a mixture of closely matched but slightly different classes. All were 1,000-tonners including *Tucker, O'Brien,* and *Sampson* classes. The *Tuckers* and *Sampsons* were 315 feet long—10 feet longer than the *O'Brien* class—but all were armed with four 4-inch guns and between eight and twelve torpedo tubes with 21-inch torpedoes.

When Taussig landed in Queenstown on May 4, he was handed a letter from Admiral Sir John Jellicoe, the first sea lord of the Admiralty, which read: "I am indeed delighted that you should have been selected for the command of the first force which is coming to fight for freedom, humanity, and civilization; we shall have our work cut out to subdue piracy."[2]

It was at dinner at the home of Vice Admiral Sir Lewis Bayly, commander of all British naval forces in Ireland, that a famous, if apocryphal, U.S. Navy legend began.

The story goes that Bayly asked Taussig how long it would take him to ready his destroyers for service. "We are ready now, sir, except, of course, for refueling!" Taussig supposedly replied.

While this bold comment illustrating the spirit of Destroyer Men is often quoted in U.S. Navy lore, Taussig makes no mention in his diary of having said anything provocative that evening. Taussig kept a meticulous diary, complaining in one early entry that he had to leave his laundry behind to make his ordered sailing time to reach Ireland.

In December 1922, Taussig wrote a *Proceedings* magazine article about the arrival of the American destroyers in Queenstown. The editor added a separate page to Taussig's article purporting that the quote at dinner was heard by an unnamed staff officer for Admiral Sims. This anonymous staff officer's account is the source of the legend.

Admiral Sims also claimed to have heard Taussig make the comment when he wrote his memoirs in 1920. Sims also had a curious observation, or criticism, of destroyers in general when he thought about Taussig's answer of: "We are ready now, sir!"

"Even under the most favorable conditions, that is an embarrassing question to ask of a destroyer commander. There is no type of ship that is so chronically in need of overhauling [destroyer]. Even in peace times, the destroyer usually has under way a long list of repairs,"[3] Sims later wrote.

Taussig discovered at the dinner that Admiral Sims had not yet convinced the stubborn Bayly of his idea to concentrate on convoy protection. Bayly insisted that the American destroyers' priority would be to sink U-boats, then provide escorts to convoys, then save the lives of U-boat victims.

"To miss an opportunity to sink a submarine means that he remains to sink other peaceful vessels and destroy more lives," Bayly told Taussig.[4]

As soon as they landed in Queenstown, the British engineers set to work, adapting their depth charge racks to the narrow sterns of the American destroyers. The Americans had never seen depth charges before, much less trained with them. Neither Taussig nor Sims make any mention in his book of the addition of 9,000 pounds of twenty to thirty 300-pound depth charges to the sterns, which changed the handling of the American destroyers, all built at least a year before the weapon's invention.

The first patrol of the American destroyers to assist the British in World War I began on May 7, 1917. It would be another six weeks before the first American foot soldiers going "over there" would land in France. The Destroyer Men of the United States Navy would be the first American servicemen to see combat in World War I.

The first patrol by the Americans was inauspicious.

Taussig reported that the first periscope his lookouts spotted turned out to be a boathook floating vertically in the water. At 11:00 p.m., he rushed to the bridge after hearing an explosion and feeling a jolt that he interpreted as a torpedo hit in the stern. It turned out that the officer on deck had released a depth charge on what he thought was a submarine. Nothing was found.

Over the coming weeks, more destroyers arrived from the United States, with some being assigned to Brest, France and Gibraltar. One division of now obsolete flivvers made it with some refueling stops. By the end of July 1917, there were thirty-seven American destroyers stationed overseas.

The U.S. finally deemed the U-boat threat so critical that it ordered the entire destroyer division stationed in the Philippines, originally intended as a guard against a feared attack by Japan, to fight the war in Europe.

On August 1, the USS *Bainbridge* (DD-1), USS *Barry* (DD-2), USS *Chauncey* (DD-3), USS *Dale* (DD-4), and USS *Decatur* (DD-5), all coal-burning 420-ton destroyers, left their base near Manila for the Mediterranean. It was an exhausting, 12,000-mile trip that would take nearly two months. The newest of the destroyers was seventeen years old and hopelessly obsolete since oil was now the standard fuel for ships. The fact that the U.S. Navy deployed virtually all of its destroyers to escort duty in the Atlantic and Mediterranean indicates just how severe a war threat U-boats were now determined to be.

Even as more American destroyers, sub chasers, armed yachts, and other vessels crossed the Atlantic for escort duty, Admiral Bayly's number one goal of sinking U-boats remained difficult to achieve. Through the summer of 1917, including the time the American destroyers were patrolling, thirty merchant ships were sunk off Queenstown itself, and not a single U-boat was damaged off the port.

It was the Germans who drew first blood against the American Navy.

On October 15, 1917, USS *Cassin* (DD-43), the lead ship in its class, sighted a U-boat and gave chase. The submarine fired a torpedo that struck the destroyer in its stern. One report said that the torpedo broke the surface twice with the shock of the surfacing, turning the torpedo to the left both times. Had luck not been with the Germans, the torpedo would have missed.

When Gunner's Mate Osmond Ingram saw the torpedo approaching the *Cassin*, he recognized the danger of the projected path and ran to the stern to release the depth charges into the ocean. Before he could release them, Ingram was killed in the torpedo's explosion. His selfless act resulted in his being the first enlisted sailor reported killed in World War I. He was also awarded the Medal of Honor. A World War II destroyer would also be named in his honor—the first destroyer named after an enlisted naval hero.

The *Cassin's* rudder was blown off and her stern wrecked, but remarkably, no other sailors were killed in the explosion. She was towed back to Queenstown for repairs, which would take nine months.

On November 9, the USS *Chauncey* (DD-3), one of the Navy's oldest destroyers, and one of the *Bainbridge* class that had laboriously made its way from the Pacific to the Mediterranean, was lost off Gibraltar. *Chauncey* collided with the fully-loaded freighter *Rose*, which sliced through the 3/8-inch thick hull of the *Chauncey* like it was butter. Twenty-one sailors, including the captain, went down with the ship. It was the first of the American destroyers lost during the war.

Launched in 1901, *Chauncey* had spent most of her life in a decommissioned state. When she was cruising around the Philippines in 1912, one of her captains was Lieutenant Frank Jack Fletcher. Thirty years later and with the rank of admiral, Fletcher would win fame as the operational commander at the World War II battles of the Coral Sea and Midway. His uncle, Admiral Frank Friday Fletcher, was the namesake of the *Fletcher*-class destroyers that began rolling off the shipways in 1942.

The USS *Wadsworth* (DD-60), a Tucker class, was Commander Taussig's flagship. *NHHC photo.*

On November 17, 1917, Taussig, the man who had brought the first American destroyers to Great Britain, left Queenstown, having been reassigned to Washington. He had steamed more than 37,000 miles on patrol and spent 143 days at sea, but had not sunk a single U-boat. He had not even seen one.

Ironically, on the very afternoon Taussig sailed east, the Americans would finally get revenge for the attack on the *Cassin*.

The USS *Fanning* (DD-37) was a three-year-old *Paulding* class weighing 742 tons that had been part of the destroyer squadron shadowing the *U-53* off Nantucket in October 1916. Not long after Taussig had left Queenstown, the convoy that *Fanning* was escorting also sailed. The careless captain of the *U-58* left his periscope up just long enough for it to be spotted by the coxswain of the *Fanning*. The destroyer rushed to the area and dropped a single pattern of depth charges that forced the submarine to the surface. The USS *Nicholson* (DD-52), an *O'Brien* class 1,000-tonner, rushed to the scene. Both destroyers fired their deck guns at the submarine, convincing the German crew to rush onto the deck with their hands in the air. Both destroyers intended to board the submarine and retrieve its codebooks, but two German crewmen had already opened the seacocks and she soon slid below the waves. One German crewman died, but the rest were saved, including one man who was only saved after two U.S. Navy crewmen dived into the cold water to retrieve him. Both destroyers shared credit for sinking the first German U-boat by the American Navy, though it was the *Fanning's* depth charges that brought the submarine to the surface.

Taussig likely did not even know of the successful sinking of the German submarine as his diary ends without mentioning it. He may not have cared. In his diary, he writes that he was exhausted and ready to head home to the United States.

Taussig would continue his service in the Navy until 1947, but the destroyer leader—who was regarded as pioneering during World War I—was now, after the war, deemed controversial. He attracted the ire of Secretary of the Navy and later President Franklin Roosevelt for more than twenty years. Taussig argued before Congress several times that the U.S. was not expanding its Navy and training its sailors for the inevitable naval war with Japan. The then-pacifist Roosevelt forced Taussig into retirement two months before Pearl Harbor, but once war with Japan started, a justified Taussig was reinstated.

Less than three weeks after the *Fanning* sunk the U-boat, the Germans would get their second revenge on the Americans.

On December 6, 1917, two ship captains who had encountered each other a year earlier several thousand miles to the east met again.

The USS *Jacob Jones* (DD-61), a new *Tucker* class, was the only member of Destroyer Division 8 that had been left behind in the initial deployment to Queenstown. The official reason was to use her as a mail ship, but another reason might have been for repairs. In February of 1917, some member of the crew opened her seacocks while she was tied up in the Philadelphia Navy Yard in an apparent act of pre-war sabotage. More than two feet of water flooded the bottom of the ship before the open seacocks were discovered and closed.

Her captain was Commander David W. Bagley, brother to Ensign Worth Bagley, the only naval officer to lose his life in the Spanish-American War when his torpedo boat, the USS *Winslow* (TB-5), was shelled in Cuba. David Bagley had followed his older brother into the U.S. Naval Academy and had other strong naval connections. His brother-in-law was Secretary of the Navy Josephus Daniels, who had ironically done what he could to slow the growth of the Navy in the pre-war pacifist Wilson administration.

On this night, the *Jacob Jones* was returning to Queenstown after escorting a convoy to Brest, France. For undetermined reasons, she was late leaving Brest. The other five escort destroyers had all sailed ahead, leaving the *Jacob Jones* alone as she sailed past the Isles of Scilly, south of the main coast of England.

Watching her through his periscope was Captain Hans Rose, commander of the *U-53*. Fourteen months earlier, Rose had boldly sailed this same submarine into Newport, Rhode Island. Two days later, he sank five freighters in international waters off Nantucket while seventeen American destroyers stood by to take off passengers and crews. One of those destroyer captains was Bagley, then commanding the USS *Drayton* (DD-23).

Rose watched the *Jacob Jones* through his periscope, more than 3,000 yards distant. He calculated that the destroyer was moving at 13 knots, far faster than he could make either under the water or running on the surface. He figured an estimated angle of where the destroyer would be nearly two miles away, then fired a single torpedo.

Commander Bagley filed a report after the action on the futility of the moment:

> I was in the chart-house and heard someone call out, 'Torpedo.' I jumped at once to the bridge and on the way up saw the torpedo approaching from about one point abaft [toward the stern] the starboard beam, heading for a point about amidships and making a straight surface run at very high speed. No periscope was sighted.
>
> When I reached the bridge, I found that the officer of the deck had already put the rudder hard left and rung up emergency speed. The ship was swinging as I personally rang up speed again and then turned to watch the torpedo. The executive officer, Lieutenant Norman Scott, left the chart-house just ahead of me and made the same estimate of the speed and direction of the torpedo.
>
> I was convinced that it was impossible to avoid being hit. Lieutenant S. F. Kalk was officer of the deck at the time and I consider that he took correct and especially prompt measures in maneuvering to avoid the torpedo. Lieutenant Kalk was a very able officer, calm and collected in an emergency. He had been attached to the ship for about two months and had shown keen aptitude.
>
> The torpedo broached and jumped clear of the water a short distance from the ship, submerged when fifty or sixty

feet away, and struck three feet below the water in a fuel-oil tank. The after compartment and engine room flooded at once, the ship settling aft until the deck was awash, then more gradually. The deck was blown clean up for a space of twenty feet. The depth-charges exploded after the stern sank. Lieutenant J. K. Richard, gunnery officer, rushed aft to try to set the charges on safety, but could get no farther than the after deck-house.[5]

The *Jacob Jones* almost got lucky. Another few seconds, and the torpedo would have missed. But it struck near the stern, exploding a fuel tank and destroying the radio mast which was located on the stern in this design.

With the wireless mast destroyed, there was no way to contact the other destroyers ahead other than firing the deck guns with star shells to try to attract the attention of their lookouts. Those destroyers must have been too far over the horizon as no lookout reported seeing any shell bursts in the sky. No destroyers turned around to aid their sister ship.

With its stern blown away, the *Jacob Jones* began to settle fast into the cold sea. Within eight minutes, she was gone. As she sank, several of her depth charges exploded with the concussion, killing some men who had survived the initial attack.

As the men abandoned ship and clambered into life rafts and boats, the *U-53* surfaced. Rose picked up two survivors from the water. Rather than putting them into the lifeboats, he kept them aboard. Rose recorded in his deck log that the American prisoners made it a point to tell him that they did not like British sailors—an odd complaint to make to the U-boat captain who had just killed many of his own shipmates.

While picking up those two survivors, Rose did something that none of the *Jacob Jones* survivors knew until they returned to Queenstown. Perhaps realizing that his torpedo had wrecked the destroyer's radio, Rose sent a wireless transmission to Queenstown, informing the base that he had just sunk a destroyer at these coordinates.

Suicidal charges from trenches against machine guns were killing thousands of foot soldiers on both sides in France, but submarine commander Hans Rose had a reputation for trying to save lives.

Rose would become the fourth most successful U-boat commander of World War I, sinking eighty-one ships totaling 220,000 tons. He and U-53 would both survive the war, and he would train U-boat commanders through 1940. The *Jacob Jones* was the only warship he sank during the war.

Bagley gathered his men into a group of life rafts, then set off in a dory rowed by several seamen. He hoped to reach the Scilly Islands, which he knew to be populated, to get help.

While the warship *Jacob Jones* never had the chance to fire her guns on an enemy, her crew acted calmly and with bravery in the face of disaster.

As the evening grew into darkness, Lieutenant (j.g.) Stanton F. Kalk, a twenty-three-year-old who had been officer on deck when the torpedo hit, swam from raft to raft, using his engineering background to convince the men to equalize the weight distribution in each raft. Kalk continued swimming, perhaps aware that he had suffered internal injuries when the depth charges had exploded beneath him. Kalk continued encouraging the men until he quietly died while hanging onto one of the rafts. He never tried to climb aboard and replace an enlisted man. One of the survivors described him as "game to the last." Once the award was created in 1918, Kalk would be posthumously awarded the Navy Distinguished Service Cross for his selfless devotion to the crew. Two other crewmen were also recognized for their bravery, staying with the sinking ship to cut loose floating mats and gather life preservers.

Two officers and sixty-two crewmen, two-thirds of her complement, went down with the *Jacob Jones;* the worst loss suffered by the U.S. Navy in World War I. A British steamer stumbled onto most of the survivors before Bagley could reach shore for help.

Admiral Sims complimented Bagley, saying, "Bagley's handling of the situation after his ship was torpedoed was everything that I expected in the way of efficiency, good judgement, courage, and chivalrous action."[6]

Both Bagley and his executive officer, Lieutenant Norman Scott, would go on to become admirals during World War II.

As more American soldiers began shipping overseas for the trenches in France, it made sense to increase the number of destroyers operating out of Brest. Eventually, Brest would be the overseas port for thirty-three destroyers compared to twenty-four based in Queenstown.

Just as Admiral Sims had suggested would happen, the convoy system of large numbers of ships protected by outlying destroyers effectively countered the U-boats. Only one ship carrying American soldiers, the SS *Tuscania,* would be attacked by a U-boat on February 5, 1918. Just over two hundred American soldiers of the two thousand onboard would be lost at sea thanks to the efforts of two British destroyers that rushed to the scene to pull survivors from the cold water. More than two million American servicemen would safely make it across the Atlantic "over there" to proclaim: "Lafayette, we are here!"

While densely packed convoys offered protection from the submarines, such formations presented their own dangers. On March 19, 1918, the brand new *Caldwell*-class destroyer, USS *Manley* (DD-74), which had only been commissioned on October 15, 1917, found itself in too close quarters with a British cruiser. The cruiser rolled down on the stern of the *Manley,* resulting in the explosion of some of the destroyer's depth charges. Those explosions ripped away some of her stern and tore into gasoline and alcohol tanks. The burning liquid flowed down into the ship, killing thirty-three enlisted men and the ship's executive officer. She would be towed back to Queenstown and eventually repaired.

The *Manley* would fight again in World War II, but she would not get the chance to fight the Germans who had wounded her in World War I. She would eventually fight against the Japanese, who were Allies of the United States in World War I.

The next month, on April 17, 1918, just under a year since the first American destroyers had sailed for Ireland, three old 420-tonners were escorting a convoy to Brest when an ammunition ship blew up. The dark night was now bright as day, with explosions and burning oil on the surface of the sea.

The captain of the USS *Stewart* (DD-13), a *Bainbridge* class, did not hesitate. He plowed into the dangerous seas to find survivors.

Two of the *Stewart's* crew, Quartermaster Frank Monroe Upton, and ship's cook Jesse Whitfield Covington, were awarded Medals of Honor for diving into the burning water to rescue a wounded man who was surrounded by gunpowder boxes that were exploding.

Danger to Destroyer Men remained through the end of the war. On October 9, 1918, the USS *Shaw* (DD-68), a new *Sampson* class at sea for just sixteen months, experienced an equipment failure when its rudder jammed. That created an immediate problem because in its path was the SS *Aquitania,* a beautiful pre-war luxury liner that had been converted into a troop ship. Aboard were eight thousand soldiers destined for France. Without hesitation, the destroyer's captain ordered "all back full." That would not avoid collision, but meant the liner's bow would slice into the destroyer's side hull rather than the destroyer cutting into the liner. The destroyer captain made the conscious decision to sacrifice his own ship and crew rather than kill unknowing soldiers.

The liner cut the destroyer into two parts, killing two officers and ten men. It would take nearly a year before the *Shaw* returned to the United States with a new bow. It would be decommissioned in the 1930s and the *Shaw* name would pass to another destroyer. On December 7, 1941, that second *Shaw's* bow would also be blown off during the Japanese attack on Pearl Harbor.

Good luck and good navigation helped avoid another tragedy.

On May 31, 1918, the USS *President Lincoln,* a former German liner, was on its way back to the United States carrying several hundred wounded men. Its destroyer escort had turned back a day earlier after passing through what had been considered a danger zone for submarines, about 300 miles from land. Without warning, she was hit by three torpedoes. The wireless operator was able to get off a distress message before the ship sank a half hour after being hit.

That night, less than twelve hours after the attack, two American destroyers, the USS *Smith* (DD-17), a coal-burning 700-tonner and lead in her class, and the USS *Warrington* (DD-30), a *Paulding* 740-tonner, arrived with their lights ablaze, ignoring the chance that a U-boat could use those lights as a target. Using nothing more than the location of the fourteen-hour-old wireless signal, the two destroyers raced more than 250 miles to reach the area where they hauled aboard 618 survivors. On the way back to Brest, they even found the *U-90*, which had sunk the *President Lincoln*. They dropped depth charges, but failed to sink it, which was lucky for the sole American prisoner the submarine had plucked from the ocean.

Once destroyers had formed into escorted convoys, the number of ships sunk decreased. The contributions of destroyers which fought in World World I are beyond significant.

The German torpedo boats made little impact in the war, even when they attacked in superior numbers such as during the two battles of Dover Straits. Neither did they affect the outcome at the Battle of Jutland, where battleships and cruisers pounded each other.

Japan entered the war in 1914, fulfilling its role set forth in the 1902 Anglo-Japanese Alliance. Japan sent one cruiser and eight destroyers to the Mediterranean in March 1917, a full month before the Americans would send their first five destroyers to Queenstown. Eventually, seventeen Japanese destroyers would escort British shipping in the Mediterranean. By the end of the war, nearly eight hundred ships carrying more than 700,000 troops had Japanese destroyer protection from German submarines.

When the American destroyer division in the Philippines moved to the Mediterranean, Japan also took on the ironic role of protecting the Hawaiian Islands, which the Americans had always considered would one day be threatened by Japan. In return for its help against Germany, Japan gained control of German territories in Asia and the Mariana,

Marshall, and Caroline islands in the Pacific. Japan would reinforce and use all those islands against the Allies in less than twenty-five years.

Of the 375 U-boats that were operational during the war, 202 were sunk. British destroyers accounted for thirty-seven kills by depth charges, sixteen by gunfire, and fourteen by ramming.

The American destroyers accounted for just one confirmed submarine kill in nineteen months of hunting, with all but one of that submarine's crew being rescued. More than one hundred American sailors died in combat against the U-boats due to one U-boat attack and several collisions with other escorting ships.

The real value that destroyers provided was in convoy escorts. Nearly 16,700 ships made some kind of voyage in the war effort. Of that number in convoy, ninety-nine percent made it safely to port. Before the convoy system was introduced, virtually at the insistence of the Americans, it had been open season on merchantmen. In April 1917, the month the Americans arrived, more than 880,000 tons of Allied ships had been sunk. The tonnage lost to U-boats decreased every month after the convoy system was instituted.

There was little for U.S. Navy battleships, cruisers, and submarines to do in World War I. The destroyers played the major role for the United States. If the U.S. Navy learned one thing in World War I that would serve it well in a war that would come along barely twenty-five years later, it was that destroyers could play vital roles in defeating an enemy.

4

The 1920s

"We have no destroyers today!"

The USS *Clemson* (DD-186), lead in its class following the Wickes class. The Clemsons had more oil storage, thus longer ranges. *NHHC photo.*

At the end of World War I, President Wilson had two seemingly conflicting goals: to put the world on a peaceful path after the "war to end all wars," and continue to make the U.S. Navy second to none in the world.

Wilson dreamed that a League of Nations would allow all countries to settle their differences with calm discussions around a table staffed with professional bureaucrats. One U.S. senator who went to the White House to hear the president's dream of everlasting worldwide peace left thinking he had spent the evening "wandering with Alice in Wonderland and having tea with the Mad Hatter."[1]

A war-weary nation would elect Republican Warren G. Harding in 1920.

To his credit, Harding made no changes to Wilson's pre-war promise and ongoing program to build up the U.S. Navy. Like Wilson, Harding and his Navy advisors may have worried that a triumphant Great Britain with a dominant and large fleet might one day again threaten the U.S. in the Atlantic just as it had in the War of 1812.

Other war planners were more worried about Japan's long-term interests in the Pacific. In 1920, the outgoing Secretary of the Navy, Josephus Daniels, warned Congress in a secret session about "the necessity of being prepared if Japan should attack us [at Guam, Philippines, or Hawaii]."[2]

In 1916, Congress approved the construction of fifty additional destroyers and fifteen more in 1917 to deal with the future threat of submarines.

The General Board of the U.S. Navy wrote in a 1917 report:

"The Destroyer is, so far as can be seen, the best form of Submarine Chaser. It is not known what the future development of the Submarine may be, but there is no doubt that it will be greatly increased in size and power...The General Board further recommends that high speed Destroyer construction with full torpedo armament be continued, to provide Destroyers for and with the fleet where the higher speed is desirable."[3]

Following the *Caldwell* class of six ships came the mass-produced four stackers, the *Wickes* (111 ships), and the *Clemson* classes (156 ships). Eleven different shipyards were employed to produce the two classes that looked much alike, with one difference being that the *Clemsons* had additional tanks for 100 tons more fuel. These two classes weighed around 1,200 tons, 200 tons more than the pre-war 1,000-tonners. They were 314 feet long with a beam of 31 feet and a draft of just over 9 feet. These newer designs still carried the same four 4-inch guns, and twelve torpedo tubes for 21-inch torpedoes. Two depth charge racks were incorporated into the design. Increased speeds were coming rapidly as designers learned more about turbines, steam pressure, and gears. The *Caldwell* class was rated at 32 knots at 18,500 horsepower, with the following two *Wickes* and *Clemson* classes rated at 35 knots and 27,500 horsepower.

During the war, the Navy had urged shipbuilders to compete with each other to produce destroyers as fast as possible. The record was set by the Mare Island Shipyard in Vallejo, California when the USS *Ward* (DD-139) was launched in less than eighteen days and commissioned in fifty-four days. The hull sections had been built in advance and then welded in place to save time. Earlier classes of destroyers often took up to ten months of construction time before they were ready for sea duty.

Even with rushed construction, only twenty-one of the *Caldwell*, *Wickes*, and *Clemson* classes of destroyers made it to Europe before the Armistice. With the war over in 1918, the Navy continued its contracts to build new destroyers but began selling or scrapping the older ships without any regard to history or sentimentality. Within two years of the war ending, all of the first twenty-one destroyers the nation had constructed between 1901 and 1909 were scrapped or otherwise sold. All were coal burners and now obsolete as the nation no longer maintained coaling stations around the world. Even the USS *Bainbridge* (DD-1), the first U.S. Navy ship to be called a destroyer, was not spared. The *Bainbridge*, which had never fired her guns in anger or dropped a depth charge, was converted into a fruit carrier. It was an inglorious end to a historic destroyer on which four future admirals had trained.

The Navy's demands upon six different shipyards to get destroyers to the war front created some construction quality problems. The *Wickes*-class destroyers built by Bath Iron Works had a range of 3,200 nautical miles, but the same class built at Mare Island Shipyard had a range 1,000 miles less. The performance difference was due to the shipbuilders' choice of boilers and turbines.

Oddly, some of the poor performing boilers were built by Yarrow Shipbuilders of Scotland, one of the pioneering destroyer builders during the early part of the twentieth century. Yarrow-built destroyers played the leading role in Japan's winning the Russo-Japanese War of 1904-1905.

By the end of 1920, 271 destroyers had been built in the United States in just five years. Since the *Bainbridge* was commissioned in 1902, 347 American destroyers had taken to sea. Few had dropped depth charges or fired their guns at an enemy. None had fired their torpedoes—the reason for the creation of the destroyer nearly fifty years earlier—at a surface enemy.

Still, some of those peacetime destroyers made history.

In the early spring of 1919, aircraft designer Glenn Curtiss delivered to the U.S. Navy four aircraft with the unlikely name "flying boats."

Almost immediately, and perhaps unwisely, the Navy admirals decided on a dramatic test of their new air arm. Within a week of delivery, the flying boats NC (Navy Curtiss)-1, NC-3, and NC-4 were on a dramatic mission to become the first aircraft to cross the Atlantic Ocean. On the first leg of the flight, four destroyers were stationed from Cape Cod to Nova Scotia to rescue the air crews if they had to ditch in the ocean. Another four destroyers watched the route from Halifax to Newfoundland.

The third and longest leg of the mission began on May 16, 1919, when the aircraft took off from Greenland for the Azores Islands. Along the way, strung out in a line and separated by 50-mile intervals, were twenty-one destroyers, all brand-new *Wickes* class. Some ships had been commissioned for patrol just days before to aid navigation by sending out wireless signals and using their searchlights as beacons. Some ships practiced their gunnery skills by firing star shells. Thirteen more destroyers monitored the route from the Azores to Lisbon, Portugal, and five from Lisbon to Ferrol, Spain. Finally, five destroyers acted as guides for the sixth and final route from Ferrol to Plymouth, England. Fifty-three different destroyers were deployed along the six legs.

The destroyers did their jobs of lighting the way over the ocean, though only NC-4 made it all the way to the Azores, 1,200 miles from Newfoundland. Both the NC-1 and NC-3 were forced down at sea. The USS *Harding* (DD-91) found the NC-1 and rescued its crew, including its pilot, Lieutenant Commander Marc Mitscher. Mitscher would later command the USS *Hornet,* the carrier from which the B-25s under command of Army General James Doolittle flew on their April 1942 bombing raid on Japan.

Only the NC-4 finished the last three legs of the flight. The entire flight of the NC-4 took thirty-three days from Newfoundland to Great Britain as the planes often had to layover to fix mechanical problems. Despite the problems, the flying boats had accomplished something no other flyers had ever done: cross the Atlantic.

While the fifty-three Navy destroyers, with their 5,300 crewmen, had not taken the risks the fifteen fliers had, the Destroyer Men gained experience they could not have obtained in any other peacetime cruise. Officers had practiced squadron navigation, keeping their ships 50 miles apart as ordered. Wireless operators contacted each other and unseen aircraft in the sky. Gunners practiced firing star shells. Captains of new ships practiced their seakeeping skills in unpredictable mid-ocean conditions rather than along familiar coastlines. All those skills would be necessary if another war broke out.

Perhaps the person most pleased with the performance of the airplanes and the destroyers was Assistant Secretary of the Navy Franklin D. Roosevelt, who had pushed the government to participate in the adventure. As president, Roosevelt would alternately try to slow, then push, the growth of the Navy.

Once the war was over, the major powers went into a period of convoluted negotiations over disarmament, coming up with formulas for how much tonnage and how many types of warships each nation should be allowed to have. United States Secretary of State Charles Evans Hughes opened the negotiations for the Washington Naval Treaty of 1922 with the declaration that he wanted all nations to suspend battleship construction for a decade and scrap all ships under construction.

"Hughes sank in thirty-five minutes more ships than all of the admirals of the world would have sunk in a cycle of centuries," was the way one newspaper reporter summed up the opening monologue.[4]

In the treaty negotiation, most attention was on building new battle-ships. The development of destroyers was not addressed.

The Japanese felt slighted during treaty negotiations because they were not treated as a major power on the same level as Great Britain and the United States. Hughes' pipe dream of total destruction of naval fleets was ignored, but the U.S. and Great Britain were allowed to build 525,000 tons each of battleships while the Japanese were allowed only 315,000 tons. Still, the Japanese won a huge concession in the 1922 treaty when the European powers were restricted from building bases in the Pacific. That guaranteed that the Japanese would grow as a Pacific power. Still, that concession could not mollify the Japanese resentment over the tonnage limitation under which they would be operating. Their hard feelings would grow over the next decade.

Even with no wars to fight, sailors could still die under combat conditions.

On September 8, 1923, the U.S. Navy suffered the worst week in its history in terms of number of ships lost in one day.

Destroyer Squadron 11 was made up of fourteen *Clemson*-class destroyers, all based in San Diego and built by the Bethlehem Shipbuild-ing Corporation in San Francisco. None of the destroyers were war veterans as they had been commissioned just weeks before the November 1918 Armistice. Having just completed the celebration of Fleet Week, the destroyers were ordered to sail back to their home port in San Diego as if they were in wartime formation. The leading flagship would navi-gate the 427-mile trip with the rest of the division following close behind.

To reach San Diego, the ships would pass through the Santa Barbara Channel, a shipping channel plagued by unpredictable currents and constant, thick fog banks. At the northern entrance of the channel was a collection of exposed, jagged rocks that had wrecked mariners since Spanish explorers had first discovered them in the 1540s. Known today as Point Pedernales, the area was called Honda Point in the 1920s. The Spanish sailors had given the area a more descriptive name nearly four hundred years earlier—the "Devil's Jaw."

Commanding the division was Captain Edwin W. Watson, an 1895 graduate of the Naval Academy who had come on board his destroyer flagship only three months earlier. Wilson ordered a return trip cruising speed of 20 knots, well short of the destroyers' top speed of 35 knots, but still 5 knots faster than the destroyer fleet had cruised for the past several years because of budgetary orders to conserve costly fuel.

The ships lined up with the USS *Delphy* (DD-261), Watson's flagship, in the van. It was his navigator's responsibility to set the course for the tight nose-to-tail formation of fourteen destroyers.

The *Delphy's* navigator could have used wireless signals continuously being broadcast from shore installations to confirm his advancing positions. But the old salts on board these destroyers were used to using the sun, stars, and landmarks to navigate rather than this newfangled technology of unseen radio waves. Most navigators in the 1920s had been trained in dead reckoning, a time-honored sailor's skill where the navigator knows his ship's starting point, forward speed, and the coordinates of where he is supposed to make his turn. In their minds, navigation was simply a math problem.

At 9:00 p.m., the *Delphy*, under orders from Captain Watson, made a left turn into what the navigator assumed was the Santa Barbara Channel. Using a compass in an open ocean during the day rarely causes problems. Finding your way on a dark, hazy night in an ocean with deadly rocks close to the mouth of the safe channel is different.

What may have affected the navigator's calculations was an earthquake a week earlier in Japan. By this time, heavy waves had traveled across the Pacific to the California coast. The navigators, even though they saw and felt the unusual waves and currents, did not change their forward speed estimates. What they did not realize was that the waves caused by the earthquake had been pushing on the destroyers and slowing their forward progress.

Within five minutes of making the left turn, the *Delphy* ran from haze into a thick fog bank. Within seconds of running into the fog, the ship crashed into Bridge Rock.

The destroyer column had not yet entered the channel when the turn was made; a navigation error of several miles due to not accounting for the slowed forward progress. Instead of turning into the 20-mile-wide channel, the division had turned into a maze of rocks just off the California coast.

Four different destroyers are visible in this aerial photo of the disaster at Honda Point off the California coast in 1923. *NHHC photo.*

The *Delphy's* officers set off sirens to warn the following ships, but since they had been in such tight formation, it did little good. The next six destroyers all crashed into rocks just yards from a narrow beach.

The eighth destroyer, USS *Percival* (DD-298), saw the danger and backed to safety. The navigator of the ninth destroyer, USS *Somers* (DD-301), had caught the navigation error and reported to his captain who made a turn to starboard, away from the beach the navigator warned must be ahead. He still hit a reef.

The tenth destroyer, USS *Chauncey* (DD-296), glided so close to the grounded USS *Young* (DD-312), now resting on its starboard side, that the survivors clinging to the port side thought they would be rammed.

The waves pushed the *Chauncey* against the still-churning props of the *Young,* slicing her open like a can opener, exposing her to the ocean just as if she had hit one of the jagged rocks. She settled near the *Young.* The *Chauncey* was an ill-fated name for a destroyer. The first USS *Chauncey* (DD-3) had sunk off Gibraltar in 1917 when struck by a British freighter. Just six years later, the ship named to replace her had sunk too.

In less than five minutes, seven of the U.S. Navy's newest and best destroyers carrying eight hundred sailors had run aground and sunk on the California coast. Two more ran aground but were able to move off and save themselves. Five more had seen the disaster unfolding in front of them and stopped before crashing. At no other time in U.S. Naval history had so many ships and men faced such peril. This deadly battle was not against a human enemy, but the sea.

Luckily, a railroad worker saw some strange lights at sea and walked to the cliff to investigate. When he caught sight of a smashed destroyer, he rushed back home and called for help. By midnight, many of the survivors had made their way ashore, climbed a steep, 100-foot tall cliff, and were huddled around a bonfire of railroad ties.

As the Destroyer Men from several sunken ships huddled around the fire, they all started singing an adaptation of a 1922 novelty tune "Yes! We Have No Bananas," made famous on the Broadway stage by singer Eddie Cantor.

"Yes, we have no destroyers. We have no destroyers today!" the men sang. A newspaper editor observed that "they sang in true jazz style."[5]

Twenty-three men died, with the bodies of six never recovered. Twenty of those lost were on the *Young.*

At a court of inquiry two weeks after the groundings, Captain Watson accepted full responsibility, explaining that he had not believed the radio bearings. He urged the court to put the full blame on him and not on any subordinates.

Still, the Navy held formal courts martial against eleven officers. Captain Watson, the division commander, and the captain of the *Delphy* were both found guilty of culpable inefficiency and negligence. The captain of the USS *Nicholas (DD-311)* was also found guilty of negligence. The other eight officers were found not guilty, but the not guilty verdicts were "disapproved" by the Navy secretary. He wanted more blame placed on the captains and navigators who had wrecked around ten million dollars worth of United States property. Perhaps most embarrassing was that the ships were now little more than junk littering the ocean. One salvage company bought the rights to all the ships for just over a thousand dollars.

The Honda Point Disaster remains the Navy's worst night for ship losses nearly a century and a world war later.

While the Americans were finishing their World War I era *Wickes* and *Clemson* destroyer classes, the British were still building their late war V and W destroyer classes, generally considered better than other nations' destroyers. These post-1916 British classes had been redesigned from earlier pre-war classes to have just two funnels, freeing up deck space. While basically the same size as *Clemson* destroyers, the later British ships produced 3,000 more horsepower and 1 more knot. The British had added a short deck so two guns could be mounted close to each other and the rear gun could fire over the front gun. The midship gun was moved aft to duplicate the bow guns. The British had also increased the gun caliber to 4.7 inches while American destroyers still had a single 4.0-inch gun fore of the bridge, two amidships, and one aft. The British would keep this design for the next decade, making improvements such as increasing horsepower to 42,000 and speed to 37 knots in the *Amazon* class launched in 1926.

While the British and Americans were finishing their wartime designs, the Japanese were coming up with post-war designs that were bigger, faster, and better armed. The *Kamikaze* displaced 1,422 tons, had a range of 3,600 miles, and a speed of 37 knots. She mounted four 4.7-inch guns and carried three tubes of 21-inch torpedoes. Only with respect to range did the *Clemson* beat the *Kamikaze*. The *Mutsuki* class of twelve destroyers in the mid-1920s increased range to 4,000 miles and added larger 24-inch torpedoes.

After the war, Germany got revenge on the Allies when the surrendered German ships were scuttled by their own crews in June 1919 at Scapa Flow, a port in Scotland where they had been interned since the end of the war. Fifty-two of the seventy-four German warships sank, including thirty-two of fifty captured destroyer torpedo boats. Most of them were salvaged and broken up within a few years.

The British were not too upset at the Germans. Sinking the fleet kept them from the bureaucratic headache of having to divide up the ships among the winning nations. The Germans considered the sinking as saving face because the ships they constructed would never sail under another nation's flag.

Germany built twelve small destroyer torpedo boats in the mid-1920s at just over 900 tons and 280 feet long. They were sleek-looking ships with a raised forecastle that extended from the bow to the bridge.

When the 1920s ended, the world seemed to be waiting for something to happen.

CHAPTER

5

The 1930s

"A destroyer is not a likely target."

With the new decade of the 1930s came a worldwide depression and a new push for disarmament. President Herbert Hoover proclaimed: "[The nation has] the largest military budget of any nation in the world today and at a time when there is less real danger of extensive disturbance of peace than at any time in more than a half century."[1]

The London Naval Treaty of 1930 between the United Kingdom, Japan, France, Italy, and the United States was yet another agreement to prevent an arms race amongst these winners of the "war to end all wars." Even though war gamers for both the U.S. and Japan were expecting a future war in the Pacific, both sides agreed to limit the size of their fleets, including destroyers. According to the treaty, destroyers could be no larger than 1,850 tons and could mount no guns larger than 5 inches.

To the dismay of naval planners, Hoover used the treaty to scuttle any plans to modernize the U.S. fleet, saying the London Treaty "has been one of the most potent factors in eliminating friction between ourselves and Japan."[2]

At the same time, the treaty required the U.S. Navy to reduce its number of destroyers. Cleverly, it seems, out of 111 destroyers in commission for scrapping, the Navy chose forty-six that had been identified as having less than satisfactory range. All these destroyers were built by Bethlehem Steel in the late war rush with British-designed Yarrow boilers, which never matched their expected performance specifications. In their place, the Navy recommissioned some better performing destroyers. In effect, the Navy was forced by treaty to reduce its destroyer fleet by one-third, but the destroyers that remained were the best performers.

Still, these ships were now more than fifteen years old in design and not comparable to the destroyers of other navies. Curiously, it was the demands of the peace activists to reduce the size of the U.S. Navy that led to a new round of peacetime modernization of the destroyer class. To his credit, Hoover did not attempt to cancel the already approved capital outlay even though he did not want to modernize a Navy he thought was useless in peacetime.

Eight new destroyers authorized in 1930 would officially be called "1,500-tonners," named after the tonnage limit as prescribed by the London Treaty. These were a step-up in size compared to the previous *Clemson* class, which came in at 1,215 tons.

The first of this new design class was the USS *Farragut* (DD-348), designed by Bethlehem Steel. The new 1,500-ton class measured 341 feet long (compared to the *Clemson* class at 314 feet long), with a beam of 34 feet (compared to the *Clemson's* 30 feet). The draft was 10 feet, one foot more than the *Clemson* class. The boilers were Bethlehem's own design, after the debacle of having used the poor performing Yarrow boilers in the construction of the *Wickes* class destroyers. The four funnels that had given rise to the fond nicknames "four stackers" and "four pipers" were now down to two thanks to an improved boiler design. The older *Clemson* could muster 27,600 horsepower while the new *Farragut* could push out nearly 43,000 horsepower.

The speed should be 36 knots with a range of 6,000 miles. The foredeck would be raised again so two guns could be mounted with the number two gun firing over the gun on the deck. This was the first time the United States had chosen this raised platform design for its gun placement, now standard with the British and Japanese.

USS *Farragut* leads a division. *NHHC photo.*

Most importantly, the *Farragut's* guns were now 5 inches in diameter, up from the 3-inch guns of the first destroyers commissioned and the 4-inch guns mounted on the 1,000-tonners and following flush deckers and four stackers. For the first time, the gun crews on the two forward guns would be somewhat protected from ocean waves and enemy fire in semi-enclosed mounts, a safer design than the open mounts with splinter shields found in older destroyers. The three guns aft of the bridge were still open to the elements, demonstrating the concern Navy designers had for topside weight.

The standard gun on a destroyer was now five inches in diameter with a barrel length of 190 inches, or 38 calibers. A caliber in this sense was determined by the formula: barrel length in inches divided by bore diameter in inches (190 inches divided by 5 inches equals 38 caliber), making this a 5-inch, 38 caliber gun. It fired a 55-pound shell about 10 miles. In contrast, the Japanese 5-inch naval gun was almost 57 inches longer, making it a 5-inch, 50 caliber gun. That longer barrel allowed its gunners to fire its 51-pound shell more than 11 miles, one mile further than the American 5-inch gun could fire its 55-pound shell. Still, the

American 5-inch gun could be loaded faster thanks to mechanization of the loading process.

For the first time, the guns were now "dual-purpose" guns, meaning they could fire at both surface targets and incoming attacking aircraft. All previous American destroyers had relied on antiquated 3-inch anti-aircraft guns to defend themselves from air attack. No German aircraft had ever fired at an American destroyer in World War I, but Navy designers were growing concerned about the technological advances of military aircraft. Still, destroyer designers underestimated the future danger of attack from the air.

The Navy planners were giddy with delight over the new destroyer design, the first completely new destroyer class in more than ten years. Speed had increased by 3 knots, the armament was now on a par with that of other nations, the guns would be supplied with ammunition by power hoists, and the destroyers' range had increased by 1,000 miles.

The old salts, sailors, and admirals alike, who had grown up sailing on the four stackers, 1,000-tonners, and flivvers, were not impressed with the 1,500-tonners. They gave them a nickname not meant to be complimentary or descriptive. They referred to the *Farragut* and the following classes of American destroyers commissioned in the 1930s as "Goldplaters." This derisive term was meant to suggest that the new destroyers were fancy, but not superior to the simpler design that had served the Navy well for the past fifteen years.

The British destroyers in the early 1930s were the *C* and *D* classes, followed naturally by the *E* and *F* classes, displacing around 1,375 tons. They produced 36,000 horsepower and were able to reach 36 knots, considerably less than the American *Farragut* class. For now, the British were stuck improving on World War I designs. It would be another few years before they would come up with a completely new destroyer.

It was not until 1934 that Germany produced a true modern destroyer, shifting their emphasis from the smaller torpedo boats they had previously favored. Known simply as the *1934* type, only four ships were built. They were 390 feet long, displacing 2,171 tons; larger than anything the Americans or British were building. The design proved to be faulty, resulting in constant machinery breakdowns. They were also top heavy, requiring the ship to keep thirty percent of her fuel as ballast. That limited range to just 1,900 miles, less than a third of what the *Farragut* could sail. Two years later, another thirteen destroyers of a slightly modified version were built. They were not much better.

It was the Japanese who were designing the most impressive destroyers in the late 1920s and 1930s. Japan had agreed to build fewer ships than the British and Americans in the Washington Naval Conference of 1920, but the treatment of their nation on the international stage as a second class power rankled their military. By the mid-1930s, Japan had abandoned all thoughts of participating in future arms limitation treaties. Japan was particularly interested in expanding its aircraft carrier and submarine fleets.

Japan's *Fubuki*, lead of its class in 1928, surprised and frightened the U.S. Navy with its large size. *National Archives photo.*

Since the 1920s, Japan and the United States had been assuming they would face each other in the Pacific. Japan's war planners saw the vast Pacific Ocean as a war asset. It adopted a "strike south" plan hinged on destroying or capturing American, British, French, and

Dutch interests in the Pacific in overwhelming attacks, leaving no footholds that would allow those forces to reinvade and reinforce. Once all regional enemy forces were destroyed, Japanese forces would then extend east, building bases from which to attack enemies making the long ocean crossing.

For the plan to work, Japan needed to build ships to overwhelm and sink whatever enemy ships lay in their path. That type of destroyer came in the late 1920s with the *Fubuki* class, followed in rapid succession in the mid-30s by the *Akatsuki, Hatsuharu, Shiratsuyu, Asashio,* and *Kagero* classes. The *Fubuki* was 388 feet long with a displacement of nearly 1,750 tons, 200 more than the *Farragut*. The *Fubuki* also produced nearly 50,000 horsepower, 7,000 more than the *Farragut* which was first commissioned in 1933, six years after the *Fubuki*. The *Fubuki* class had a range of 5,000 miles, 1,000 miles less than the *Farragut*.

Most disturbing to the other nations' war planners was the Japanese destroyer's armament. The *Fubuki* mounted six 5-inch guns in three twin-gun weatherproof gun houses, with two of those mounts aft of the bridge and one forward of the bridge. The *Fubuki* was the first destroyer class of any nation to fully protect her gun crews from both salt spray and steel splinters.

She also had nine torpedo tubes for 24-inch torpedoes, with the ability to reload each tube for a total of eighteen torpedoes. That compared to a total complement of eight 21-inch torpedoes carried by the *Farragut*. Those tubes could not be reloaded. In an era when torpedoes were still expected to be a destroyer's long-range weapon, the newest American destroyer had fewer than half the torpedoes of a Japanese destroyer six years older.

After the *Fubuki*, the largest destroyer of its time to enter service, the Japanese retreated somewhat to 1,680 tons for the following *Akatsuki* and 1,490-ton *Hatsuharu* classes, launched in 1932 and 1933 respectively. In 1935, a typhoon severely damaged many Japanese ships while on maneuvers, creating a round of redesign and modifications making these latest destroyer models more stable and seaworthy. The Allied fleets in the Pacific would bear the brunt of those nature-inspired redesigns for the first two years of the coming war.

Partially in response to the Japanese super destroyers and partly because the 1930 London Treaty allowed it, the U.S. laid down eight 1,850-ton destroyers in 1933 and 1934 called the *Porter*-class destroyer leader. For the first time, the Navy mounted eight 5-inch guns in fully enclosed twin mounts. However, that increase in firepower per mount was somewhat offset by their being single-purpose guns meant only for ship-to-ship or ship-to-shore shelling. While the single-gun 5-inch mounts of the *Farragut* class could also elevate high to defend against aircraft, the twin-gun 5-inch mounts of the *Porters* could elevate no higher than 35 degrees. It would be another few years before naval designers came up with the technology to mount dual-purpose 5-inch guns in twin mounts.

The *Porters* were 381 feet long with a beam of 37 feet and a draft of 13 feet. They produced 50,000 horsepower with a range of 6,500 miles, 1,400 miles more than the *Fubuki*. The class still had just eight 21-inch torpedo tubes, but they could be reloaded.

In 1934, the U.S. Navy began taking orders for sixteen new destroyers headed by the USS *Mahan* (DD-364), which added four torpedo tubes for a total of twelve 21-inch torpedoes. Since the Navy had already exhausted its allotment of destroyer leaders with the *Porter* class according to the 1930 treaty, the *Mahan*-class destroyers were smaller at 341 feet and 1,500 tons. Still, thanks to engineering advances in turbines, the *Mahans* produced 50,000 horsepower and were rated at 36 knots. Gone, however, were the twin 5-inch single purpose guns in fully enclosed mounts that the *Porters* had. Each *Mahan* had five 5-inch dual- purpose guns in semi-enclosed mounts. Anti-aircraft protection was still being ignored as planners gave her only four .50 caliber machine guns. Those would prove inadequate soon enough.

USS *Mahan* (DD-364) was the lead of its Goldplater class. *NHHC photo.*

Next year brought an improvement in the *Mahan* class with the two-ship class headed by the USS *Dunlap* (DD-384), which introduced improved shell handling and a fully enclosed gun mount on the forward guns, though the aft guns would still be protected by splinter shields.

After *Dunlap* came the four-ship class of the USS *Gridley* (DD-380), a 340-foot-long class with greatly improved high pressure boilers. That space-saving allowed these destroyers to mount sixteen torpedo tubes for 21-inch torpedoes—the most any American destroyer would ever mount. The *Gridleys* had a range of nearly 7,500 miles and produced 50,000 horsepower. By this time in the 1930s, American ship engine designers were surpassing all other navies in producing efficient power plants. This class needed just one smokestack tied to all the boilers. Only twenty years earlier, most of the American destroyers needed four stacks.

In 1936, the U.S. fulfilled its treaty-sanctioned thirteen destroyer leaders with the five ships based on the USS *Somers* (DD-381). They were similar to the *Porters*, weighing 1,840 tons and mounting eight single-purpose 5-inch guns in twin-gun mounts. The *Somers* class added two

1-inch anti-aircraft cannons, but those would soon prove inadequate and eventually be replaced. The class could carry twelve torpedoes.

The 1936 London Treaty was supposed to further limit the building of naval fleets through 1942, but when Japan refused to participate, it must have given the other nations pause about the coming future. Even the signers of the treaty left themselves plenty of options to ignore the provisions in the treaty they were signing. For instance, battleships were supposed to be limited to 14-inch guns, but the United States started construction of two battleships with 16-inch guns. The 1936 treaty allowed the larger guns under an "escalator clause" because Japan, which had signed the 1930 treaty, had refused to participate in the second treaty. Battleships were supposedly limited to 35,000 tons displacement in the 1936 treaty, but were soon ballooning to 45,000 tons.

Neither the 1930 nor the 1936 treaties had much effect on the design and construction of destroyers other than keeping displacement of destroyer leaders below 1,850 tons. Naval destroyer designers could live with that displacement.

Starting in 1936 came the last of the 1,500-ton weight destroyers for the United States with the manufacture of ten ships based on the USS *Benham* (DD-397). These destroyers looked like the *Gridley* class, but internally, they were using three boilers operating at higher pounds per square inch instead of the four boilers of the *Gridleys*. The *Benham* class kept the sixteen torpedo tubes first placed on the *Gridleys*.

The last class of American destroyers authorized and commissioned before the U.S. entered World War II was led by the USS *Sims* (DD-409). Coming in at 1,570 tons, the twelve destroyers were the last class to have all the firerooms in one location, which had always made that area vulnerable in the event of a torpedo hit. Later designs would split the fireroom into two locations in hopes that if one fireroom were hit, the second could continue to operate. The *Sims* class would finally enclose all 5-inch gun mounts.

The improvements made in American destroyers, from the last of the four stackers, the USS *Pruitt* (DD-347) commissioned in 1920, to the last of the *Sims* class, the USS *Buck* (DD-420) in 1939, was a testament to American engineering. The *Pruitt* had a range of 4,900 miles and 26,500 horsepower, a top speed of 35 knots, and main armament of four 4-inch guns and twelve 21-inch torpedo tubes. Just twenty years later, the *Buck* could cruise more than 6,500 miles with 50,000 horsepower and mounted five dual-purpose 5-inch guns in enclosed mounts that could turn faster than the old 4-inch guns that were open to the elements. Speed had increased only 2 knots with the modern destroyer, but the creature comforts for the sailors were much improved.

Following the *Sims* were three classes that started construction in 1939 and continued construction through the mid-war years, even though the newer designed *Fletchers* were also under construction. The *Benson, Bristol,* and *Gleaves* classes were all closely matched, weighing 1,620 tons, mounting five 5-inch guns, and carrying up to ten torpedo tubes. Ninety-six versions of these three classes would enter service between 1940 and 1943.

Curiously, naval designers still did not believe destroyers would become the targets of enemy aircraft as even the newest models were still limited to four .50 caliber machine guns. The Bureau on Construction Repair even argued against the need for dual-purpose guns on destroyers.

"Due to its small size and great maneuverability, a destroyer is not a likely target for high altitude bombers, and direct gunfire defense for it against these bombers would not be necessary. Against dive bombers the machine gun is a better defense," reads a 1933 report from the Board of Construction & Review.[3]

The Board wanted to save the weight of dual-purpose 5-inch guns so the destroyer could carry more torpedoes.

The Chief of Naval Operations, Admiral William Pratt, did not like the idea of limiting gun power to the torpedo. Though the destroyer as a ship type had been created to launch torpedoes against enemy capital ships, Pratt had other ideas.

With Japan clearly in mind, Pratt wrote in response to the Bureau of Construction & Review report: "The most probable campaign of war which will confront this nation will include an overseas operation, conducted at a distance from home waters....our fleet will be constantly at sea, constantly exposed to torpedo attack, and at a greater distance from adequate docking and repair facilities...The CNO cannot recommend any design of destroyer which subordinates the gun to the torpedo...he wants our destroyers to have an even better chance of sinking enemy destroyers than they have of destroying our own."[4]

One of the advantages the Navy would give its ships was a means to find its enemies before they came into sight.

In 1937, the U.S. Navy began experimenting with radar (radio detection and ranging) with the installation of search radar on the USS *Leary* (DD-158). The following year in 1938, the battleship USS *New York* (BB-34) installed a working model and engaged in exercises where some destroyers made a night torpedo run at the battleship. The future radar operators watched as the destroyers advanced in the darkness. At 5,000 yards, the battleship switched on its searchlight and spotted the attacking destroyers. In one exercise, radar had proven itself.

As new American destroyers were commissioned each year, Navy planners wisely began to look at the older destroyers with the intention of modifying them for other uses rather than scrapping them.

The U.S. Marines were particularly interested in finding ways to better deploy their men who were, after all, supposed to be amphibious assault troops. In 1938, the Marines settled on a craft called the "Eureka" boat as the ideal means of landing their men ashore. The Eureka was developed by a Louisiana boat builder, Andrew Jackson Higgins, who catered to the lumber and oil industries which needed shallow-draft. Once the war began and it was learned that the Japanese used a landing craft with a bow ramp that could be lowered, Higgins modified the Eureka into what would be called the LCVP (Landing Craft, Vehicle, Personnel), more commonly called the "Higgins" boat. The Higgins boat could carry thirty-six men or a Jeep right onto a beach. The ramp could be lowered, the men disembarked, and the boat could be on its way back to ships for another load within a few minutes.

On February 1, 1939, the USS *Manley* (DD-74), a *Caldwell*-class destroyer commissioned in October 1916, reentered service as *APD-1*, the Navy's first fast attack transport. This was more than a figurative second chance at life for the *Manley*. During World War I, she had caught fire after a collision with a British ship, resulting in the second worst loss of life on a wartime American destroyer. Only the heroic actions of her crew had saved the ship from exploding.

The modifications were relatively simple. The torpedo mounts amidships were removed, leaving deck space to add derricks for two landing craft on both sides. Below decks, two boilers were removed, creating living space for around two hundred Marines, but the removal of the boilers also reduced the ship's speed from 36 knots to 25 knots. The destroyer's standard 4-inch guns were replaced with rapid-firing 3-inch guns. Once the Marines demonstrated how quickly they could load into their landing craft from a short net draped over the side of the destroyer, thirty-one other World War I era destroyers, all *Wickes* and *Clemson* classes, were modified to carry infantrymen.

At the same time the Marines were considering the destroyers, so too were Navy aviators.

Fourteen *Clemson*-class destroyers were modified in the late 1930s into seaplane tenders (AVD) by removing two boilers, two stacks, anti-aircraft guns, and torpedo tubes. Instead of adding living space, the Navy added fuel tanks holding up to 50,000 gallons of aviation fuel. The seaplanes serviced would primarily be PBY Catalinas, which would play major roles in flying long-range aerial patrols.

In 1939, following the start of the war in Europe, the Navy began converting another seventeen *Clemson* and *Wickes* destroyers into high-speed minesweepers (DMS). Since the minesweeping equipment was so heavy, only one boiler was removed, leaving the four pipers with three stacks instead of their signature four. While many minesweepers were adapted from other types of ships, and others were purpose-built, the DMS flush-decker destroyers kept their stinging guns should any enemy ship challenge them on the ocean.

If destroyers could find mines, they could also lay them. By 1939, fourteen more *Clemson*-class destroyers were modified into destroyer minelayers (DM) to carry up to eighty mines. Little modification was necessary other than removing the torpedo tubes and substituting them with racks of mines.

Seventy-seven *Wickes* and *Clemson*-class destroyers, twenty-year-old ships effectively obsolete by 1941, would be converted to continue serving their country during World War II.

The British designed what was probably their best destroyer in 1937— the *Tribal* class. At 1,824 tons and 377 feet long with a beam of 36 feet, the *Tribal* classes produced only 44,000 horsepower, but could make 36 knots with a range of 5,700 miles. They were armed with four enclosed mounts holding twin 4.7-inch guns. While the Americans and Japanese were still loading up on torpedoes, the *Tribal* had only a single four tube launcher for 21-inch torpedoes. Twenty-seven *Tribals* would be built from 1937 through 1945.

Free of having to comply with any treaties, the Japanese began designing bigger and better armed destroyers in 1937 with the *Asashio* class, which came in at 1,961 tons and 388 feet long compared to the United States' largest destroyer at the time, the USS *Sims* class, at 1,570 tons. The ten destroyers of the *Asashio* class carried six 5-inch guns in three twin gun houses. It also carried eight torpedo tubes with reloading capability for 24-inch torpedoes. This was the first Japanese class destroyer with sonar, though their war planners were still reluctant to install radar.

The *Asashio* class was equipped with the latest in torpedo technology. The Japanese had perfected oxygen as a fuel oxidizer, substituting it for the compressed air used by most other nations. The practical effect of using oxygen was the Japanese 24-inch Type 93 torpedo, which left little wake. It was later dubbed the "Long Lance" by an American historian. An incoming torpedo of this type was almost impossible for lookouts to see on the ocean since carbon dioxide, the byproduct of oxidizing the fuel, was absorbed into the sea water.

With a maximum range of 22 miles and a normal range of 13 miles, the Type 93 torpedo's top speed of 50 knots gave the Japanese destroyers a distinct—if theoretical—advantage over their expected enemy, the United States. Modern American destroyers carried the 21-inch Mark 15 torpedo with an effective range of 3.5 miles, a maximum range of 8.5 miles, and a standard speed of 26 knots. The Type 93's warhead was over 1,000 pounds, while the Mark 15 carried a warhead of 825 pounds.

Coming along behind the *Asashio* class in 1939 was the *Kagero* class at 2,033 tons and 389 feet long. The nineteen ships of this class also carried the now standard six 5-inch guns and sixteen Type 93 torpedoes fired from eight torpedo tubes. Larger and better armed than any American destroyer, it lacked only one weapon the American destroyers now routinely employed: radar.

In the spring of 1939, the world still seemed to be waiting for something to happen.

CHAPTER

6

Atlantic Theater
1939-1941

"Keep on engaging the enemy."

When Japan attacked and sank the USS *Panay,* a river gunboat, on the Yangtze River in China on December 12, 1937, President Roosevelt treated the deaths of three U.S. Navy crewmen and the wounding of forty-three others as an unfortunate incident. The president accepted Japan's explanation that pilots who bombed the gunboat mistook the three American flags on the boat for Chinese flags.

Still, Roosevelt realized he had to prepare for a potential war. Within a few days of the *Panay* attack, Roosevelt sent an officer to Great Britain to begin talks about cooperation on the oceans. The diplomat later remembered the instructions the president had given him: "We had to make preliminary arrangements to explore what could be done for communicating with each other, for establishing liaison, intelligence, and other things, so if war did come we would not be floundering around for months until we got it together."[1]

Roosevelt, notorious for being unfocused when it came to making decisions, had taken one small step in supporting Great Britain. However insignificant it was to send one aide to London with a vague message of cooperation, it was a major step forward when compared to the months

71

before entering World War I when Navy planners were speculating whether the United States could fight a third war against the British instead of a first one with the Germans.

Just as in World War I, the U.S. government in the late 1930s turned to its Navy to plan for a coming war.

The Great Depression had a silver lining: the U.S. Navy now had experienced seamen. Reenlistment rates were nearly eighty percent as men stayed in the service because it was steady work.

That did not mean they were ready to fight a war. Only one U.S. destroyer had sunk a U-boat during World War I. Now, twenty years later, gunnery practice in the Great Depression was limited due to the prohibitive cost of ammunition. When American destroyers practiced finding and sinking friendly submarines, they rarely succeeded because there were too few men trained in using sonar, a device still in experimental stages in 1937.

As the Nazis gained political power in Europe and the Japanese gained vast territory in the Far East, Roosevelt grew more nervous. In the fall of 1938, he created the Atlantic Squadron of seven cruisers and seven destroyers "to discover and turn back a sudden raid into the Caribbean."[2]

A year later, within days of Germany invading Poland, starting the war, Roosevelt began what he called "Neutrality Patrols." The deployment of destroyers to patrol off the East Coast was ordered so quickly that some ships put to sea with half their normal wartime complement of 106 men. Thirteen of the seventeen destroyers ordered on patrol didn't have torpedoes and half lacked machine guns. All of the destroyers deployed in the Atlantic in 1938 were old four stackers since most of the new Goldplaters had been assigned to Pacific Ocean ports in anticipation of fighting the Japanese.

The president's idea of a neutrality zone was a line 1,000 miles east of the major port of Charleston, South Carolina. It was an impossibly large area for a small force of ships to patrol, but Neutrality Patrols would take on an added air of necessity for the United States after

Germany invaded Poland on September 1, 1939. Great Britain and France reacted by declaring war on Germany.

The United States still saw itself as a neutral country, but made it clear that any belligerent ships from any country were not welcome in the western hemisphere. It was an empty threat for now; Great Britain was focused on forcing German ships to stay in their ports, and Germany did not want to provoke the United States into entering the war on the side of the British and French.

It did not take long before British destroyers and an old British battleship proved their worth in the new war. At the same time, the British ships proved how thoroughly inadequate the Kriegsmarine—the German surface navy—was, even as its army was smashing through Europe.

The fault of the German Navy's weakness lay with one man. In the years prior to 1939, German Fuhrer Adolf Hitler prioritized the building up of his army and air force while neglecting to give equal regard to his navy. Germany had built several powerful "pocket battleships" like the *Bismarck,* and was continually developing better, longer-ranging submarines, but Hitler saw little need to design and construct good and plentiful cruisers and destroyers.

That shortsightedness would embarrass Hitler early in the war.

On March 1, 1940, Hitler ordered an invasion of Norway to protect access to iron ore being mined for Germany in northern Sweden. During the winter, much of the sea route from Sweden to Germany was clogged with ice, but a railroad ran from southern Sweden to the ice-free port of Narvik, Norway. Hitler's war planners convinced him that if Narvik were captured and held, Germany would have year-round access to the iron ore. Hitler committed ten German destroyers built in 1934 and 1936 to deliver an invasion force to capture Norway.

On April 9, 1940, the German force sailed into Vestfjord, Norway, and its destroyers made short work of the two old Norwegian vessels at the Narvik docks with two virtually point blank salvos of torpedoes. Nearly three hundred Norwegian sailors died without doing any damage to the German destroyers. The German destroyers took the town without loss. They then moored to wait for refueling from a single tanker traveling with them.

On April 10, the day after Germany's successful taking of Narvik, Great Britain's 2nd Destroyer Flotilla of one *Grenville* class and four *H-Class* destroyers entered the mouth of Vestfjord under the cover of a blinding snowstorm.

This would be the first test of German destroyers against British destroyers in more than twenty years. All of the ships on both sides were less than four years old, and it would be the first combat any of their crews had seen.

On paper, the Germans had all of the advantages. The ten German destroyers were *Type 34* and *Type 36* classes, ranging between 2,171 tons to 2,411 tons, and 390 to 410 feet long. The British flagship, HMS *Hardy* (H-87), weighed 1,465 tons, but the other four British destroyers facing the German destroyers were only 1,340 tons and 323 feet long. The German destroyers also had five 5-inch guns each compared to each *H*-class destroyer armed with four 4.7-inch guns. Each destroyer could lay mines, but none were fitted with depth charge racks.

In reality, the German destroyer classes were mechanically unsound in the engine compartment. Because their steam turbines operated at extremely high pounds per square inch pressures, they suffered constant failures of valves, seals, and steam tubes—critical design flaws that did not become evident until the war started. They also had short ranges, less than 2,000 miles compared to the *H*-class, with a range of 5,500 miles. Finally, their designers had designed them for speed, but not for extended battles. The destroyers had little storage space for ammunition.

The British commander eased toward Narvik, not knowing his five ships were outnumbered two-to-one. The British approached as silently as possible in a line at 4:30 a.m., with torpedo tubes pointed to starboard and port, waiting to see targets.

Lieutenant G.R. Heppel, on board the flagship HMS *Hardy,* spotted the docked destroyers amid some cargo ships and said to his commander,

Captain Bernard Warburton-Lee, "There's a torpedo target like I've never seen in my life."[3]

Warburton-Lee calmly replied, "Well, get on with it then."

The *Wilhelm Heidkamp's* (Z-21) stern was blown off when the first torpedo hit its aft magazine. Among the eighty German sailors killed in the blast was the flotilla commander, a loss that may have slowed the regimented German response to the attack as subordinate officers waited for orders that never came.

Warburton-Lee then ordered more power to his engines, which threw off the aim of Heppel, who missed all of the remaining ships with his second salvo of torpedoes. The second British destroyer in line, the HMS *Hunter* (H-35), torpedoed the German destroyer *Anton Schmitt* (Z-22) before following the *Hardy* out of the harbor.

That left the HMS *Havock* (H-43) to take its turn. Its three torpedo salvos hit two merchant ships and the *Anton Schmitt* again. The second explosion caused that destroyer to heel over onto a third one, the *Herman Kunne* (Z19). That destroyer's engines seized from the shock of the close hit on the other destroyer. As the *Havock* turned to leave, a German sentry on board a merchant ship emptied his revolver at the bridge of the *Havock*. He was the first German to answer the attack with any sort of return fire.

Now came the HMS *Hotspur* (H-01) and HMS *Hostile* (H-55) firing into the harbor now choked with smoke from burning ships. Remarkably, one German ship had been missed by all of the torpedoes and gunfire—the tanker.

In less than an hour, the five British destroyers had sunk eleven merchant ships and two German destroyers, and had heavily damaged another destroyer. None of the attacking force had suffered so much as a scratch as they turned to leave and head for the open ocean.

What the British did not know was that five other German destroyers were not docked at Narvik. Those ships were now belatedly streaming toward the action.

The British destroyers ran first into three German destroyers coming in from the northeast, then another two from the west. Luckily for the British, the three Germans coming from the northeast were low on fuel and their leader chose not to directly engage. He turned away rather than fight, leaving two fresh and fully fueled Germans.

At first, Warburton-Lee mistook the incoming pair of large German destroyers for two British cruisers he thought were coming to help. It was an understandable mistake as Warburton-Lee had no idea any Germans were in front of him, and the oncoming ships were so much larger than his own.

German destroyers like the *George Thiele* (Z2) were plagued with fuel-thirsty engines and poor ammunition storage. The *George Thiele* was sunk at the Battle of Narvik in 1940. *NHHC photo.*

When the two German destroyers swung broadside to his leading ship, Warburton-Lee finally realized his mistake. Still, he thought he was engaging at least one German cruiser because the German destroyers were 75 feet longer than his own ship and nearly 1,000 tons heavier.

Warburton-Lee signaled to the other British destroyers at nearly 6:00 a.m. to "keep on engaging the enemy," an oddly calm signal for a flotilla commander with fresh enemies in front and behind him.

With its fourth salvo, the German destroyer *George Thiele* (Z-2) hit the bridge of the *Hardy*, wounding nearly everyone there, including

Warburton-Lee. Despite his wounds, the ship's paymaster scrambled from the wrecked bridge to the wheelhouse, where he was able to steer the burning ship onto the shore so the bulk of its crew could abandon ship. Warburton-Lee would be the first person posthumously awarded the Victoria Cross in World War II.

The *Havock* now attacked the *George Thiele*, hitting it in the forward boiler near its ammo bunker. Still, the *George Thiele* fought on, hitting the *Hunter* with a torpedo and some shellfire, setting her on fire. Coming behind was the *Hotspur*, which rammed the *Hunter* in the confusion and smoke. As the *Hotspur* backed away, the *Hunter* capsized, but not before her one operating gun got off one more angry round at the *George Thiele*. As the *Hotspur* passed by the remaining German destroyer—the *Bernd von Arnim* (Z11)—the British destroyer got off five shell hits, which damaged the German destroyer's boiler. The other three German destroyers, which had not fired a shot, chose not to engage the three badly damaged British destroyers as German naval doctrine was to preserve one's ship if a battle seemed lost or nearly over.

The British Admiralty had lost two destroyers and three others were badly damaged, but the lure of demolishing the surviving German destroyers was great. Three days later, a larger force of nine destroyers and the old battleship HMS *Warspite* (03) arrived at the mouth of the fjord. Sending a battleship with a draft of 33 feet into narrow, shallow waters was a risk, but the British might have considered the old veteran of the Battle of Jutland expendable as she was commissioned in 1913 and now obsolete compared to the newer German cruisers and battleships. Instead of attacking at night, the British came in full daylight since they were also backed by airplanes from the aircraft carrier HMS *Furious* (47).

This time, the Germans had two U-boats on guard, but one was sunk by an airplane launched from the *Warspite*, and another submarine ran aground on a rock ledge. With the U-boats sidelined and the German destroyers low on fuel and ammo and backed into a port with only one way out to the open ocean, the British expected a complete victory—something they had failed to achieve three days earlier.

One British officer described the hour-long battle "like shelling peas." The *Warspite* had plenty of time to bring her 15-inch guns to bear on the German destroyers, as her guns had a range of 33,000 yards compared to the German destroyers' 5-inch guns with ranges of 19,000 yards. The eight German destroyers that survived the first Battle of Narvik three days earlier were either sunk by British gunfire or scuttled by their own crews. Three British destroyers were damaged but able to withdraw.

Strategically, the two naval battles meant little as the British were unprepared to follow up with a ground invasion of Norway. Still, it was a bright spot for the United Kingdom; a stunning defeat of the German Navy just six months after the German Army had rolled into Poland to begin the war. Of the twenty-two German destroyers in its entire fleet in 1940, ten of them were sunk in the course of three days at the loss of only two British destroyers.

The crew of the old *Warspite*, which had been hit 150 times at the Battle of Jutland, had proved that old battleships still could fight. The crews of the new British destroyers proved their ship designs were rugged enough to stay afloat after many German 5-inch gun hits. The British also now knew that German destroyers were poorly designed with fuel-thirsty engines and too little ammunition storage, meaning they would not be a formidable force on the open ocean. Even the British naval flyers had reason to be proud of the battle. A biplane from the *Warspite* had sunk a U-boat; the first time in the war an aircraft had sunk a submarine.

The news of Great Britain's thrashing of Germany's destroyers at Narvik did not impress the United States. Remarkably, in the spring of 1940, President Roosevelt killed a bill before Congress that would have increased the nation's shipbuilding. On one hand, the president was promising the British he would work with them on the seas, while on the other, he was crippling his own Navy's ability to do just that.

It took the surrender of France before the president realized that a German threat could exist to the United States. Once again, he radically changed his mind, and supported, however lukewarmly, the

Two-Ocean Navy Act of July 1940, which called for the expansion of the fleet by seventy percent. A total of 115 destroyers were approved for construction.

With the fall of France in mid-June, Great Britain now stood alone facing Germany. Prime Minister Winston Churchill made it clear to President Roosevelt that the British needed help right away.

By the summer of 1940, Roosevelt and Churchill had agreed on a plan to send fifty 1918-era *Caldwell, Wickes,* and *Clemson*-class destroyers to Great Britain in exchange for ninety-nine year leases of British ports in the Caribbean. The president dismissed the pacifists in Congress by explaining that any threat to the Caribbean would be a violation of the Monroe Doctrine. It was a clear violation of the president's pledge to his own citizens to stay neutral in the European conflict, but the Destroyers for Bases Agreement went into effect in September 1940.

Most of the American destroyers, with their now antiquated 4-inch, single-purpose guns and twelve 21-inch torpedo tubes, had not been on the ocean in years. Still, even though the British had scores of more modern destroyers in service, the addition of fifty more ships to patrol home waters was welcome.

The United States' generosity in giving away fifty destroyers may not have been as generous as it seemed. One American officer, knowledgeable about the destroyers' poor condition after being laid up for so long, said: "The British will go bankrupt trying to keep those boats in oil."[4]

The British renamed the new ships "*Town* class" after towns that shared the same name in both Great Britain and the United States. Forty-three went across the Atlantic, with seven joining the Canadian Navy. While getting the ships was popular with the British public, not all British seamen who were assigned to them were happy. The ships wallowed in the heavy seas common in the North Atlantic were fuel-thirsty compared to modern British destroyers, took very wide turns for their relatively small size, and lacked sonar. The seamen even complained about the American mattresses in the crew quarters, preferring their centuries-old tradition of setting up hammocks.

Within a month of the Destroyers for Bases Agreement, Hitler signed the Tripartite Pact of 1940, which sealed the understanding that Japan would help Germany by keeping the Americans busy in the Far East should war come between Germany and the United States.

In January 1941, the British and Americans held meetings planning for a mutual defense. One American admiral wrote to his fleet commanders: "...our entry into the war now seems to be when and not whether."[5]

By March, the ships in the Neutrality Patrol were pulled back into port from their far-flung, boring patrols to be refitted and organized into task forces. In October 1938, the Atlantic Squadron had included thirty-five old four stacker destroyers. Just two and a half years later in April 1941, the Atlantic Squadron had 159 ships, including seventy-eight destroyers. The majority of those destroyers were now Goldplaters built in the 1930s.

Though large in size, the Atlantic Squadron was not ready for combat. The destroyer crews had little experience in finding and sinking submarines. Their gun crews had not practiced. Their commanding admiral created their working motto when he told them: "We must do what we can with what we have."[6]

It was on April 11, 1941 that one destroyer did what it could with what it had. The incident could have incited America's entry into the war eight months sooner had anything really happened.

The USS *Niblack* (DD-424), a *Gleaves* class, had left Halifax, Nova Scotia, on April 7 with the mission of dropping off naval experts in Iceland to see if the island could be used as a naval base. On April 10, the *Niblack* heard a distress signal from a Dutch freighter that had been torpedoed. By 8:00 a.m., the survivors were on board when the sonarman heard what sounded like a submarine moving toward them. Commander Dennis Ryan dropped three depth charges. No oil slick came to the surface.

Commander Ryan broke off the attack "with a curious mixture of disappointment and relief," he wrote in his deck log.[7]

No U-boat commander reported being attacked on that day, so the inexperienced sonarman likely misidentified a whale or school of fish.

When the *Niblack* returned from its scouting mission to Iceland, Ryan reported the supposed contact to his commander. That officer chose not to report the supposed contact to his superiors considering nothing had happened other than that three depth charges had been dumped off the back of the destroyer. No debris had surfaced, so no one could tell if a submarine had been destroyed or damaged.

Ship crews talk. By summer, a pair of newspaper columnists speculated that President Roosevelt had staged the *Niblack* incident to create an excuse for entering the war. The president, who had not heard about the depth charging since his staff admirals had not heard about it, furiously denied the implication. Commander Ryan was now forced to report directly to the Chief of Naval Operations about his depth charge attack. He kept his command, and the incident was soon forgotten. On the plus side, destroyer captains now knew their commanders would back them up if a real U-boat fired on them.

The HMS *Bulldog* (H-91) played a secret role in the war by capturing a German Enigma machine from a submarine in 1941. *Royal Navy photo.*

On May 9, 1941, two vintage destroyers in the service of Great Britain proved that even old ships still had great military value.

Just after noon, two merchant ships were sunk in a convoy being escorted by destroyers, including the HMS *Bulldog* (H-91), an old *B*-class destroyer commissioned in 1931, and HMS *Broadway* (H-90), formerly the USS *Hunt* (DD-194), a *Clemson* class built in 1920. A corvette dropped some depth charges, as did the *Broadway*, which forced the *U-110* to the surface less than 100 yards from the *Bulldog*. Most of the U-boat crew ran to the deck. Believing the U-boat crew was attempting to man their deck gun, the *Broadway* rammed the submarine, but struck only a glancing blow. Before the *Broadway* could fire on the submarine, the captain of the *Bulldog* signaled to stop the attack.

Recognizing the opportunity to capture an intact Type IXB U-boat—the latest model being used by the German Navy—the *Bulldog's* captain quickly put a landing party into a boat and rushed them to the submarine. Meanwhile, the U-boat's survivors were stashed below the deck of the corvette so they could not see that their submarine, presumably with charges set to blow it up, still floated.

Sublieutenant David Balme drew the duty to "recover all codebooks and papers" he could find.[8]

He rightfully worried that the submarine had been rigged to explode, or that other members of the submarine crew waited for him below decks. He drew his revolver, though he admitted: "I'd never fired it in my life…I felt there must be someone below trying to open the seacocks, or setting detonating charges, but no one was there…she was left to us as the greatest prize of the war."[9]

Balme remembered: "Everything was lying about just as if one had arrived at someone's house after breakfast, before they had time to make up the beds…A coding machine, too, was plugged in as though it had been in use when abandoned. It resembled a typewriter; hence the telegraphist pressed the keys, and reported to me that the results were peculiar."[10]

He had recovered a complete Enigma machine, a device using rotors that the Germans believed rendered their naval codes unbreakable. He would find the July codes for the machine in a sealed envelope on the captain's desk. Balme did not mention in his post-war memoirs if he realized at the time what he had discovered. He did say, however, that hundreds of men aboard the two destroyers had seen the submarine boarded. All of them were sworn to secrecy and word never leaked out that the Enigma machine had been captured.

The original idea of capturing the submarine to thoroughly examine it in a dry dock would have been the wrong thing to do. Had the submarine been towed the 400 miles to Iceland, there was the potential that German spies would see it and then pass on the disturbing news to Germany that the sub's Enigma machine and codebooks may have been captured. If that had happened, the Germans might have redesigned the Enigma machine or rewritten the codes.

Luckily for the British, the *U-110* sank while under tow, probably from weakened bulkheads giving way from the depth charging. The value was not in the new submarine, captured after only two patrols, but in the decoding machine the seaman thought looked like an odd typewriter.

And, while no one knew it at the time, the British had gotten a sort of revenge with the sinking of the *U-110*. Her captain, Kapitänleutnant Fritz-Julius Lemp, had commanded the *U-30,* which had sunk the unarmed passenger liner SS *Athena* on September 1, 1939, the first official day of the war. Twenty-eight Americans were among the 128 dead.

By coincidence, 128 Americans were killed in 1915 when a German U-boat torpedoed the unarmed British liner *Lusitania*. President Roosevelt in 1939, just like President Wilson in 1915, did not declare war against Germany in retaliation for the lost American civilian lives.

The capture of the *U-110's* Enigma machine was so secret that Churchill did not even notify President Roosevelt about it until ten months later in January 1942 when Churchill and Roosevelt met in person.

Both the *Bulldog* and the *Broadway* would survive the war, damaging the Germans in several other engagements, but both of their crews likely never knew how much they had done to win the war so early in the conflict.

In early June 1941, President Roosevelt made another step toward provoking the Germans when he sent a force of several thousand Marines to occupy Iceland, relieving the British who had earlier occupied it. Destroyers escorted the forces, but the Marines landed from traditional troop ships rather than from the four stackers converted into fast attack transports in 1938.

Hitler noted the encroachment, but still refused to order attacks on American warships. At the same time, he let it be known that he would not punish a U-boat captain if he torpedoed an American ship by mistake.

Roosevelt, growing more comfortable with the idea that he would soon have to deal with Germany, wrote in July 1941 to his chief of naval operations: "...the presence of any German submarine or raider should be dealt with by action looking to the elimination of such threat of attack on the line of communication [to Iceland] or close to it."[11]

Once the Iceland base at Reykjavik was established, supply ships began to make the run, escorted by American warships. Still, the president was reluctant to escort British ships across the full expanse of the Atlantic, even though his chief of naval operations was urging just that sort of warlike measure after Germany invaded Russia in July.

In June and July 1941, the first of the 115 destroyers authorized by the Two-Ocean Navy Act of July 1940 were laid down in yards around the nation. It was two months after the *Niblack* had dropped depth charges and the same month the nation began escorting British convoys. These would be the ships most citizens of the United States would identify with when thinking of destroyers in this war. Using this one design, 175 would be commissioned—the most of any destroyer class from any country. All of them would be needed to win the war that began for the United States in six months. They would fight in all of the oceans of the world.

The design of the *Fletcher* class, named for Admiral Frank Friday Fletcher of the early twentieth century, uncle of Admiral Frank Jack Fletcher of World War II, began during the construction of the sixty-six members of the *Gleaves* class of 1939 through 1942. While the *Gleaves* was successful, it was also somewhat top-heavy, requiring lead to be added to its keel for better stabilization.

The *Fletcher* design had big advantages over the *Gleaves* design because the United States was now totally free of any international treaty restrictions on tonnage or weapons.

The *Fletcher* weighed 2,050 tons. It was 376 feet long with a beam of 39 feet and a draft of 17 feet. The *Gleaves* was only 348 feet long with a beam of 36 feet and a draft of 13 feet. The *Fletcher* could produce 60,000 horsepower and make 36.5 knots, compared to the *Gleaves* with 50,000 horsepower and 37.4 knots. Their main armament was identical: five 5-inch dual purpose guns. The *Fletchers* were originally equipped with 1.1-inch automatic cannons for anti-aircraft defense, while the *Gleaves* started with .50 caliber machine guns. These guns would later be replaced by 20-millimeter Oerlikon cannons. The *Fletchers* would also be equipped with six to ten 40-millimeter Bofors guns, ten 21-inch torpedo tubes, two depth charge racks, and six K-gun depth charge projectors.

When measured against four stacker destroyers built in the 1920s, the last time the United States had ordered such large numbers of the same class, the *Fletchers* were enormous. The *Clemsons* were 314 feet long and 31 feet wide with a draft of 9 feet. A *Clemson* weighed almost half that of a *Fletcher*. A crew on a *Clemson* consisted of 122 officers and crew compared to a *Fletcher's* complement of 329.

One big advantage the *Fletchers* would have over its enemies is that all of them had radar and sonar installed.

At about the same time the *Fletchers* were being built, the Japanese were building the *Yugumo* class that was roughly equivalent in size at 391 feet long, a beam of 35 feet, and a displacement of 2,077 tons. The Japanese continued their design of gun placement with one double-gun house forward and two aft. They carried eight torpedo tubes with one reload for a total of sixteen torpedoes, compared to the *Fletchers'* ten tubes.

A substantial difference was that the *Yugumo* class was not initially equipped with radar and only nineteen were built. More than nine times that number of *Fletchers* would find their way into the war.

On August 9, 1941, Roosevelt met with Churchill for the first time on board the HMS *Prince of Wales* (53), docked in Argentia, Newfoundland. It was a secret mission. The president employed a body double posing as him fishing off the coast of Maine to keep the newspapers from speculating on his whereabouts if he disappeared from the public eye. Roosevelt was delivered to the British battleship by the USS *McDougal* (DD-358), a *Porter*-class destroyer.

Churchill proved to be a persuasive man at their first in-person meeting. The resulting Atlantic Charter, a document creating a broad outline for war goals should the U.S. enter the war, included a side agreement that the United States would begin to escort British convoys across the Atlantic.

It was a huge, provocative step for the United States, though it fell short of what the British had hoped would be a major commitment of resources. Roosevelt left the meeting worried that the American people would feel he was now helping the British too much and putting U.S. destroyers in the sights of German U-boats.

It did not take long before Roosevelt's worries became real.

On September 4, 1941, the USS *Greer* (DD-145), a *Wickes*-class destroyer commissioned just six weeks after the end of World War I, was about 125 miles southwest of Reykjavik carrying mail and supplies to the Marines now operating in Iceland. Just before 9:00 a.m., a British bomber signaled to the destroyer that it had spotted a U-boat on the surface just 10 miles away. Commander George W. Johnson set a course for the U-boat with the intention of tracking it, but not attacking it. As he interpreted his orders, he had no authority to attack as he was not escorting a convoy, so there should not have been reason for the U-boat to attack him.

For more than three hours, the *Greer* tracked *U-652* but did not attack. Meanwhile, the British bomber dropped four bombs which startled the submarine's crew. Finally, the U-boat turned toward the *Greer* and fired two torpedoes, both missing. Now that it had been attacked, the *Greer* dropped seventeen depth charges over the course of nine hours, but never saw any evidence of a hit. She soon resumed her voyage to port and the *U-652* surfaced to recharge her batteries. Other than frayed nerves, neither the American destroyer nor the German U-boat suffered any damage.

Nothing really happened during the naval engagement, but on September 11, 1941, President Roosevelt said in a fireside chat: "These Nazi submarines and raiders are the rattlesnakes of the Atlantic. The time for active defense is now...our patrolling vessels and planes will protect all merchant ships—not only American ships but ships of any flag—engaged in commerce in our defensive waters."[12]

Whether real or imagined, U.S. destroyers made contact with what they thought were U-boats over the next several days. On September 14, while on the way to Reykjavik, the USS *Truxtun* (DD-229) spotted a U-boat pop out of a fog bank just 300 yards away. The U-boat crash-dived. The destroyer's depth charges did not bring it to the surface. The embarrassed crews of three destroyers admitted their inexperience allowed them to miss what could have been an easy kill had they been able to train just one gun at such pointblank range. It was the closest Hitler's U-boats had come to being attacked by Americans. He had ordered his U-boat captains to avoid contact if possible, but if attacked, they could retaliate.

On September 16, 1941, Convoy HX 150 left Halifax, Nova Scotia with fifty ships escorted by HMCS *Annapolis,* formerly the USS *Mackenzie* (DD-175). The next day, the convoy was met by two *Gleaves*-class destroyers, the USS *Ericsson* (DD-440) and USS *Eberle* (DD-430), as well as four stackers USS *Upshur* (DD-144), USS *Dallas* (DD-199), and USS *Ellis* (DD-154). The destroyers, all of which could make 35 knots, plodded along at the pace of the slowest merchantman: 9.25 knots. On September 25, the convoy was turned over to British destroyers—which had all been American destroyers twenty years earlier—HMS *Churchill,* HMS *Chesterfield,* and HMS *Broadwater.* The first convoy escorted across the Atlantic made it safely thanks to the protection of new and old American destroyers now serving in both navies.

The USS *Kearny* (DD-432) was a *Benson* class torpedoed by a U-boat in October of 1941. *NHHC photo.*

On October 17, 1941, Convoy SC 48, a convoy of fifty-three ships, was off Iceland. The ships were defended by seven British corvettes and seven destroyers, including the USS *Kearny* (DD-432), a *Benson* class barely one year old. Starting just after 8:00 p.m., the convoy was attacked by several U-boats. One nervous British corvette captain cut across the bow of the *Kearny*, forcing her captain to stop in mid-ocean to avoid a collision. The surfaced *U-568* saw the destroyer drifting, took his opportunity, and fired three torpedoes at the *Kearny*. The U-boat captain had not strictly obeyed his orders. The *Kearny* had not yet attacked him, but it was on its way to look for him.

One torpedo hit the *Kearny* in the starboard side in the forward fireroom, killing seven men on duty and another four seamen on decks above as the explosion swept upward. Twenty-two seamen were wounded.

Several hours later, the HMS *Broadwater,* the former USS *Mason* (DD-191), a *Clemson* class, became the first of the *Town*-class destroyers to be torpedoed, just over a year after being transferred to the British navy. An American officer, still attached to the *Broadwater,* lost his life. She was sunk by the *U-10*. After this sinking, her twenty-second victory, the *U-10* was assigned as a training vessel for other U-boat crews.

After the first convoy had made it across the Atlantic with no losses, what had happened to SC 48 was shocking to war planners. Ten merchant ships out of fifty-three, one destroyer, and one corvette were sunk by five different U-boats, and the *Kearny* was damaged. No U-boat had even been seen, much less attacked. While convoying was supposed to be safer than traveling alone, this one attack proved destroyer crews did not yet know how to find and sink U-boats.

Roosevelt reacted with another oddly calm fireside chat, especially given that eleven Americans had died. "We have wished to avoid shooting. But the shooting has started. And history has recorded who fired the first shot. In the long run, however, all that will matter is who fired the last shot," the president said.[13]

The USS *Reuben James* (DD-245) was a *Clemson* sunk in October of 1941 by a U-boat. *NHHC photo.*

Despite his mildly threatening speech, the President made no active moves to declare war on Germany.

The USS *Reuben James* (DD-245) was twenty years old and tired in October 1941. Unlike some of the other *Clemson*-class destroyers which had been decommissioned and laid up for years, the *"Rube"* had been in almost continuous service in the Atlantic, Mediterranean, Caribbean, and Pacific oceans before joining the Neutrality Patrol in 1940. She was among the Atlantic Fleet's most traveled destroyers when she was assigned to escort HX 156, a convoy of forty-three merchant ships, leaving Argentia, Newfoundland on October 23.

On October 30, she was ordered to check out a contact. As she steamed into the darkness, the sky was brightening behind her, making her stand out to the *U-552* running on the surface. Rather than submerge and wait for a merchant ship, the U-boat captain, who had already sunk thirteen merchantmen by this time, could not resist such an easy target. He fired two torpedoes from the short range of 1,000 yards.

One torpedo smashed into the destroyer's port side, just forward of her number one funnel, almost in the same spot where the *Kearny* had been hit on the starboard side a few weeks earlier.

The *Kearny,* a newer ship with a hull made of 5/8-inch thick tempered steel, survived its torpedo strike with buckled plates and flooded compartments. The *Reuben James,* with a hull made of thinner, 3/8-inch rolled steel, did not. The *Rube*'s forward section exploded and sank almost immediately, likely because the forward magazine ignited.

As the stern started to sink, the ship's own depth charges exploded, killing a number of men who had stayed with the stern as long as they could. Out of a crew of 143 men and officers, just forty-four survivors were picked up. No officers survived. The USS *Niblack* (DD-424), the *Gleaves*-class destroyer that had dropped depth charges on what it thought was a U-boat back in April 1941—the first overt action the U.S. had taken against Germany—rescued thirty-five of the survivors.

Just as he had with the attack on the *Kearny,* President Roosevelt had a muted public response which reflected the public's own seeming disinterest in the attack. Even some of the Navy's admirals seemed impartial to the loss of their own men.

Admiral Ernest King wrote: "I suggest we go slow in the matter of making heroes out of those people who have, after all, done the jobs they are trained to do."[14]

The president did not ask Congress for a declaration of war. In fact, when asked at a press conference, he pointedly said he would not break off relations with Germany. The commander in chief, who had given a

fireside chat detailing his anger of how the USS *Greer* had been unsuccessfully attacked without loss of life, did not follow up with a fireside
chat about how the USS *Reuben James* had been sunk with the loss of
nearly one hundred Americans.

Curiously, it was a pacifist singer, Woody Guthrie, who would react
most publicly to the sinking, writing a song where he asked: "What were
their names? Did you have a friend on the good Reuben James?"[15]

After two and a half years of war, the British were justifiably proud
of what they had done. Their destroyers and an old battleship had sunk
nearly half of German's entire complement of destroyers in 1940. They
followed up that celebrated victory the next year with the top-secret
capture of one of Germany's most prized pieces of communications
equipment.

The Americans, from whom the British wanted help, had accomplished very little other than seeing that increasing numbers of merchant
ships had safely reached English ports. American destroyers had been
torpedoed twice, with one heavily damaged and one sunk. Despite scores
of depth charges being dropped into the North Atlantic, the United States
had not even scratched the paint on a U-boat.

Politically, the Americans found themselves in the same pacifist
frame of mind they had been in before being dragged into World War I.
The American government and the American people did not want to
know about an undeclared war being fought off the coast of Iceland.

It would take something dramatic to wake up the president and the
American people. It would take an attack on American property.

7

Pacific Theater 1941

"Suddenly and deliberately attacked."

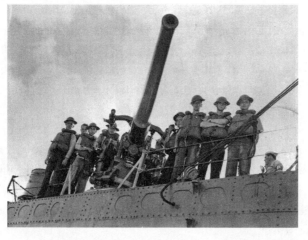

The gun crew of the starboard midship's 4-inch gun of the USS *Ward* (DD-139), which sank a Japanese midget submarine outside of Pearl Harbor on December 7, 1941, before the Japanese started their air attack. *NHHC photo.*

It was an American destroyer, not a Japanese airplane, that fired the first shot in the war between those two nations on December 7, 1941.

While the nation would be told by President Roosevelt's radio address that the "United States was suddenly and deliberately attacked by naval and air forces of the Empire of Japan," it was the USS *Ward* (DD-139) that suddenly and deliberately attacked and sank a vessel of the Imperial Japanese Navy. That sinking came more than an hour and a half before the first Japanese aircraft dove on Pearl Harbor to torpedo, bomb, and strafe the U.S. Navy's Pacific Fleet.

Had the *Ward's* account of the submarine's sinking been passed up the chain of command faster, the crews of the berthed American ships would have been waiting for the Japanese aircraft when they first zoomed in over the harbor. The Pacific Fleet would still have been severely damaged. However, an hour and a half warning given by a twenty-three-year-old *Wickes*-class destroyer commissioned in 1918 would have alerted all those other ships to put up a vigorous aerial defense. The Japanese would certainly have lost many more than the twenty-nine aircraft that were shot down that day.

Lieutenant William Outerbridge, an experienced officer with fourteen years of sea service, had taken over command of the *Ward* just two days earlier on December 5, 1941, after serving as executive officer on the USS *Cummings* (DD-365), a newer *Mahan* class. At 6:30 a.m. on December 6, 1941, the *Ward* got underway to relieve the USS *Chew* (DD-106), another *Wickes* class, which had been patrolling the defensive sea area—the entrance to Pearl Harbor.

It was 3:42 a.m. on Sunday, December 7, when lookouts on the USS *Condor* (AMc-14), an ugly fishing trawler repurposed into a coastal minesweeper, thought they spotted a periscope in the dark water. They reported it to *Ward* by blinker. The *Ward* looked and listened with sonar but found nothing. Outerbridge thought it was a false alarm and did not report his search.

At 6:30 a.m., the supply ship USS *Antares* (AG-10) reported a suspicious object that seemed to be following it as the submarine net protecting the harbor was lowered for ships entering or leaving. At 6:37, Outerbridge saw the object himself and called his destroyer to general quarters at 6:40. At 6:45, Outerbridge, without asking for orders from his superiors, fired his first round from the number one 4-inch gun at a range of 100 yards at the conning tower of what he believed to be either a small Japanese or German submarine. The destroyer's second shot hit the conning tower from a range of just 50 yards. As the sub sank beneath the waves, *Ward* dropped depth charges.

"The submarine sank in 1,200 feet of water and could not be located with supersonic detector," Outerbridge wrote in his after action report.[1]

Outerbridge reported at 6:45 a.m., radioing to his commandant: "We have attacked, fired upon, and dropped depth charges on a submarine operating in defensive sea area."[2]

Outerbridge's report was passed around to several officers, including Pearl Harbor's highest-ranking officer, Admiral Husband Kimmel, who later testified that he was not sure Outerbridge had actually seen anything. Despite Outerbridge's precise language, the *Ward*'s sinking of the submarine did not excite his superiors. They thought the *Ward* had made a false contact, so they did not raise a general alarm.

One hour and five minutes later, the first of 363 Japanese aircraft dropped out of the skies to attack the moored fleet. Just six weeks earlier and on the other side of the world off Iceland, one American destroyer had been sunk and another damaged with the loss of more than 110 sailors' lives. The loss of those American lives in the Atlantic had not moved President Roosevelt and Congress to declare war.

This air attack by Japan would.

Thirty destroyers in four divisions were present at Pearl Harbor during the attack. Four of the destroyers were left over from World War I. The oldest destroyer in the port was the USS *Allen* (DD-66), a *Sampson* class that had hunted U-boats from Queenstown, Ireland. The next oldest were three *Wickes*-class destroyers commissioned in the 1920s. The other twenty-six destroyers were divided among *Farragut, Porter,* and *Bagley* classes.

Other than the *Ward*, the *Bagley*-class USS *Helm* (DD-388) was the only warship underway when the Japanese attacked at 7:50 a.m. She was already in the harbor deperming (demagnetizing) buoys when she saw a second submarine. As the *Helm*, unaware of the *Ward*'s encounter with the first submarine, turned to attack, this second submarine hit a reef and floundered. One crewman crawled out of the two-man sub. The *Helm* was now responsible for capturing the first Japanese prisoner of war, and for Japan's third naval death before the first aircraft had been shot down. When the *Helm* came under air attack, she responded with both her 5-inch guns and .50 caliber machine guns, but her captain later reported that "the fire was slow due to the necessity of breaking ammunition out of magazines and belting all but a small amount."[3]

The first warship to leave her berth during the attack was the USS *Henley* (DD-391), another *Bagley*-class destroyer inadvertently called to general quarters by an inexperienced sailor who had meant to play call to muster over the ship's intercom. Rather than wait for his commanding and executive officers to come aboard, the officer on deck ordered the *Henley* underway.

Not far behind her was the USS *Monaghan* (DD-354), the last ship built of the *Farragut* class, commissioned in April 1935. As she left the harbor, the *Monaghan* encountered a third small Japanese submarine. It rammed the submarine and then dropped depth charges with a detonation so shallow that the destroyer was lifted out of the water. Following the *Monaghan* was the USS *Dale* (DD-353), another *Farragut,* which came under heavy aircraft attack once she reached the mouth of the harbor as the Japanese aircraft were now trying to sink an American ship in the channel. The *Dale* escaped damage and shot down three attacking planes.

An hour later, the second wave of Japanese fighters and bombers arrived. This time, the Navy was ready for them.

Another old *Wickes* destroyer, the USS *Breese* (DD-122/DM-18), opened up with her 3-inch anti-aircraft gun. Her captain reported firing forty-five rounds, hitting a dive bomber just aft of the cockpit. The ship also fired 1,700 rounds of .50 caliber rounds, which her captain pointedly found ineffective in his after action report.

"The anti-aircraft battery of this vessel is considered inadequate," wrote Captain A.B. Coxe, Jr. Still, Captain Coxe believed shooting at the Japanese planes helped his crew's morale: "The following landing force equipment was used to augment the anti-aircraft battery; and although its effectiveness is doubtful, it served as a means of satisfying the offensive spirit of the crew, 3", .330 caliber Lewis machine guns, 3 Browning automatic rifles."[4]

Coxe made a typo in his report. He meant to say his men used three .303 caliber Lewis machine guns, a British machine gun invented in

World War I with a distinctive round magazine on top of the barrel. The Browning Automatic Rifle, commonly called the "BAR," was normally carried by soldiers. It carried just twenty rounds in a box magazine, but Coxe's sailors were using everything they had to defend themselves.

Just after 9:00 a.m., a flight of Japanese bombers noticed the battleship USS *Pennsylvania* (BB-38) had not been hit. While the primary target was the battleship, three destroyers in dry dock beside her were also bombed. Within a half hour, USS *Cassin* (DD-372), USS *Downes* (DD-375), and USS *Shaw* (DD-373), all *Mahan* class, were burning. The *Cassin* would roll down on top of the *Downes*. Nearby, in another dry dock, the foreword magazine of the *Shaw* was hit, resulting in a spectacular explosion of boiling smoke and fire captured by a photographer at the very instant of ignition. The photo would become one of the iconic images of the ferocious attack.

Ironically, the damage suffered by the three destroyers taught the Navy lessons it would use in repairing ships in the future. All the vessels were loaded with fuel oil, 5-inch shells, torpedoes, and depth charges, even though they were in dry dock and not going anywhere. When the bombs hit, those flammables started fires that could not be extinguished with the firefighting equipment on hand at the dry dock. New regulations were issued to remove flammables from ships undergoing repairs.

Both the *Cassin* and *Downes* were refloated to get them out of the important dry dock, but they never fought again. Salvageable equipment was sent back to Mare Island in California and installed in new destroyers commissioned with the same names. The hulls of the original destroyers were scrapped in Pearl Harbor.

Remarkably, the *Shaw*, which seemed to disintegrate judging by the photo, was not destroyed. The explosion of her magazine blew off the bow, but the rest of the ship was salvageable. On February 9, 1942, she sailed for Mare Island with all of her guns as well as her superstructure removed to save weight. A temporary bow had been welded in place, but it slowed the ship to a crawl. She made it back to the United States, where a new bow was welded in place. She returned to Pearl Harbor in late

August 1942. A destroyer that seemed to have been destroyed at Pearl Harbor would fight the rest of the war, earning eleven battle stars.

Twenty-nine Japanese aircraft were shot down during the attack; nine in the first wave and twenty in the second wave. The crews of various destroyers claimed to have shot down at least eight Japanese planes.

Lieutenant Commander Herald F. Stout, commander of the *Breese*, had no doubt his crew hit one Japanese airplane with their 3-inch anti-aircraft gun. The gun crews had been missing the incoming Japanese because they had never fired on real airplanes attacking at several hundred miles per hour. Their practice had always been against towed canvas targets. Once the gun crews started shortening the anti-aircraft shell fuses to make the rounds explode quicker, the *Breese* brought down an airplane.

"It fragmentized the bastard. The engine kept right on going, but the plane disintegrated in a ball of fire with parts of it coming down like leaves from a tree in autumn. Yeah, we got the S.O.B," Stout said in a 1964 interview.[5]

A third wave attack meant to target fuel tanks and dry docks was contemplated by the Japanese, but rejected due to concern that the Americans were now ready with anti-aircraft guns. Another concern was that returning planes would have to land on carrier decks in darkness; something they had not practiced.

The Japanese sank four battleships and damaged four others, damaged three cruisers, wrecked two destroyers and damaged two others, and sank six auxiliary ships. A total of 169 American aircraft were destroyed, most of them on the ground. More than 2,300 American servicepeople were killed.

The Japanese understood that unless the American ships were blasted to pieces, they likely were not gone forever. Pearl Harbor was a repair facility with dry docks, so if the ships were sunk at their berths, they could be refloated and repaired. The Japanese attack had several purposes. The first goal was to destroy the fleet in the harbor, with the secondary goal of damaging the fleet so heavily that the United States would be unable to oppose Japanese ground gains in the Pacific theater for many months. Another goal was to destroy the repair facilities and fuel tanks, but it was abandoned when the third strike was called off. The final goal turned out to be a pipe dream: to demoralize the American public into forcing its government to ignore Japanese victories thousands of miles away from the United States.

The "date that will live in infamy," as President Roosevelt described it, galvanized a divided nation into one ready to fight a war in two different directions thousands of miles apart.

While the attack was devastating, it was not catastrophic to the Pacific Fleet. Only the USS *Arizona* (BB-39) and USS *Oklahoma* (BB-37) were total losses among the battleships. That does not count the USS *Utah* (BB-31), an obsolete World War I era battleship used by the U.S. as an anti-aircraft ship. She was sunk by the Japanese, who thought her to be operational. Six damaged battleships were refloated or repaired and would get into the war within a matter of months.

All three of the U.S. carriers in the Pacific fleet—USS *Enterprise* (CV-6), USS *Saratoga* (CV-3), USS *Lexington* (CV-2), and the destroyers escorting them—were away from port during the attack, so the most dangerous ships to Japan were untouched for the moment.

Of the eight heavy and light cruisers at Pearl, only two were greatly damaged. Both were repaired and in action within months.

Just two of the thirty destroyers at Pearl were destroyed. Two damaged destroyers would be repaired.

At the time of the attack, naval doctrine in all warring nations was caught in the middle of historical thinking and planning for the future. Battleships had been the focus of fleet construction for sixty years. At the beginning of the war, Japan had twelve battleships compared to the United States' seventeen, with eight at Pearl Harbor.

Most of the battleships on both sides were constructed after World War I, with fewer constructed through the 1930s, when both nations were still flying biplanes. Then, in just three hours, Japan proved that a massive force of modern airplanes could wreck an entire fleet of capital ships using well-placed bombs and torpedoes. Battleships would still be used by both sides in shore bombardments and a handful of surface battles, but the 14-inch, 16-inch, and 18-inch naval guns mounted on heavily armored platforms were no match for skilled airmen.

A look at the number of battles in which each class of ships was engaged during the Pacific war might indicate that the Japanese targeted the wrong classes of war ships at Pearl Harbor.

Any American ship that fired on an enemy, or who was fired on by the enemy, was awarded a battle star by the Navy as a means of boosting morale.

Counting only the battleships that went back into service after Pearl Harbor, they earned forty-one battle stars during the rest of the war. Most of those were for naval bombardments of islands. Only two battles, Guadalcanal on November 15, 1942, and Leyte Gulf on October 25, 1944, pitted American battleships against Japanese battleships. Though USS *South Dakota* (BB-57) was heavily damaged at Guadalcanal in 1942, no American battleship was sunk during the war after Pearl Harbor.

All the cruisers at Pearl Harbor continued fighting in the war, accumulating eighty-one battle stars with only the USS *Helena* (CL-50) being sunk in battle at the Battle of Kula Gulf in July 1943.

Instead of targeting the bigger ships, the Japanese might have survived longer if they had gone after the tin cans.

Of the thirty destroyers at Pearl Harbor during the attack, twenty-eight would continue to fight in the war, accumulating 257 battle stars, including many ship-to-ship battles as well as shore bombardment and aerial battles against kamikazes late in the war. The fifteen destroyers away from Pearl Harbor on the day of the attack escorting the carriers *Lexington* and *Enterprise* would participate in battles that would win them 105 battle stars. The six *Clemson*-class destroyers converted to minesweepers and seaplane tenders present at Pearl Harbor during the attack would win twenty-three battle stars. The nine *Wickes* and *Clemson*-class destroyers converted to minesweepers that were based at Pearl

Harbor, but at sea on the day of the attack, would win fifty-three battle stars. Even the old *Sampson* class USS *Allen* (DD-66), commissioned in 1917, and which would remain unconverted, would win a battle star that day and continue her service as a convoy escort for the rest of the war. At the end of the war, she was the longest serving destroyer in the U.S. Navy, with nearly thirty years of service.

The fifty-five Pearl Harbor-based destroyers, counting those that had been converted to minesweepers and seaplane tenders, would win 438 battle stars over the rest of the war. The American battleships considered so important to the Japanese would win forty-one battle stars.

Just three days after the attack, Admiral Kimmel realized that the battleship losses, however temporary, necessitated an entirely new battle plan. He expected destroyers to play a key role.

"With the losses we have sustained, it is necessary to revise completely our strategy of a Pacific War. The loss of battleships commits us to the strategic defensive until our forces can again be built up. However, a very powerful striking force of carriers, cruisers and destroyers survives. These forces must be operated boldly and vigorously on the tactical offensive in order to retrieve our initial disaster," Kimmel wrote in a report to the secretary of the Navy.[6]

Dauntless dive bombers from the carrier *Enterprise* drew first blood on the Japanese navy by sinking the submarine *I-70* on December 10, 1941, using two 1,000-pound bombs.

A more impressive retaliation for the Pearl Harbor attack came four days later when the Japanese attacked Wake Island on December 11, 1941. That day also proved to be an indication of how little punishment some older model Japanese destroyers could take.

Marine gunners, manning a hidden battery of 5-inch shore defense guns, waited and watched as the *Hayate,* a *Kamikaze*-class destroyer launched in 1922, came within 4,500 yards of Wake Island, apparently believing Japanese aircraft had destroyed the American shore guns. Within two minutes of the Marines opening fire and with just the third salvo, the 1,422-ton destroyer blew up. Rattled, the Japanese fleet commander ordered a withdrawal of his ships to get them out of range of the Marines on shore. But that did not help one destroyer. The *Kisaragi,* a newer *Mutsuki* class launched in 1925, was hit by a single 100-pound bomb dropped by a Marine F4U Wildcat operating from Wake Island. Within five minutes, this destroyer blew up and sank. Only one Japanese crewman survived out of 326 on both destroyers.

Satsuki was a *Mutsuki* class used extensively as a destroyer transport, much like the American converted *Wickes* and *Clemson* classes were converted to Fast Attack Transports (APDs). *NHHC photo.*

The second destroyer's sinking revealed a weakness in older Japanese designs that would not be corrected until mid-war, when they would be refitted. Even though the Japanese navy had just proved the devastating effect of aircraft attacks on ships, the *Kisaragi* had only four machine guns for anti-aircraft defense. The Wildcat probably dove on the ship and released its bomb before even coming into machine gun range.

At this early point in the war, detailed analysis of the vulnerability of Japanese destroyers was not at the top of the U.S. Navy admirals' minds; fighting off amphibious troops was. Wake fell to the Japanese on December 23, 1941, and would remain in Japanese hands for the rest of the war.

One day after the fall of Wake, an American destroyer would sink a second Japanese submarine; or the U.S. Navy may have claimed the sinking to boost morale back home.

Details are sketchy, but the USS *Drayton* (DD-366), a *Mahan*-class destroyer escorting the *Enterprise* during the attack on Pearl Harbor, was escorting a four-ship convoy to Palmyra Island when it picked up a sound contact around 2:40 p.m. on December 24, 1941. It dropped three depth charges and observed oil and debris almost immediately. The destroyer swung around and dropped three more. A scooped up towel drenched in the oil from the ocean smelled like diesel. That was one method destroyers used to check if their depth charges had destroyed a sub. If the debris did not smell of oil, it could be pieces of the exploded depth charge coming back to the surface.

The *Drayton* dropped another three depth charges when Captain Laurence Allen Abercrombie heard a shout: "'Look, a submarine!' It was too, the bow of an enormous submarine, the full 50 feet of it, pushing up through the water slowly at a steep 70 degree angle, dripping oil, the net cutter at the bow looking like a set of teeth and the diving planes at its side showing the characteristic Jap shape."[7]

Abercrombie ordered his surprised deck crew to fire, but he remembered only the machine gunners got off any rounds before the sub slid back under the sea. He reported feeling and hearing explosions under the ocean "heavier and deeper than our own depth charges," adding that "the last barrage must have set off something within the sub itself."[8]

A diary kept by Chief Henry Clyde Daniels of the *Drayton* collaborates what Abercrombie wrote, though Daniels recalls that the number one and number three 5-inch guns put four rounds apiece into the submarine, while the captain wrote that only that the .50 caliber machine guns got into action.

"She sank with a big hissing sound. So long, you yellow bastards. Repaying debt for Pearl Harbor. Picked up convoy and continued on our way," reads Daniels' diary entry.[9]

Abercrombie was awarded his first Navy Cross for the action, and his second in October 1942.

Chief Daniels' diary entry matches Abercrombie's post-war account written with famed writer Fletcher Pratt. However, neither the U.S. Navy nor the Japanese navy published a post-war list showing the sinking of a Japanese submarine on that date.

The year 1941 ended with the U.S. Navy reeling from the attack at Pearl Harbor. It would be months before the heavy ships damaged at Pearl could be refloated, and for other help to arrive from the United States. Until then, it would be up to a thrown together force of old four stackers, newer destroyers, a handful of cruisers, and three carriers to face emboldened Japanese.

Despite the admonition from Admiral Yamamoto that Japan would awaken "a sleeping giant" of American industrial prowess with its attack at Pearl Harbor, the ability of the United States to defeat the Japanese in the Pacific was not at all clear to the United States at the end of 1941.

CHAPTER

8

Atlantic Theater 1942

"American beacons and searchlights visible at night."

When the war started for the United States in December 1941, the U.S. Navy had 170 destroyers in service: forty-five based at Pearl Harbor, thirteen in the Asiatic Fleet based in the Philippines, twenty-one on the Pacific West Coast or elsewhere along the Pacific down to the Panama Canal, and ninety-one with the Atlantic Fleet. Counting eight destroyer minelayers, eighteen destroyer minesweepers, fourteen destroyer seaplane tenders, and six high-speed destroyer transports which had been converted from *Caldwell, Wickes,* and *Clemson*-class destroyers, the total destroyer force on the opening day of war for the United States was 216 ships.

The United States' offensive capability, with its entire destroyer force, was not overwhelming. Of all 170 destroyers, seventy of them, or forty-one percent of the entire ready fleet, were designed and built before 1922. Adding in the forty-six pre-1920 destroyers that had been modified into minesweepers, minelayers, seaplane tenders, and fast attack transports in the late 1930s while still keeping some of their destroyer armament, fifty-four percent of the nation's 216 destroyers were of World War I era design. Just forty-six percent, or one hundred destroyers out of 216, could be considered modern, designed in accordance with the provisions of the 1930 London Treaty, which limited tonnage.

More American destroyers would soon be on the way, but were not yet at sea. The first destroyer class after the treaty weight restrictions had been discarded in the mid-1930s was the *Fletcher* class. The keel for the class name ship, the USS *Fletcher* (DD-445), was laid down on October 2, 1941, just two weeks before the USS *Kearney* (DD-432) was torpedoed in the North Atlantic. Twenty-two *Fletchers* were under construction on December 7, 1941, but would not be ready for commissioning until the summer of 1942.

The country with the most destroyers was Great Britain. The British, having been at war for two years, had 184 destroyers and fifty-two more under construction. More than half of them were modern, but also counted were fifty World War I era destroyers transferred by the United States to Great Britain.

The Japanese had sixty-eight destroyers in service when the war started, but many of them had been laid down in the 1920s. Another sixty-four were commissioned during the war, about one-third of the number of *Fletcher*-class destroyers.

The Germans had only twenty-two destroyers in 1939 and lost ten of those in 1940 at the Battle of Narvik. Germany had put its faith in building U-boats, large battleships, and cruisers with the expectation that they would sail into the middle of Allied convoys.

Just as the U.S. Pacific Fleet ended the year with the disaster at Pearl Harbor, the Atlantic Fleet's year started poorly in 1942.

February 18, 1942 saw the first sinking of an Atlantic Fleet destroyer since war was declared. The USS *Truxtun* (DD-229), a *Clemson*, had run aground off Greenland. The Germans were nowhere near, but Mother Nature was adversarial enough. Of the 156 officers and crew, only forty-six survived the raging seas. Counting the dead crewmen of the *Kearny* and the *Reuben James,* both torpedoed in October 1941, the Atlantic Fleet had lost more than two hundred Destroyer Men within four months. No tin can had fired a shot, launched a torpedo, or damaged any German vessel with a depth charge.

Throughout 1941, Hitler had steadfastly refused his naval commanders' entreaties to place U-boats off the American coast in anticipation of the coming war. Hitler's admirals already considered the U.S. deployment of destroyers as escorts of convoys to Great Britain to be an act of war against their nation, but the Fuehrer feared that if he put U-boats closer to U.S. shores, it would tip the scales, leading the United States to declare war against Germany. Hitler wanted to avoid appearing aggressive, and he reasoned that when Britain finally surrendered to him, an unthreatened American public would pressure their government into avoiding war since Europe was already under German control.

To Hitler, the United States' vast industrial potential would be neutralized if Germany could defeat Great Britain without angering the United States through any aggressive move. He had been correct until now in believing that the United States wanted neutrality. Two American destroyers had been torpedoed by U-boats with one sunk, but President Roosevelt and Congress had still not declared war against Germany.

That strategy ended on December 7, 1941. Germany's treaty with Japan required Hitler to declare war on the U.S., which he did on December 11. By that time, his admirals' plans to smother the U.S. coast in U-boats was no longer immediately viable. A large number of U-boats had already been sunk by British forces, and others were committed to stopping the convoys supporting British ground advances in North Africa. Only six U-boats were immediately ordered to American shores, but these first six were commanded by some of Germany's most experienced commanders.

The first commercial shipping kill that caught Americans' attention came on January 12, when a British passenger steamer was sunk 300 miles east of Cape Cod. It was still in international waters, but within weeks, more U-boats would cross the Atlantic and start creeping closer to the shore.

In February, U-boat attacks on shipping became more frequent. Destroyers based with the Eastern Sea Frontier in New York City were finding more lifeboats and making what they thought were more sound contacts on submarines. Even the pilots of American passenger airliners were reporting U-boats on the surface of the ocean as they came in for landings at various airports along the Eastern Seaboard.

The USS Jacob Jones (DD-130), a *Wickes* class, was sunk off Cape May, New Jersey in February of 1942, the only American warship sunk in Continental U.S. waters. *NHHC photo.*

It was only a matter of time before the effects of war would be noticed by American civilians, who until then had been reading only about distant combat thousands of miles away.

The USS *Jacob Jones* (DD-130), a *Wickes* class, had started construction just a year after the first *Jacob Jones* (DD-61), a *Tucker* class, was sunk in December 1917 off the southern coast of England. Since the first *Jacob Jones* was the only American warship lost during World War I to enemy action, the Navy honored it by immediately giving its name to the next destroyer in line to be completed. The second *Jacob Jones* was commissioned just two years after the first ship's sinking. With the war over, it was decommissioned in 1922, then brought back into continuous service in 1930.

Now with twelve full years at sea, including Neutrality Patrol and convoy duty, the *Jacob Jones* was one of the most used of the Atlantic Fleet destroyers. Based in New York harbor as part of the Eastern Sea Frontier, she was commanded by Lieutenant Commander Hugh Black. After putting to sea after midnight on February 22, Black thought he made a U-boat contact immediately outside of New York's harbor. That was alarming. If U-boats were already coming close to the nation's largest city and most important port, they were becoming bolder faster than anyone had expected. The *Jacob Jones* dropped fifty-seven depth charges, a full load, in twelve runs. An oil slick rose to the surface, but there was no wreckage.

The Eastern Sea Frontier commander argued that no submarine would operate in such shallow water at the mouth of the harbor, and the oil slick must have originated from an existing sunken wreck. Captain Black argued that his sonarman heard propeller noises and the sound contact moved; something an underwater wreck does not do. Still, the *Jacob Jones'* contact was dismissed as false. Other destroyer commanders grumbled that the *Jacob Jones* must have attacked a submarine, but post-war checks of German U-boat records do not show a submarine lost on that date.

Still, U-boats were venturing close to New York City's harbor, with some submarine commanders marveling at how the brightly lit city was making it easy to see potential shipping targets at sea. The *Jacob Jones* truly could have made a submarine contact, but did not sink it in any case.

Five nights later, the *Jacob Jones* was patrolling about 30 miles east of Cape May, New Jersey, some 100 miles south of New York City. Other than finding the floating hulk of a freighter empty of crew, the patrol was routine.

At 5:00 a.m. on February 28, two torpedoes tore into the port side of the destroyer as it was heading south. With the shoreline as a backdrop, the first rays of dawn had illuminated the *Jacob Jones* for the *U-578*.

The first torpedo may have exploded the destroyer's magazine as it had blown off the section of the ship just aft of the bridge. The second torpedo hit 40 feet forward of the fantail. In seconds, the ship had separated into three sections. All but one of the officers was killed.

Twenty-five sailors were able to launch rafts, but fourteen of them were in a single raft near the stern when the ship's depth charges exploded as it sank. Most of those men were killed by the concussion.

Within an hour, the rest of the ship had sunk. By 9:07 a.m., alerted by an aircraft on routine patrol that had spotted the wreckage, a search boat, *Eagle 56*, reached the area. Only twelve out of a crew of 113 were saved, with one dying on the way back to Cape May.

The similarities in the sinking of the two *Jacob Joneses* in two different wars were striking. The first was the only U.S. warship lost in World War I. The second would be the only one lost to enemy action off the coast of the continental United States. Both were sunk by U-boats in darkness. Both lost crewmen to exploding depth charges that were left armed in anticipation of imminent action. Both ships lost the majority of their crews. One difference was that the first *Jacob Jones* was sunk by a skilled U-boat commander with seventy-nine ships to his credit in World War I. The second destroyer was sunk by a commander who would have only five kills in five patrols. His submarine would not come back from a patrol in the Bay of Biscay in August 1942. Both U-boats would sink only one warship each. Both would be destroyers.

The USS *Buchanan* (DD-131) was one of fifty destroyers given to Great Britain in 1940. She was renamed the HMS *Campbeltown* (I-42) and sunk on a raid on the French coast. *NHHC photo.*

Ironically, it would be an American-built destroyer in German disguise that would first avenge the United States' loss of the *Jacob Jones*.

The USS *Buchanan* (DD-131), another *Wickes* class just one hull number after the *Jacob Jones*, had been in and out of commission several times since her initial commissioning in 1919. She was formally transferred to the United Kingdom in September 1940 as one of the fifty destroyers in the Destroyers for Bases Agreement. She was recommissioned as a *Town* class, the HMS *Campbeltown* (I-42).

The port city of Saint-Nazaire, on the Loire estuary, which empties into the Atlantic Ocean in eastern France, had one of the world's largest dry docks for the servicing of ocean liners. It was also large enough to hold the German battleship *Tirpitz* in the likely event that the sister ship to the now sunk *Bismarck* would one day need hull repair.

British naval planners envisioned blowing up the dry dock, forever forcing *Tirpitz* to stay near its home port in Norway within range of British ships rather than changing ports to France, where it would be better protected.

Naval bombardment of Saint-Nazaire was rejected because of how far inland the dry dock was from the open ocean. Aerial bombardment was rejected as too inaccurate. That left only a direct assault.

Planners settled on a ruse. They would send a flotilla of small vessels loaded with commandos, which would be attached to a ship disguised as a German destroyer coming into port. That destroyer, loaded with more than four tons of explosives, would ram into the dry dock. Once all of the commandos on board the destroyer had been evacuated, the explosives would be detonated by preset timers.

The British destroyer chosen for conversion into a German destroyer was the hard-luck *Campbeltown*, which had spent almost as many months in port being repaired from three collisions as it had at sea protecting convoys.

The type of German ship chosen for the *Campbeltown* to impersonate was the *Type 23* torpedo boat. Nothing could be done about size discrepancies—the torpedo boat was 285 feet long compared to the *Campbeltown's* 314 feet length. But the silhouette of the German ship could be duplicated by removing two of the *Campbeltown's* four stacks and cutting the remaining two stacks into the rakish shape used by the *Type 23*. Other modifications included gutting much of the interior to reduce weight so the destroyer could pass over outlying sandbars rather than through the main channel. Her 4-inch guns, torpedoes, and depth charges, all offensive weapons, were removed in favor of a single 12-pounder cannon and eight 20-millimeter Oerlikon cannons. Those would come in handy fighting German soldiers on the docks.

Campbeltown, two escorting destroyers, and a flotilla of sixteen small vessels loaded with 256 British Army commandos left Falmouth, England, at 2:00 p.m. on March 26. At nearly midnight the following night, British bombers began a diversionary attack to draw attention to the sky and away from the sea. The flotilla made its way over the sandbars, but was challenged and illuminated by search lights at 1:22 a.m. on March 27.

Even though the *Campbeltown* was flying the German ensign and it answered a challenge in the correct return code, the ruse did not work. When the Germans began firing on the flotilla, the *Campbeltown* increased its speed to 19 knots, as fast as it could run with the removal of half of its boilers. It rammed the gates of the dry dock at 1:34 a.m. Just as had been anticipated, the *Campbeltown's* momentum carried it into the dry dock. The timer on the explosives was set and the commandos jumped onto the dock to begin fighting for their lives.

The explosion was supposed to have occurred at 4:30 a.m., but it failed. For reasons unknown, the explosives hidden in the destroyer's bow finally went off at noon, more than seven and a half hours late. More than forty German soldiers who were still carefully searching the ship for explosives were killed.

Just as planned, the dry dock was extensively damaged and would not be back in service until 1947. The *Tirpitz,* the battleship that worried the British, never ventured out into the southern Atlantic or English Channel because she never acquired the option of repair at a friendly French port. She stayed in Norway and was eventually sunk by British bombers in 1944.

The raid had been successful, but at a high cost of men. The plan for the commandos to board the small vessels after wrecking the docks had fallen apart when most of those vessels were spotlighted and sunk on their way into the harbor. Out of 622 commandos and sailors who started on the mission, only 228 made it back home. The rest were killed or captured.

Other former American destroyers turned over to the British would be sunk during the war, but the *Campbeltown* was the only one intentionally sacrificed.

The U.S. Navy would get its own revenge on the Germans on April 14, just two and a half weeks after the Saint-Nazaire raid, and six weeks after the loss of the *Jacob Jones*. It would be the first victory of the war in the Atlantic Theater for the U.S. Navy, but it would also disturb coastal residents because the victory would come almost within sight of their beaches.

The USS *Roper* (DD-147), a *Wickes* class, sank the first U-boat by an American destroyer off Nags Head, North Carolina in April of 1942. *NHHC photo.*

The USS *Roper* (DD-147), a *Wickes* class commissioned in 1919, had been at sea continually since 1930 and was one of the Atlantic Fleet's most traveled destroyers, having served as far away as China. Now based in Norfolk, Virginia, she had not seen any U-boats, but her wary crew knew they were off the coast. The *Roper* had already achieved fame by rescuing a baby born in a lifeboat. The mother was so grateful that she gave her child the middle name "Roper." The story of the rescue made national newspapers and weekly news magazines; a bit of good news in a world gone mad with war.

Just six minutes after midnight while cruising about 18 miles away from the village of Nags Head, off the Outer Banks of North Carolina, the *Roper's* radar picked up a ship some 2,700 yards south of the destroyer. Soon, the sonarman made the same contact. At first, *Roper's* captain, Lieutenant Commander H.W. Howe, believed he was tracking a friendly United States Coast Guard craft. To be on the safe side, Howe called his crew to general quarters and commanded them to man their guns as he approached the ship. After a torpedo passed along his port side, the *Roper* switched on its searchlight and confirmed a large submarine just 300 yards distant. Machine gun fire cut down the submarine's crew rushing to man their deck gun and one of the destroyer's 4-inch guns hit the conning tower as it was going down.

Believing the submarine captain had submerged in order to either escape or scuttle, Howe dropped eleven depth charges in the water. Twice, the *Roper* passed through the survivors in the water, but Howe reported that he did not stop to pick them up out of concern of a second U-boat lurking nearby. By 9:32 a.m., the *Roper* had recovered the bodies of twenty-nine men, likely killed by the concussion of the depth charges. The *Roper* steamed back to Norfolk so authorities could examine the bodies and their effects. It was the first time any U-boat crew, dead or alive, had been seen by the Navy in World War II. The bodies would later be buried in a naval cemetery in Norfolk.

The boat was the *U-85*, a Type VIIB and 753-ton submarine just a year old on its fourth patrol. Only twenty-four of this type were built. A diary recovered from one of the crewmen reported that the submarine had spent the night of April 13 off New York, noting "American beacons and searchlights visible at night."[1] That entry at least gave credence to the *Jacob Jones'* captain's report and his claims that he found a submarine at the mouth of New York's harbor six weeks earlier.

The *U-85* was the first German submarine lost in Operation Drumbeat: Germany's major offensive along the Atlantic coast to find and sink American shipping heading to Great Britain. Operation Drumbeat was so effective that U-boat crews informally named the six month offensive the "Second Happy Time," meaning they were happy that so many Allied ships were sunk off the American coast.

The *U-85* sank just 110 feet down, but the U.S. Navy made what would seem in retrospect to be a halfhearted effort to enter its wreck. One hard hat diver reported seeing "occupation money" floating inside the submarine when he pulled open a hatch. He apparently went no further because the submarine's Enigma machine was not recovered until 2001 by sport divers.

If the U.S. Navy had put more effort into exploring the submarine, it would have captured an Enigma machine of its own, not long after the British navy had captured its first one.

The hard hat diver's mention of "occupation money" and some writers' noting of the crew bodies in civilian clothes apparently launched rumors which persist today that the *U-85's* true mission was not to sink shipping, but to drop German spies off North Carolina's coast. Those stories seem to be without merit. It is true that German submarines had dropped off spies and saboteurs along the American coast during the war, but it seems unlikely that the *U-85* was one of them. The names of the crew of forty-four are known from records. No extra passengers were recorded to be on board. The *U-85* had sunk shipping earlier in its patrol, seeming to have been its primary mission.

When caught by the *Roper,* the *U-85* was proceeding due south 18 miles off a barrier island, hardly the location where spies in rubber boats might be offloaded. Even if the presumed spies had reached Hatteras

Island, they would have had to drag a rubber boat overland and then paddle another several miles over sound water to reach North Carolina's mainland. There, spies would have found nothing of interest—no large towns, defense plants, or even a railroad to take them to targets of interest. Finally, there was no standard German submariner uniform. Many crewmen wore civilian clothes, such as the thin checkered shirts and shorts seen in photos of the dead *U-85*'s crew. The diary recovered from the submarine even reports that the crew was "all stripped bare" at some points during the patrol due to "abominable heat."[2]

Howe's actions in continuing his attack rather than capturing the crew has been criticized. But Howe reasoned in his after action report that there could be a second submarine waiting for the destroyer to go dead in the water, which is what he would have had to do to pick up survivors. Critics say he could have captured the submarine on the surface, but all witnesses reported it began going down after he fired on it. The Navy gave Howe a Navy Cross and he retired as a rear admiral.

The USS *Blakely* (DD-150), a *Wickes* class, survived being torpedoed in May of 1942 and cruised to a safe port despite its bow being open to the ocean. *NHHC photo.*

The next month, a *Wickes*-class destroyer demonstrated just how tough the old four pipers were.

The USS *Blakeley* (DD-150) had been decommissioned twice since 1919 until finally being recommissioned in 1939 and assigned to the Neutrality Patrol. On May 25, 1942, she was on patrol off Martinique in the Western Caribbean when a single torpedo tore 60 feet off her bow. The captain of the *U-156,* who had already sunk thirteen ships and damaged three others in just three months, radioed his base for permission to finish her, but that request was denied.

For the next four hours, the *Blakeley* cruised with its shattered, twisted bow section open to the sea, which was now held back by just a thin bulkhead. She was steered by varying her shaft speeds to rudder control until she could make a safe port. It was an amazing feat of seamanship. In port, a wooden bulkhead was wedged in place to strengthen her forward area. She then sailed to another port in Puerto Rico, where a better replacement was welded into place. With a little more assurance that she was now seaworthy, she sailed for Philadelphia. There, the bow of a decommissioned destroyer was permanently welded into place. By September 1942, the *Blakeley* was back on convoy duty in the Caribbean.

The twenty-three-year-old destroyer continued to serve her country until 1945. She had only one encounter with her enemies, so she received only one battle star for the action that should have sunk her. But that one action proved to other Destroyer Men that even an old ship, if manned by a determined young crew, could sometimes survive almost sure sinking.

On October 30, the HMS *Petard* (G-56), a P-class British destroyer at sea only since July, made its place in history.

The *Petard* depth charged the *U-559* to the surface near the mouth of the Nile River. Three men went below to retrieve both the new four-rotor Enigma machine being used by the German Navy as well as the codebooks for it. The codebooks were retrieved, but the machine itself may have been with the officer and sailor who never made it out of the hatch before the submarine sank below the waves. The most important codebook retrieved dealt with how to encode the weather conditions, which were often rebroadcasted by the Germans without any coding. That gave British code breakers a means of matching up open information to coded information.

Two British destroyers, the *Bulldog* in 1941 and the *Petard* in 1942, had made important contributions to the deciphering of the codes Germany was confident would never be broken.

The year ended with a destroyer scraping the bottom of a river to complete its vital mission.

Operation *Torch*, the invasion of North Africa in November 1942, was something of a forced operation pushed upon generals and admirals by Roosevelt and Churchill, who were anxious to blunt Germany's advance on Russia. The military men were finally ordered to plan for the invasion despite their misgivings; the U.S. Army and Navy had not yet been molded into a fighting force.

The Americans aimed to take advantage of the fact that French Morocco, a protectorate in North Africa controlled by the Vichy French, was less heavily defended than other areas under German control.

The Navy men in Task Force 34, who would transport the hastily trained soldiers to North Africa, were equally green, with fewer than half having been to sea before being assigned to this task force. More than forty destroyers would screen what was then the largest invasion force in history, with more than 110 ships crossing the Atlantic in a tight convoy formation.

Several old four stackers played major roles in the landings.

The USS *Cole* (DD-155) and the USS *Bernadou* (DD-153), both *Wickes*, drew the assignment to land troops at the small port of Safi. The destroyers were not the fast attack transports (APDs) that would commonly be used in the coming Pacific island hopping campaigns, but some top weight was removed from the destroyers by cutting down their masts and funnels. The two destroyers moved into the harbor at nearly 4:00 a.m. with the *Bernadou* running right into a wharf rather than beside it. The *Cole* was able to dock without mishap.

The destroyer with the most interesting mission during Operation *Torch* was the USS *Dallas* (DD-199), a *Clemson*, later renamed *Alexander Dallas* to avoid confusion as cruisers were named after cities.

The *Dallas*, which had been modified by removing her original 4-inch guns and some of her superstructure including her masts, was tasked with capturing the airfield at Port Lyautey. The *Dallas* would take a detachment of Army Rangers 12 miles up the Wadi Sebou River in a hoped-for surprise attack. It would be a surprise because the French who were protecting the airfield believed the river was so narrow and shallow—only 17 feet deep—that it would serve as a natural obstacle practically guaranteeing that no invasion force could ever reach them.

What the French had not counted on was the *Dallas* having an empty draft of 9 feet, perhaps 11 feet if fully loaded with the Rangers.

Still, the *Dallas* had to make it over the sandbar across the river. When she pushed her way over the sandbar with her engines running fast enough to produce 26 knots on a calm sea, her captain later noted in an after action report that "a glance over the side showed...that we were making less than five [knots]."[3]

The attack strategy did not work out in reality as it had been planned back in the States. The *Dallas* twice rammed a boom stretched across the river mouth, but did not break it. Finally, a navy party cut the boom and the *Dallas* started upriver.

At her wheel was her captain, Lieutenant Commander Robert Brodie, Jr., and beside him stood a Frenchman, Rene Malavergne, a river pilot native to the area who had returned to free his homeland. As Malavergne issued orders to the helm, and the *Dallas* steamed from one side of the river to the other, her keel often struck the bottom of the river. One shell from a nearby French fort fortuitously landed close enough to lift the stern out of the mud and back into deeper water.

At one point, the *Dallas* steered between two sunken freighters, running at full speed to keep moving against the current with just a few feet to spare on each side. As Brodie cleared the two sunken wrecks, he spun the wheel to keep from running into the river bank.

It took four hours to go just 12 miles upriver to the airfield; a trip that should have taken only half an hour on the open ocean. The *Dallas* grounded just off the airfield, but the seventy-five Rangers were able to land in rubber rafts and capture the airfield without a loss. Despite Malavergne being a French civilian, both he and Brodie were awarded Navy Crosses.

It was a somewhat empty victory. The airfield was so pockmarked with shell holes that many of the P-40s launched from a carrier and flown to the airfield were damaged trying to land. The *Contessa*, a shallow-draft freighter loaded with aviation fuel that had followed the *Dallas* upriver, also grounded and was unable to land its cargo of fuel until after the battle was over. Still, both the *Dallas* and the *Contessa* had completed their missions to capture the airfield.

The British navy ended 1942 with a tremendous victory over Germany at the Battle of Barents Sea on December 31.

Sailing from Scotland, Convoy JW 51B consisted of fourteen merchant ships carrying tanks and other vehicles, fighters, bombers, and aviation fuel bound for Russia. The convoy was protected by six destroyers.

Spotted by a U-boat, the convoy was targeted by a force of two German cruisers and six destroyers operating from a captured port in Norway. The flagship cruiser was the *Admiral Hipper,* which weighed 16,170 tons and was armed with eight 8-inch guns that could throw shells weighing 269 pounds 20 miles. The cruiser *Lutzow* weighed 12,630 tons and was armed with six 11-inch guns that could throw a shell weighing 660 pounds 19 miles.

The German destroyers were *Friedrich Eckoldt* (Z-16), *Richard Beitzen* (Z-4), *Theodor Riedel* (Z-6), Z-29, Z-30, and Z-31. All were Type 1934As and Type 1936As, weighing between 1,625 tons and nearly 2,600 tons. Most carried four 5-inch guns which could throw 61-pound shells nearly 10 miles. While formidable-looking, these classes still had engine problems, range limitation, and little ammunition storage. On top of that, their bows plunged into head seas so badly that their turrets had electrical problems with their wiring shorting out.

The British destroyers were the HMS *Obdurate* (G-39), HMS *Achates* (H-12), HMS *Orwell* (G-98), HMS *Oribi* (G-66), HMS *Onslow* (G-17), and HMS *Obedient* (G-48). Two corvettes, a minesweeper, and two trawlers rounded out the protecting escorts. Five of the six were O-class destroyers weighing 1,540 tons and measuring 345 feet long. The destroyers were armed by nothing larger than 4-inch guns throwing a 31-pound shell no more than 9 miles.

Every British destroyer was outweighed by every German ship, and every British destroyer was outgunned by every German ship.

The battle should have been no contest. The German commander had no doubt he could destroy the entire convoy and its escorting destroyers with the superior range and weight of his larger guns.

The battle opened at 8:00 a.m. with the British destroyers feigning a torpedo attack, scaring the German cruisers from moving in closer. The British destroyers successfully engaged the German cruisers for more than three hours before two British cruisers, operating in the same waters, arrived to make the odds even. The cruisers were able to damage the *Admiral Hipper* with their long-range guns. At one point, two German destroyers tried to form up on a light British cruiser, confusing her with the *Admiral Hipper*. One of them, *Friedrich Eckoldt*, was immediately sunk with all hands.

The *Achates* came under cruiser fire but continued to stay at her post, laying smoke to hide the convoy until she sank. A British minesweeper was also sunk, but not a single freighter was touched in a battle that lasted over four hours. The German force, with its heavy cruiser *Admiral Hipper* damaged, simply ended the attack and turned back with the arrival of more British cruisers.

When Hitler learned that two of his heavy cruisers, one at 16,000 tons and the other at 12,600 tons, plus six of his destroyers, had sunk only one puny 1,300-ton British destroyer and a minesweeper, he flew into a rage. The rage grew even worse when he learned that the entire convoy of fourteen merchant ships bound for Russia had also escaped with only a few steel splinters in their hulls.

Hitler demoted the head of the German Navy, Admiral Erich Raeder, who had always been a proponent of large surface fleets. Hitler replaced him with Admiral Karl Donitz, who had long championed U-boats. For several days, Hitler insisted he would scrap the entire Germany surface fleet and use its salvaged steel to make more U-boats, but Donitz talked him out of that drastic measure.

While it had taken the arrival of British cruisers to damage the attacking German cruisers, it was the six gallant destroyers protecting the convoy that had kept the superior German force at bay for more than three hours before the British cruisers could steam into range.

British Destroyer Men had much to celebrate and German Destroyer Men had much to embarrass them. In two battles in two different years, Narvik in 1940 and the Barents Sea in 1942, an outnumbered force of British destroyers had soundly defeated two superior forces of German destroyers.

The year 1942 ended with the U.S. Army establishing a firm foothold in North Africa. Three old destroyers from World War I had played key roles in establishing that beachhead. One old American destroyer given to the British had completely wrecked a dry dock, spoiling the plans of the Germans to service its most formidable battleship. Two British destroyers had played key roles in capturing Enigma machine codebooks. Six British destroyers had saved a convoy from being sunk and forced a change in the top command of the German Navy.

No one realized it at the time, but destroyers were becoming indispensable to the war effort.

Pacific Theater 1942

"Courageous abandon against fearful odds."

The *Asagumo* was an *Asahio* class, a ten-ship class commissioned in the late 1930s. All class members were sunk during the war. *NHHC photo.*

The Japanese navy had most of the advantages when the Pacific War began in earnest in 1942. It had twelve battleships compared to none for the U.S., considering all eight in the Pacific were now out of commission at Pearl Harbor. The Japanese had ten fleet aircraft carriers in Pacific waters while the United States had three. Japan had forty-four cruisers of all weights compared to nineteen cruisers for the U.S. Navy.

Only when comparing total destroyer numbers did the Japanese come close to matching up with the Americans. But the statistics were deceiving.

Japan had 108 destroyers in service at the start of the war, but forty of them were commissioned in the early 1920s with more than a dozen deemed too unseaworthy to do much more than patrol home Japanese waters. Twenty-one ships belonging to two classes, *Kamikaze* and *Mutsuki,* would be used extensively as destroyer transports, but were considered obsolete as front-line destroyers.

Counting just those ships ready to battle the Americans on an even basis when the war started in December 1941, Japan had sixty-eight destroyers in six classes. All of them were formidable, starting with the nineteen copies of the *Fubuki* class which first were commissioned in 1928. Following were four copies of the *Akatsuki* class, six of the *Hatsuharu* class, ten of the *Shiratsuyu,* and ten of the *Asashio* class, ending in April 1941 with the commissioning of the last of the nineteen ships of the *Kagero* class.

Those sixty-eight destroyers weighed between 1,750 and 2,033 tons. All of them carried five to six 5-inch/50 caliber guns in three twin weatherproof gun mounts. These Japanese 5-inch guns were longer than the guns the Americans used, allowing them to throw a shell more than one mile further. The Americans had been disturbed at the appearance of the *Fubuki* in 1928 and had every reason to worry about the construction of the following classes over the intervening fourteen years.

The U.S. Navy went to war in the Pacific with seventy-nine unconverted destroyers (DD) in all Pacific ports. That number did not count the converted four stackers, eight minelayers (DM), thirteen minesweepers (DMS), and six seaplane tenders (AVDs) that were assigned to the Pacific Ocean. Six fast attack transports (APDs) would soon be transferred to the Pacific Fleet from the Atlantic Fleet. Counting those converted destroyers that still had some of the speed and sting of their original design, the United States had or soon would have 112 ships in the Pacific that were either destroyers or started their service as destroyers.

The seventy-nine American destroyers outnumbered the sixty-eight front-line destroyers the Japanese had in the Pacific, but a closer look shows problems with the comparison.

Of the seventy-nine American destroyers carrying the DD designation, forty-five, or fifty-seven percent, were built in the 1930s. The other thirty-three destroyers, or forty-three percent, were built just after the end of World War I, including all of the thirteen destroyers stationed in the Philippines and Borneo as part of the Asiatic Fleet.

All sixty-eight Japanese front-line destroyers had great advantages over the forty-three percent of the American destroyers constructed in the early 1920s. The American *Clemson*-class destroyer weighed 1,215 tons compared to the *Fubuki* at 1,750 tons. The *Clemson* had four 4-inch guns with an effective range of five miles in open mounts that offered their crews little protection from the sea or shell splinters. The *Fubuki* had six 5-inch guns with a maximum range of 11.5 miles mounted in three water-tight gun houses. The *Fubuki* had nine 24-inch torpedo tubes compared to the *Clemson,* with twelve 21-inch torpedo tubes.

Even though fifty-seven percent of the United States' destroyers in the Pacific were considered modern, raw statistics show they may still have been outclassed by Japanese destroyers. The *Mahan* class for the United States, the most numerous at Pearl Harbor, weighed 1,500 tons and was armed with five 5-inch guns in four semi-enclosed gun mounts. By the end of 1941, Japan had launched eighteen ships of the new *Kagero* class, which weighed 2,000 tons and were armed with six 5-inch guns in three-gun houses and eight 24-inch torpedo tubes. Those tubes could also be reloaded. The *Gridley*-class of destroyers, successors to the *Mahan* and the newest destroyer design that the Americans had in service in December 1941, still weighed 1,500 tons and were armed with four 5-inch guns and sixteen 21-inch torpedo tubes.

Even when comparing the more modern American destroyers against the Japanese destroyers, the Japanese had the edge. The Japanese 5-inch/50 caliber guns' maximum range was 11.5 miles firing a 51-pound projectile, compared to the American 5-inch/38 caliber range of 10.3 miles firing a 55-pound projectile. The Japanese would use 24-inch diameter torpedoes with a 1,000-pound warhead compared to the Americans using 21-inch torpedoes with an 825-pound warhead.

One area where both Americans and Japanese destroyers were equally inadequate was the woeful lack of air defenses. The *Gridley* and *Mahan* classes were both equipped with only four .50 caliber machine guns on deck. The comparable *Kagero* class had better anti-aircraft guns—four 25 millimeter cannons. But due to a slow rate of fire, these proved to be little better than the American machine guns. The older *Fubuki* class had only two 13-millimeter machine guns.

While the United States' attention was still riveted on the attack on the Pacific Fleet at Pearl Harbor in December, it was the little recognized Asiatic Fleet that was most in danger of Japanese attack in January 1942.

The Asiatic Fleet had been a force in the Philippines since 1902, in place nearly forty years longer than the Pacific Fleet, which had moved from California to Pearl Harbor in 1940. Many future World War II admirals such as Chester Nimitz and Jack Fletcher had learned the Philippine waters while commanding destroyers from the port at Cavite on the island of Luzon. For more than a decade in the 1930s, the Asiatic Fleet had been a force in China until the advancing Japanese had forced the ships out of their mainland China ports and back to the Philippines and Balikpapan, a port on the island of Borneo.

Over time, the prestige of the Asiatic Fleet had dwindled, despite it being commanded by a four-star admiral. In January, the force consisted of only two cruisers, thirteen *Clemsons*, twenty-nine submarines, two tankers, four seaplane tenders, and a variety of other support vessels. Despite being directly in the path of any Japanese advance through the Pacific since the mid-1930s, the fleet had not been assigned any of the new *Mahan* and *Gridley* destroyers based at Pearl Harbor.

Admiral Thomas Hart, commander of the Asiatic Fleet, described his *Clemsons* in Destroyer Squadron 29 as: "Old enough to vote; not only inadequately armed for the warfare of the day, but sadly in need of overhaul, [but] manned by rock-hard veterans of the China Station who, under relentless, nerve-racking pressure, fought them with fierce determination and courageous abandon against fearful odds."[1]

The Japanese did not have perfect timing when they attacked the Philippines on December 8—the same day as Pearl Harbor, but over the International Date Line. The sailors on the destroyers based at Cavite and Manila heard about the attack on Pearl by radio. Two destroyers at Manila were able to get up steam and escort two oilers and a seaplane tender out of the harbor before the Japanese airplanes arrived. Left behind at Cavite was the USS *Peary* (DD-226), which was being repaired after an earlier collision with the USS *Pillsbury* (DD-227). The *Peary* was hit by a bomb, but not sunk. After repairs, she put to sea.

The *Peary* and *Pillsbury* eventually escaped Cavite with the *Peary* making Darwin, Australia on January 3, but only after being attacked by both Japanese and Australian airplanes along the way. One sailor was killed by the concussion of an Australian bomb, resulting in an early use of the term "friendly fire" in the *Peary's* deck log.[2]

"The [*Peary*], bedraggled-looking ship, the smoke stacks full of holes, the bridge half gone, no mast except a boat spar, camouflaged in various ingenious ways, had reached a haven," reads an anonymous report filed by an officer with Destroyer Squadron 29 in March 1942, describing the *Peary* as he saw her.[3]

The *Pillsbury* headed to Balikpapan, where it joined forces with the rest of the *Clemsons*, American cruisers, and surviving British and Dutch ships to form the ABDA (American British Dutch Australian) Command on January 15, 1942. In a move many American officers would question, Dutch Admiral Karel Doorman, who had spent most of his career behind a desk rather than at sea, was given command of the sea forces of ABDA.

ABDA's combined forces included two heavy cruisers, seven light cruisers, twenty-three destroyers, forty-six submarines, and several auxiliary ships. While the force looked formidable on paper, its area of operation was equal in size to the Atlantic Ocean, and it was isolated in waters now controlled by the Japanese. Most distressing was that the force had little air cover protection as it had no carriers, and the American ground-based airplanes in the Philippines had been virtually wiped out in the first strikes. The only friendly forces in the air were a few scattered Dutch bombers.

By comparison, Japan had six carriers patrolling in the Western Pacific looking for the last vestiges of resistance like ABDA.

For the rest of January, the American destroyers did what they could, acting as an isolated forward force without any hope of reinforcements coming from any direction. Their only source of supplies and fuel were a few scattered ports not yet taken.

One bright spot came on January 20, when the USS *Edsall* (DD-219) picked up a sound contact as it escorted a small convoy into the port of Darwin. Working with an Australian corvette, the *Edsall* dropped depth charges and was rewarded with the surfacing of a large swirl of oil: evidence the *I-124,* an obsolete Japanese minelaying submarine, had been killed. It would be the first confirmed Japanese submarine sunk by an American destroyer in the war (not counting the *Drayton's* claimed but unconfirmed kill on December 24, 1941). The Australians would also claim credit as they too dropped depth charges in the area.

Indonesia's oil wells developed by the Dutch were captured by Japanese forces on January 21, 1942, with the taking of Tarakan Island. Now Balik-papan became their objective. A force of twelve Japanese destroyers and sixteen transports was dispatched to take the port recently evacuated by ABDA.

The USS *Paul Jones* (DD-230), USS *Pope* (DD-225), and USS *Parrott* (DD-218) were all members of the ill-fated Asiatic Fleet. *NHHC photo.*

All that ABDA could muster quickly against the invasion was four *Clemsons*: USS *John D Ford* (DD-228), USS *Pope* (DD-225), USS *Parrott* (DD-218), and USS *Paul Jones* (DD-230). Just before 3:00 a.m. on January 24, the four ships steamed undetected into the Balikpapan Harbor. Their captains could not believe their luck. The oil refineries on shore were burning, having been blown up by the retreating Dutch. Two transports were also burning, struck the previous afternoon by some of the few remaining Dutch bombers. Smoke covered the harbor, which helped screen the approach of the American ships with the fires on shore also backlighting the anchored transports.

Ten Mark 8 torpedoes in two salvos were loosed by two destroyers at the point-blank distance of 1,000 yards, but none of them exploded. A third salvo by the *Parrott* finally hit a transport. The Mark 8 torpedoes were World War I era torpedoes with a warhead of 466 pounds. Once the torpedoes were fired, the destroyers started firing their 4-inch guns.

"At one time I could count five sinking ships. A third time we reversed course and ran through the demoralized convoy...The water was covered with swimming Japs. Our wash overturned several lifeboats loaded with Japs. Other ships looked like they were covered with flies. Jap soldiers were clambering down their sides in panic...So far I believed the Japs had not discovered that we were in their midst. Attributing the torpedoes to submarines and believing we were their own destroyers," wrote a gunner officer on the *Ford* after the attack.[4]

Luckily, none of the more modern Japanese destroyers ever made contact with the Americans as they all had heavier, farther ranging guns than the 4-inch guns on the *Clemsons*.

In a battle lasting three hours, the four *Clemsons* sank four Japanese transports and a patrol craft. They could have sunk more transports as all of their Mark 8 torpedoes were fired at short ranges, but the torpedoes either missed or failed to explode. The torpedoes may have missed because the destroyer captains did not slow down from 24 knots before firing. They also might not have exploded because American torpedoes—including the Mark 8s carried by the *Clemsons*, the Mark 14s carried by submarines, and the Mark 15s, which replaced the Mark 8s—all suffered from the quality control problems of running too deep, too shallow, or not exploding at all when they hit a target.

The Battle of Balikpapan was not decisive. The Japanese had already captured the port and offloaded their troops and supplies. What the battle accomplished was boosting the morale of the Asiatic Fleet. It had won its first true engagement in the war—the first time the United States had fought a sea battle since the Spanish-American War. The sinking of a Japanese submarine off Darwin might have to be shared with the Australians, but this was an all-American victory.

The reality of ABDA's isolated situation soon undermined the morale boost.

"We scraped barrel-bottom for food stores. As for repairs, some of those shabby old cans got along with practically nothing but bailing wire and chewing gum," wrote an unnamed sailor who had been with the fleet.[5]

After the thrill of Balikpapan in January, February 1942 proved disastrous for ABDA.

On February 19, the *Peary*—the plucky little destroyer that had earlier survived being bombed twice by Japanese aircraft and once by Australian aircraft—was swarmed by more than two hundred Japanese aircraft in Darwin's harbor, the first time Australia itself was attacked by the Japanese. Five bombs landed on the ship, killing eighty-eight of its crew. Witnesses watched as the machine gunners on board continued shooting at the enemy until they sank beneath the water. The *Peary's* captain would be nominated for a Navy Cross for his actions.

Starting on February 18, ABDA tried to stop the invasion of Bali at the Battle of Bandung Strait. Early in the engagement, both submarines and aircraft tried to attack the Japanese fleet but were driven off. On the night of February 19, three ABDA Dutch cruisers, six American destroyers, and one Dutch destroyer met the four Japanese destroyers escorting two transports. With heavier ships and larger numbers, the ABDA force should have made short work of the Japanese destroyers, but the multinational force had not counted on the practiced night fighting skills of the Japanese.

For decades, the Japanese navy had planned on two strategies for defeating the Americans. One was to hit the Americans with a big devastating attack as they had done at Pearl Harbor. After that blow, the Japanese intended to pick off the remaining enemy forces in smaller night battles, where they would use their superior optical sights, searchlights, and torpedoes.

The four Japanese destroyers—*Asashio, Oshio, Michishio,* and *Arashio*—were all from the modern 1930s *Asashio* class, giants at 2,370 tons compared to the *Clemsons* they faced at 1,215 tons. The calm Japanese captains used this battle as practice for bigger battles still to come.

Within minutes, the Dutch destroyer HNLMS *Piet Hen* was hit by a torpedo and immediately sunk. Three hours later, another Dutch cruiser and four American destroyers arrived to again stalk the Japanese destroyers. The Dutch cruiser HNLMS *Tromp* was severely damaged, as was the USS *Stewart* (DD-224) by Japanese shell fire. All four Japanese destroyers were hit, but only lightly damaged. While a Dutch cruiser is credited with doing most of the damage to the Japanese destroyers, the American destroyers, firing their antiquated 4-inch guns, also made some hits while successfully avoiding the Japanese destroyers with their longer-range 5-inch guns.

Bandung Strait was an embarrassing loss and exposed the fact that ABDA could do little to blunt the Japanese anywhere in the region.

The *Stewart* put into the port of Surabaya, Java, for repair but was abandoned by her crew as the Japanese were closing in on that port. Scuttling charges were set. No American ever expected to see the *Stewart* again, but she would resurface later in the war under a different flag.

The sinking of the Dutch destroyer by a single Japanese torpedo fired from a long distance should have raised eyebrows among the ABDA commanders, but no one realized just how deadly this particular type of torpedo was this early in the war. This was the first time the Japanese had sunk an opposing ship with a torpedo launched from one of its own surface ships.

The torpedo was the Type 93, nicknamed "Long Lance" after the war by an American naval historian. It was 24 inches in diameter, nearly 30 feet long, weighed nearly 3 tons, and used compressed oxygen to help burn the alcohol fuel to power the 1,000-pound warhead to its target. The torpedo had a maximum range of nearly 22 miles, though the Japanese rarely attempted such distances. Because the mixing of alcohol and oxygen releases carbon dioxide, a gas readily absorbed by water, the Type 93 had a most dangerous advantage: it could leave a wake with few bubbles, making it almost impossible for lookouts to see it coming.

The Allies would see many more Type 93s fired from surface ships, and its sister, the Type 94, fired from submarines during the war.

Torpedoes were not the only things the Americans, British, and Dutch had to worry about. Of equal concern was smothering Japanese air cover.

On February 26, the USS *Langley* (AV-3), formerly the nation's first aircraft carrier converted to a seaplane tender, was caught by Japanese dive bombers off Indonesia. Her crew was transferred to the USS *Edsall* (DD-219), and the badly damaged ship was sunk by the USS *Whipple* (DD-217).

The next day, February 27, would be an even worse day.

The ABDA fleet of one Dutch cruiser, two British cruisers, one Australian cruiser, one American cruiser, two Dutch destroyers, three British destroyers, and four American destroyers had barely refueled in Surabaya, Java when they were ordered to find the Japanese. The fleet they would face was somewhat larger, with four cruisers and fourteen destroyers.

The Battle of the Java Sea would be the largest and last battle for the ABDA fleet, and would again deeply embarrass ABDA. Partial blame for the disaster could rest on the language barrier existing between the Dutch and American officers. Each nationality in ABDA also used different methods of issuing signals to their ships. Doorman had intentionally removed the float planes from his cruisers while the Japanese observation aircraft roamed the skies during the entire engagement. Doorman had intentionally blinded his own force in an effort to save weight on his cruisers.

The battle began at 4:20 p.m. Within eleven minutes, the first Japanese shell smashed into the Dutch commander's flagship cruiser. Within an hour, two Dutch destroyers had been sunk by Japanese cruisers' long-range and effective firing. No Japanese ships had even been hit.

With darkness approaching, the four American *Clemsons*—USS *John D. Edwards* (DD-216), USS *Alden* (DD-211), USS *John D. Ford* (DD-228), and USS *Paul Jones* (DD-230)—were ordered by Doorman to attack. Two of the destroyers had participated in the successful late-night Balikpapan raid, but now they were facing Japanese cruisers and destroyers that could see them in the twilight.

As the World War I era American destroyers, armed with nothing larger than 4-inch guns, steamed toward Japanese cruisers with 8-inch guns and destroyers with 5-inch guns, a sailor on the bridge of the *Alden* broke the tension: "I always knew these old four-pipers would have to go in and save the day!" The bridge erupted in laughter.[6]

The four American destroyers missed with all of their torpedoes and retreated back to Surabaya to refuel and rearm as best they could while the main fleet pressed on to confront the rest of the Japanese fleet. Before the day ended, ABDA had ceased to exist. Three cruisers and three destroyers had been sunk, with the Japanese suffering only a slightly damaged destroyer, hit by a single 4-inch shell from one of the American four stackers. Doorman himself died when he chose to go down with his sinking cruiser flagship.

Within two days, three American destroyers were picked off in separate engagements. *Edsall* was sunk by two Japanese battleships and two cruisers on March 1 in the Indian Ocean. Its captain proved to be adept at evading Japanese salvos. The frustrated Japanese sailors fired more than 1,300 14-inch shells at the *Edsall* without stopping it. It took an attack by dive bombers to finally slow the *Edsall* so it could serve as target practice for the battleships.

The *Pope* went down the same day after taking many bombs from dive bombers during the Second Battle of the Java Sea. The next night, *Pillsbury,* trying to make it to Australia, was sunk with all hands by two Japanese cruisers.

All three sinkings were so isolated from other American forces that the U.S. Navy was not sure what had happened to the destroyers until after the war, when captured Japanese navy records were checked. It was not until the 1950s that the fate of all of the crews was determined. None of the more than three hundred crew members survived the attacks from the battleships, heavy cruisers, and dive bombers.

Of the thirteen four stackers in the Asiatic Fleet through March 1942, eight would survive the rest of the war, with two of them fighting in the Atlantic. Five would be assumed lost within four months of the opening of the war along with at least four hundred crewmen. One destroyer, the *Stewart,* would be assumed destroyed in the dry dock where its crew left it. While they had unwillingly served under foreign leadership as part of the ABDA Command, the crews of the *Clemsons* acquitted themselves well during battle, sinking several Japanese transports and damaging much newer and larger Japanese destroyers.

During the Battle of Coral Sea from May 4-8, no surface ships ever saw or fired on each other, but destroyers played the major role in rescuing sailors from the sea. Three destroyers rescued nearly 2,800 men from the sinking USS *Lexington* (CV-2). Not a single carrier sailor was lost to drowning at sea thanks to the destroyers.

Emboldened by their ability to easily brush aside the ABDA in February and March, the Japanese moved eastward in May, intending to occupy Port Moresby in New Guinea. From Port Moresby, the Japanese could mount better attacks on Australia. As three Japanese carriers advanced, their aircraft chanced upon the USS *Sims* (DD-409) escorting a tanker on May 7. The *Sims,* commissioned in 1939, was the lead ship in her class of twelve 1,570-ton destroyers. She had not been at Pearl Harbor, so this was her first action. It was also her last. Thirty-six dive bombers swarmed her and the tanker. It would be the first loss of a modern 1930s era American destroyer in the open Pacific.

One month later, a destroyer would play a major role in determining the winner of the carrier-dominated Battle of Midway fought June 4-7, 1942. Some naval historians count the Battle of Midway as the turning point of the war in the Pacific after which the Americans were on a path to defeat the Japanese.

Ironically, a Japanese destroyer can be credited with making the battle the turning point.

Arashi was a *Kagero*-class destroyer commissioned in November of 1940. On the morning of June 5, the USS *Nautilus*, a submarine, had stumbled onto the Japanese fleet steaming east toward Midway. A Japanese cruiser spotted its periscope and ordered the *Arashi* to attack and sink the submarine, lest it be successful in targeting the advancing fleet or surfacing and radioing its position. For at least an hour, the *Arashi* dropped depth charges, but was never able to injure the *Nautilus*. By 9:40 a.m., the destroyer broke off its attack and set a course to return to the fleet. The destroyer's captain left at a flank speed of 38 knots, either unaware or uncaring that his high speed was leaving a deep, wide wake that could be spotted from miles away by any plane that should be looking down.

One was. At 9:55 a.m., Lieutenant Commander Wade McClusky, Jr. was leading a flight of thirty-three Dauntless dive bombers at 19,000 feet as he searched for the Japanese carriers. When he saw the ship's wake, he realized it could only be Japanese from the direction it was headed. He guessed the wake was made by a cruiser because it was so large, another indication that the newest *Kageros* were much larger than most American destroyers.

McClusky was so far behind the enemy's wake that he realized the destroyer's lookouts could not see him. Rather than close in to attack this lone, tempting target, he ordered his flight to throttle back. He wanted to see where the wake was heading. The dive bombers could not do this for long. They had been in the air for more than two hours and were reaching the end of their fuel window to return to the USS *Enterprise*. Just five minutes after spotting the *Arashi's* wake, McClusky spotted the wakes of many ships. The *Arashi* had pointed to the four-carrier Japanese fleet like a huge arrow on the Pacific's surface.

McClusky's dive bombers soon had two of the four Japanese carriers ablaze. Two more would go down during the Battle of Midway. Had McClusky not spotted the large destroyer acting like an arrow on the ocean surface, the war might have turned out differently.

Commander Watanabe Yusumasa, captain of the *Arashi*, had picked up a downed American pilot in the ocean, brutally interrogated him, then had a crewman bash him with a fire ax and toss him into the ocean. Using information taken from the pilot, the Japanese carriers launched one last attack against the American carrier USS *Yorktown* (CV-5), a ship the Japanese thought they had sunk at the Battle of the Coral Sea. Yusumasa did not survive the war, so no war crimes were filed against any other members of the crew.

Nor did the *Arashi*—one of the most important destroyers in the history of the Pacific theater. She would be sunk fourteen months later in the Battle of Vella Gulf, along with two sister destroyers.

The Japanese submarine *I-168* would achieve some measure of revenge for the disaster at Midway when it would send a spread of four torpedoes at the crippled carrier USS *Yorktown* (CV-5) and the USS *Hamman* (DD-412) on June 6. The *Hamman* had rescued some eight hundred sailors from the *Lexington* the previous month and more from the *Yorktown* on this day. She was standing close to the carrier providing electrical power when the torpedo hit. She sank in less than four minutes, killing eighty crew members, including some killed by her own exploding depth charges. The *I-168* barely survived depth charging by destroyers and made it back to Japan for repairs. She would be sunk the following year by an American submarine.

On August 7, the U.S. Marines landed on Guadalcanal in the Solomon Islands, the first offensive operation of ground forces by the United States in the Pacific Theater. The troops originated from Espiritu Santo in the New Hebrides, an island about 610 miles to the southeast. For the rest of the war,

Espiritu Santo would be a major port from which American destroyers would sail against the Japanese moving from north to south toward Guadalcanal.

While these first troops on Guadalcanal disembarked down 30-foot-long cargo nets strung from the tall sides of troop ships, other Marines bound for the nearby island of Tulagi used much shorter nets strung from the lower decks of four stackers converted to fast attack transports (APDs).

A total of thirty-two World War I era destroyers—seventeen *Wickes*, fourteen *Clemsons*, and one *Caldwell*—would be converted to *APDs* just before and during the war. Halfway through the war, dozens of modern *Buckley*-class destroyer escorts would also be converted into *APDs*.

While the name was not official, their crews nicknamed the *APDs* "all-purpose destroyers." The first six commissioned *APDs*, transferred from the Atlantic Fleet, were all engaged to run back and forth from Espiritu Santo in the New Hebrides to supply the Marines and Army soldiers with food, fuel, and ammo during the six-month struggle to take and keep Guadalcanal. *APDs* seven through thirty-six would be converted after the successful use of the first six during the Guadalcanal campaign.

The USS *Gregory* (DD-82/APD-3) was sunk off Guadalcanal in the company of the USS *Little* (DD/APD-4) in September of 1942. *NHHC photo.*

The first *APD*, the USS *Manley* (DD-74/APD-1), the only 1,000-tonner *Caldwell* to be converted, had already proven itself to be one tough ship in

World War I. She lost more than a third of her crew from a fiery accident in 1918, and almost sank while being towed to Ireland for repairs. After laying up for eight years from 1922-1930, she had been constantly at sea.

Manley, USS *Colhoun* (DD-85/APD-2*),* USS *Gregory* (DD-82/APD-3), USS *Little* (DD-79/APD-4), USS *McKean* (DD-90/APD-5), and USS *Stringham* (DD-83/APD-6), all laid down before 1918, played active, exhausting roles in keeping the supplies landing on Guadalcanal. For days on end, the destroyers would make the 50-mile trip from Tulagi Island off the southern coast of Florida Island to Lunda Point on the northern coast of Guadalcanal.

Three of the first six *APDs* were sunk during the desperate struggle to hold Guadalcanal. Three weeks after landing the 1st Marine Raider Battalion, the *Colhoun* was attacked by dive bombers after dropping off supplies. Half of her crew was killed. On September 5, the *Gregory* and *Little* were staying at sea on the north coast of Guadalcanal on the night of September 5 rather than risk running aground on shoals by returning to Tulagi through the haze. As they watched a Japanese force on their radar, confident that their radarless enemies could not see them, a U.S. Navy Catalina dropped a string of flares over what it thought was a Japanese submarine. The flares silhouetted the two old destroyers for the surprised Japanese. It was no match: three Japanese destroyers, each armed with at least five 5-inch guns against two American destroyers, each armed with three 3-inch guns. Within half an hour, the two *APDs* were sunk. The ships were so close to shore that some of the crews were able to swim to Guadalcanal.

The USS *Little* (DD-79/APD-4) was sunk along with the *Gregory* when a U.S. Navy aircraft accidentally illuminated them in range of Japanese ships. *NHHC photo.*

"With little means, the ships performed duties vital to the success of the campaign," Admiral Chester Nimitz said when he heard of the sinking of the *Little* and *Gregory*.[7]

Eleven of the original thirty-two four stacker conversion *APDs* would be sunk or damaged beyond repair during the war, including one sunk in a collision with another American destroyer in September of 1944, and one by kamikaze in May of 1945. The first *APD*, the *Manley*, won five battle stars and was scrapped in 1946 after completing a service life of more than fifty years. The thirty-two four stacker *APDs* accumulated 203 battle stars in World War II, with the USS *Schley* (DD-103/APD-14), amassing the most with eleven.

The Japanese also converted otherwise obsolete destroyers into armed transports. Twenty-one *Momi*-class and twelve *Mutsuki*-class destroyers were used to deliver and resupply their troops at Guadalcanal. The *Momi* destroyers, built about the same time as the American four stackers, were smaller, weighing 864 tons compared to a *Wickes* class at 1,154 tons. The *Mutsuki* class was 1,315 tons. Both classes were modified by reducing numbers of guns so that more troops could be carried and dropped off by the Toku Daihatsu landing craft, which had a droppable, bow-mounted ramp later duplicated in the Higgins boats.

The First Battle of Savo Island, just northeast of the eastern tip of Guadalcanal, was fought on August 9. It remains one of the worst defeats of the U.S. Navy considering the American forces outnumbered those of the Japanese by nearly three to one. The American and Australian force consisted of six heavy cruisers, two light cruisers, and fifteen destroyers, matched up against five heavy cruisers, two light cruisers, and just one destroyer for the Japanese.

The USS *Blue* (DD-387), a *Bagley* class, played an unwitting role in the battle when it failed to spot the approaching Japanese fleet either on radar or visually. There is some speculation that Savo Island's own radar echo cloaked the Japanese ships, considering the fleet came within a mile of the *Blue* without being seen by American lookouts.

It was up to the USS *Patterson* (DD-392), a *Bagley* class, to open the battle when it alerted by radio and blinker around 1:45 a.m.: "Warning! Warning! Strange ships entering the harbor!"[8] She fired star shells at the Japanese column, but it was too late. The Japanese ships had already picked out American and Australian cruisers as their targets, now illuminated by flares dropped by accompanying floatplanes.

Confusion dominated the American and Australian fleet, with the USS *Bagley* (DD-386) possibly hitting the HMRS *Canberra,* an Australian cruiser, with at least two torpedoes. In less than two hours, four Allied cruisers and two destroyers had been sunk, taking 1,077 lives. The Japanese lost only 129 lives with slight damage to three light cruisers. The battle was an obvious tactical victory for the Japanese, but a strategic defeat considering the objective had been to destroy the American troop transports still landing men and supplies on Guadalcanal. The Japanese fleet commander turned around out of fear that American aircraft based on nearby carriers would reach his fleet at daybreak. What he did not realize was that the American carriers had pulled back out of concern they were the real targets of the Japanese attacking force.

The Japanese fleet commander was disciplined by his superiors, but they were confident in their night fighting skills and were convinced no other American ships would dare oppose them after the humiliation of Savo Island.

They were wrong.

Two months later, the Americans would get some measure of revenge for their sloppy performance at the First Battle of Savo Island when they fought the Battle of Cape Esperance, also known as Second Battle of Savo Island, on October 11-12.

In command of Task Force 64 was Admiral Norman Scott, who had been executive officer of the USS *Jacob Jones* (DD-61), the only destroyer lost in World War I to a U-boat attack. Scott had done what he could to prepare his ships' crews to fight at night by making them stand night watches. It was a woefully inadequate attempt to make things even with the Japanese, who had spent years practicing night fighting.

The battle opened with both naval commanders being confused about who was in front of them. Scott was unsure if the opening fire of his ships was directed at the Japanese. The Japanese commander was just as confused. He thought his own column was firing at him when it was American ships, which scored a bridge hit to kill the Japanese commander.

USS *Duncan* (DD-485), a *Gleaves*, misinterpreted the battle plan and attacked the entire Japanese column alone when the rest of the American ships were turning away in a planned maneuver. She scored a torpedo hit on a Japanese cruiser and a destroyer before being hit herself by shells. Shell hits were recorded on both sides of the *Duncan*, indicating that in the confusion, she was fired on by the Japanese and her fellow American ships, which had not expected one of their own to be so far forward in the battle. The impetuous *Duncan*, which had rescued more than seven hundred sailors from the sinking carrier USS *Wasp* (CV-7) on September 16, now had to have her own crew rescued. Most survived.

One Japanese cruiser and one destroyer were sunk during the battle. The first Japanese destroyer lost in ship-to-ship combat with the Americans in the Pacific War was the *Fubuki*, the lead of the twenty-ship class that had shocked the U.S. Navy in 1928 with its huge size of 1,750 tons.

No American naval commander realized the irony of the *Fubuki's* destruction at such an early point in the war. The destroyer class that had terrified the U.S. Navy fourteen years ago had been destroyed within a few minutes by the combined 8-inch and 5-inch shells of American cruisers and destroyers.

Again, the Americans had fought an ill-coordinated battle, sometimes hitting their own ships, but they were learning.

During the battle, the *Duncan* or the USS *Buchanan* (DD-484) fired the first 1930s-designed Mark 15 torpedo to hit a Japanese ship, more than nine months after a 1911-designed Mark 8 torpedo had sunk a Japanese transport at the Battle of Balikpapan.

Within a year of the war's opening, the Mark 15 torpedo, a close match to the Mark 14 carried by American submarines, replaced the shorter, lighter Mark 8 on newer American destroyers built after the mid-1930s. The older four stacker destroyers would continue to use the Mark 8, as would patrol torpedo (PT) boats.

Newer technology did not mean better technology.

The Mark 8 was 21 inches in circumference and 21 feet long with a top speed of 21 knots carrying a warhead of more than 400 pounds. The Mark 15 was 24 feet long with a top speed of up to 45 knots carrying a warhead of 825 pounds.

The Mark 15's improvements in speed and warhead weight over the Mark 8 meant nothing. The ship class of destroyers was developed to deliver the torpedo, which was virtually worthless as manufactured by the Americans.

Both the Mark 14 fired by American submarines and Mark 15 torpedoes performed poorly for more than a year after their first use in combat, running too shallow, too deep, or not exploding when they did hit the hull of a Japanese ship. At first, the U.S. Navy brass in charge of manufacturing torpedoes back in the States blamed poor marksmanship on furious destroyer and submarine captains who insisted they were making hits. Investigation proved the captains were correct that all American torpedo models had manufacturing defects, particularly with the warhead's detonator. Remarkably, all during the 1930s when a war seemed imminent, the Navy, acting as its own contractor and manufacturer, had not bothered to test the torpedoes to make sure they actually exploded.

In late September, the first of the *Fletcher*-class destroyers, the USS *Nicholas* (DD-449), arrived at Espirtu Santo. It was a wartime coincidence that the tide-changing Battle of Midway opened on the same day—June 4, 1942—that the *Nicholas* was commissioned into service after construction at Bath Iron Works in Maine.

The *Fletchers* were designed in 1939, ordered in 1941, and began to hit the waves in the summer of 1942. They displaced 2,050 tons compared to the 1,507 tons of the preceding *Sims* class, and were 376 feet long compared to 348 feet for the *Sims*. By widening the *Fletchers* to 39 feet, designers solved the top-heavy problems of the *Sims,* which were 36 feet wide at the beam.

The men still serving on the World War I era *Wickes* and *Clemsons* must have been in awe and were probably envious when they saw what must have looked like the giant *Fletchers.* The old four stackers weighed 1,215 tons and were 314 feet long with a beam of 31 feet.

The classes of destroyers developed in the 1930s carried the same five 5-inch guns as the *Fletchers,* though the *Fletchers* carried ten 21-inch torpedo tubes compared to twelve tubes for the *Sims.* The major difference in fire power between the 1930s destroyers and the *Fletchers* was that the *Fletchers* were designed with much heavier anti-aircraft guns while the original *Sims* only had four .50 machine guns, the early *Fletchers* were equipped with four 1.1-inch anti-aircraft guns, and six to ten 20-millimeter Oerlikon cannons. The 1.1-inch anti-aircraft guns proved susceptible to jamming, so they were soon replaced by 40-millimeter Bofors guns.

At the beginning of World War II, counting only American destroyers designed and built in the 1930s, there were twelve based on the *Sims* design, sixty-six *Gleaves,* eighteen *Mahans,* four *Gridleys,* thirty *Bensons,* ten *Benhams,* eight *Bagleys,* eight *Porters,* eight *Farraguts,* and five *Somers.* Before the end of the war, these destroyers would be joined by 175 *Fletchers.*

The Japanese had no way of knowing how many *Fletchers* would be coming into the Pacific in so short of a time, but the warnings of Yamamoto about the industrial capacity of the United States were proven correct even as Japan was technically still winning the battles in mid-1942.

From August through the rest of the year, the waters between Guadalcanal and Florida Island saw heavy naval combat. Savo Sound, at the southern end of the New Georgia Sound, would be nicknamed Iron Bottom Sound because of the number of ships sunk there. The New Georgia Sound was called "The Slot," because it served as a shipping lane running northwest through all of the Solomon Islands to Rabaul, a supply base and port held by the Japanese on New Britain about 660 miles north of Guadalcanal. Stopping the Japanese supply ships and transport destroyers coming down The Slot became the months-long goal of American destroyers operating out of Espiritu Santo, about 610 miles south of Guadalcanal.

The Battle of Santa Cruz Islands, a three day battle stretching from October 25-27, was another tactical victory for the Japanese. No surface ships engaged each other. A Japanese submarine sank the USS *Porter* (DD-356), and the carrier USS *Hornet* (CV-8) was sunk by Japanese dive bombers. The loss of the *Hornet* was devastating. The damaged USS *Enterprise* (CV-6) was now the sole American carrier in the Pacific.

One bright spot for American sailors during and after the battle was watching the USS *Smith* (DD-378), which downed six Japanese airplanes, extinguish the fires on its bow by cruising into the wake of the battleship USS *South Dakota* (BB-57). The *Smith* survived and won a Presidential Unit Citation for staying in the fight despite her fires.

As the new *Fletchers* began arriving, the crews of the old destroyers showed the newcomers how war was conducted. On November 10, the USS *Southard* (DD-207/DMS-10), a *Clemson* converted to a mine-sweeper in 1940, encountered the Japanese submarine *I-15* running on the surface. The submarine dove. For nearly six hours, the *Southard* made depth charge runs before the *I-15* broke the ocean's surface then sank below it.

That same day on the other side of the world, Americans landed in North Africa, the first time American ground troops were deployed in the European theater. The United States was now fighting back hard in two different parts of the world less than a year after the Pearl Harbor attack.

The Japanese objective during the Guadalcanal campaign was simple: either recapture or destroy Henderson Air Field on Guadalcanal to eliminate the American air threat to constantly incoming Japanese transport ships. For the past four months, the Japanese had been running transport destroyers and some light cruisers to the island at night to keep its troops supplied. But those ships were not equipped to offload the heavier guns and tanks their army needed to dislodge the Americans. Only transports with cranes could handle the heavy loads, but they took extra time to unload. By daylight, the American aircraft at Henderson Field could target the transports. Henderson Field had to be recaptured and held by the Japanese to end the American threat to resupply.

The American objective was also simple: sink all Japanese supply ships so Henderson could be saved. American resupply to their troops always came in the daylight because the Japanese ships owned the night-time seas around Ironbottom Sound.

The Japanese and American objectives were both the opposite and overlapping. The Japanese were confident they owned the night ocean, but needed to eliminate the daytime threats of American air attacks from Henderson Field. The Americans thought they could win daylight air battles, but their ships needed to also successfully engage the Japanese ships at night—their favored resupply regimen.

It was the Naval Battle of Guadalcanal on November 12-15 where the *Fletchers* got their baptism of fire.

The Japanese fleet of two battleships, ten cruisers, sixteen destroyers, and eleven transports had no expectation of meeting the Americans on the dark night, which was somewhat remarkable since the Americans were becoming increasingly bolder in confronting the Japanese in the darkness. The American force of two battleships, five cruisers, and twelve destroyers was somewhat outgunned, but it had the advantage that some of its destroyers were *Fletchers,* fresh from the U.S. shipyards and equipped with the latest versions of radar.

Curiously, Admiral Daniel J. Callaghan put the most modern destroyers in the rear of his column instead of in the van, where their radar could see further.

The two fleets virtually ran into each other in the darkness, an encounter so surprising to the Japanese that most of their ships' guns were loaded with high explosive shells designed to shell Henderson Air Field rather than the armor-piercing shells needed to fight other ships.

The Japanese first illuminated the cruiser USS *Atlanta* (CL-51) with powerful searchlights and then eliminated her, killing Admiral Scott. Next came the destruction of the USS *Cushing* (DD-376), a *Mahan,* which fired several torpedoes at the battleship *Hiei* for a range of just 1,000 yards. Three torpedoes hit, but if they exploded, the *Hiei's* below water armor absorbed them. The *Cushing* went down, smothered by Japanese shell fire.

The USS *Laffey (*DD-459), a *Benson,* tried the same torpedo attack. She was also too close, and her torpedoes hit the *Hiei* and bounced off before they had a chance to arm. The *Laffey* was hit by torpedoes and 14-inch shells from the *Hiei.* She too went down.

Next up was the USS *Sterett* (DD-407), a *Benham*-class, and the USS *O'Bannon* (DD-450), a brand-new *Fletcher* in its first real fight. Both destroyers fired torpedoes from a point blank range of just 1,200 yards at the *Hiei,* a 36,000-ton battleship launched in 1912, but which had been upgraded with better armor and guns. None of the torpedoes stopped her, but 5-inch shells hitting her superstructure killed a large number of the bridge crew and wounded Admiral Kobe, who was directing the battle.

Inexplicably, during the opening minutes of the attack, Admiral Callaghan ordered his ships to cease firing; an order most his fleet's gunners ignored as the Japanese were shooting at them. Callaghan's flagship, the cruiser USS *San Francisco* (CA-38), did cease fire. The Japanese did not issue any similar order and numerous hits on the cruiser's bridge killed Callaghan and his staff.

Both Admiral Callaghan and Admiral Scott would be posthumously awarded Medals of Honor for this confused action.

The USS *Barton* (DD-599), a *Benson,* stopped dead in the water to avoid a collision with the cruiser *Helena.* That made the American destroyer a tempting target for some Japanese destroyer torpedo man. She took two torpedoes and sank in seven minutes with most of her crew. Coming along behind *Barton* was the USS *Monssen* (DD-436), a *Gleaves.* Illuminated by star shells her captain thought were mistakenly fired by friendly ships, he turned on his destroyer's lights believing it would prove to the ships firing on him that he was American. It did. Within seconds, Japanese search lights illuminated his ship, resulting in thirty-seven shell hits.

The USS *Fletcher* (DD-445) was at the rear of the column as Admiral Callaghan had ordered. Using her superior surface radar, which could have been used to report Japanese locations sooner and better had she been leading the column, the *Fletcher* began firing at Japanese ships deep within its formation.

Once again, the Japanese admiral commanding the column turned his force around rather than continue with his mission to destroy Henderson Field. The battle was over, a tactical but costly victory for the Americans since the Japanese had withdrawn their forces. Four American destroyers and two light cruisers were lost compared to two Japanese destroyers and one battleship. Though the Japanese turned back before achieving their mission, the battle proved yet again that the Imperial Japanese Navy was still the master of the night ocean, even though its ships still did not have radar and the Americans did.

Admiral Halsey recognized what had just happened with a letter: "To the superb officers and men on the sea, on land, in the air, and under the seas who in the past five days have performed such magnificent feats for our country. You have won the undying gratitude of your country and have written our names in golden letters on the pages of history. No honor for you could be too great, my pride in you is beyond expression. Magnificently done. May God bless each and every one of you. To the glorious dead, hail heroes—may you all rest with God."[9]

While Halsey's letter was welcomed by the battered Destroyer Men, it did nothing to improve the Mark 15 torpedo. Of the thirty torpedoes fired by the American destroyers during the Battle of Guadalcanal, none exploded. Some hit Japanese battleships and destroyers but did not sink them.

Within three weeks, the Japanese were back, once again trying to reinforce their troops on Guadalcanal. This time they were more desperate. Until now, the destroyers used by the Japanese as resupply ships had been older models, much like the *Clemson APDs*. On this mission, the Japanese loaded supplies onto the decks of their frontline destroyers, seemingly a hindrance if the destroyers needed to make sudden movements.

Once again, the Americans were waiting for them, this time with destroyers which had the latest radar watching the approach from the head of the column rather than at the rear. The destroyers spotted the Japanese column 13 miles, or 23,000 yards, distant. On paper, the fleets were unbalanced, with the Americans waiting with five cruisers and four destroyers, and the Japanese approaching with eight destroyers.

The Battle of Tassafaronga—sometimes called the "Fourth Battle of Savo Island"—was fought during the night of November 30, just south of Savo Island. Once again, it was an embarrassing night action loss for the Americans. Catching the Japanese unawares, the American destroyers fired twenty torpedoes and missed with all of them, partially because the fleet commander delayed approval of a request to fire when the Japanese were unaware of their presence.

The Japanese destroyers fired at least thirty-six Type 93 torpedoes in return. Within a few minutes, three American cruisers were hit by the spread. The entire battle lasted less than thirty minutes. Once again, the Japanese admiral commanding the fleet lost his nerve and turned back despite that American warships had been severely damaged.

The Japanese tried several more times to deliver food to their infantrymen, once just dumping barrels of food overboard from destroyers in hopes it would wash ashore within their army's reach. Instead, American aircraft recognized the barrels for what they were and strafed them in the daylight, sending them to the ocean floor.

By mid-December, the Japanese high command reached the decision to evacuate their troops from Guadalcanal instead of resupplying them. It was a curious decision. The Japanese navy had continually embarrassed the American Navy throughout 1942. With the exception of the Battle of Midway in June, Japan had performed well in all of the major engagements. All of those battles had been at night just as the Japanese had practiced and expected to fight according to their decades old war plan against the Americans.

In most of the battles that the Americans had tactically won, it was not because of overwhelming numbers or good shooting on the part of the Americans. The American victories came when nervous Japanese commanders pulled back after some hard fighting, sometimes with victory within their grasp. The fighting men of the Imperial Japanese Navy had done their jobs, but their commanders too often turned back rather than continue fighting to a firm resolution of the battle.

Seventeen American destroyers and a half dozen cruisers had been sunk just in the vicinity of Guadalcanal in the second half of 1942. Even without the advantage of radar, the Japanese destroyers and cruisers were still getting the best of the Americans thanks to the Type 93 torpedo.

The Japanese army generals were furious when their superiors back in Japan decided to abandon the island. The generals laid the blame for their starving soldiers on the failure of the Japanese navy to defeat the U.S. Navy, which, though often bumbling, was growing stronger in numbers of fighting ships and developing better night fighting skills.

What the Japanese generals on Guadalcanal were not thinking about was what the admirals back in Tokyo were. Angered by the Pearl Harbor attack, the Americans were now furiously building hundreds of brand new ships to replace the ones resting on Ironbottom Sound. The Japanese could not match that ship production. The Japanese admirals realized that if they continued to lose valuable ships doggedly resupplying their soldiers on Guadalcanal, the Americans would eventually win the war through sheer industrial might without ever leaving one little island in the Solomons. The Japanese navy wanted to husband its resources and fight stand-up naval actions elsewhere, not be bogged down acting as a rice delivery service to a small, jungle-covered island.

When 1942 ended, barely a year after the Pearl Harbor attack, the naval war in the Pacific had already become a war of attrition, which Admiral Yamamoto had warned his countrymen they could not win.

Atlantic Theater 1943

*"Wiped out every exposed member of the
sub's crew topside."*

In 1943, the Allied forces were fighting two entirely different sea wars in the Pacific and the Atlantic.

In the Solomon Islands in the Pacific, Japanese and American cruisers and destroyers pounded each other regularly from air bases and ports 1,100 miles from each other with the combat zone halfway in-between. A column of ships from either side could leave port in the morning and be in combat later that night. A flight of aircraft could sometimes find an enemy ship to strafe, bomb, or torpedo within an hour of taking off. Combat was almost like two neighborhood street gangs slugging it out before returning to their side of the street. All might be peaceful on the ocean until one side made a move to reinforce and resupply their own troops.

In the Atlantic, the battlefield was nearly 4,000 miles wide and divided into three distinct combat regions: along the American Atlantic coast, the British and European coasts, and the great swath of the Atlantic between the two coasts out of range for land-based aircraft. Any day or night could bring a U-boat attack on a freighter sailing alone or a convoy escorted by warships.

For the first two years of the war, 1939-1940, Allied convoys, escorted by a handful of warships commanded by inexperienced captains, were frequently overwhelmed and confused by U-boat wolfpacks. The submarines would sometimes penetrate the convoy's presumed protection ring and attack, leaving the escorting ships looking for them outside the ring where they were expected to be. This period was known to the Germans as the "First Happy Time."

Through mid-1942, when the Germans were conducting Operation Drumbeat, German U-boats enjoyed the "Second Happy Time," when they could find unescorted Allied shipping off the American coast, often backlit by coastal towns' streetlights. In just nine months, German U-boats accounted for more than six hundred Allied ships while losing just twenty-two submarines.

By 1943, a new kind of ship, the destroyer escort, was available to augment the destroyers now escorting huge convoys over hundreds of routes.

Designed specifically to escort slow-moving convoys, which rarely made more than 10 knots per hour, destroyer escorts' top speed was just 21 knots compared to destroyers' top speed of 34 knots. All six classes of destroyer escorts produced starting in late 1942 and early 1943 displaced around 1,200 tons and were around 300 feet long. Armament consisted of three 3-inch guns, three torpedo tubes, varieties of 40-millimeter and 20-millimeter anti-aircraft guns, plus depth charges and a new weapon, the hedgehog.

Hedgehogs, invented by the British and also used by the Americans, were twenty-four shells launched at the same time toward the front of a destroyer. They exploded on contact with a submarine's hull. *Royal Navy photo.*

Developed by the British in 1941, the hedgehog fired twenty-four 65-pound shells forward of the ship in a wide semi-circle. The sinking shells would only explode if they hit a submarine's hull, so crews knew immediately if a salvo were successful. As an added bonus, any salvo of hedgehogs that did not explode against a sub's hull would not disrupt the water, which meant sonar echoes could continue to be tracked. Exploding depth charges ruined a sonarman's ability to hear, sometimes allowing a U-boat to slip away from contact.

At first, British ship captains were reluctant to use the hedgehog out of concern that its small 65-pound explosive charge was ineffective compared to 300-pounds of explosive in a depth charge. But once deployed in large numbers, the hedgehog proved much more effective than the World War I technology of the depth charge. One British study found a kill ratio of six hedgehog attacks to one U-boat kill compared to sixty depth charge attacks to one U-boat kill.

The British employed a wider array of convoy escorts than the Americans including 205-foot-long corvettes, 238-foot-long frigates, 299-foot-long sloops and destroyers of various classes.

By 1943, the Germans were waiting with wolfpacks of as many as twenty U-boats instead of the lurking single submarines deployed early in the war. In April, there was one wolfpack of fifty-five U-boats lying in wait for one large convoy. While the Allies would often be trying to find the submarines using destroyers launched during World War I, the U-boats coming on line in 1943 were improved, modern versions of their most numerously produced Type IX and Type VIIC submarines. More than five hundred of the VIIC submarines would be built. Type XIV supply submarines, called "milch cows," were developed to fuel submarines at sea.

The year started terribly for the Allies.

Convoy TM 1 was a convoy of nine tankers carrying petroleum products, including furnace oil. It left Trinidad for Gibraltar in early January, escorted by one destroyer and three corvettes. The protective ratio of one escort to two tankers was exceptional, but it did little good.

Discovered by one U-boat, the convoy soon was met by nine other submarines, which began their attacks on January 8. Over the next four nights, seven of the nine tankers were sunk with only minor damage to two U-boats from depth charges.

Lessons were being learned on both sides.

The destination of Convoy SC 118 was Liverpool. The convoy set sail on February 4 with sixty-four freighters protected by three destroyers, two cutters, and four corvettes. Thirteen U-boats were looking for the convoy when a merchantman accidentally fired an illumination shell, giving away the convoy's position. The *U-187* saw the burst and radioed the position. That signal was picked up by the convoy's escorting destroyers using their High-Frequency Direction Finder (HF/DF or "Huff Duff"). By comparing signals, the escorts were able to find the submarine. It was sunk by the HMS *Beverly* (H-64), formerly the *Clemson*-class USS *Branch* (DD-197), and the HMS *Vimy* (D-33), a V-class destroyer built in World War I. The *U-187*, a Type IXC/40, had only been completed six months earlier and was on her first patrol. The *Vimy* had also sunk a submarine in 1942 and rescued nearly three thousand soldiers from Dunkirk in 1940.

When Convoy SC 118 finally reached Liverpool, eight of the sixty-four freighters, or twelve percent, had been sunk at the cost of three U-boats—a fifteen percent loss. While carelessness had revealed the position of the convoy, the skillful use of Huff Duff had proved effective in finding U-boats.

What happened with Convoy ONS 5 during the last two days of April and the first week of May 1943 would mark the crucial turning of the Battle of the Atlantic for the Allies. U-boats would continue to menace Allied ships through 1945, but from May 1943, their losses would mount and the tonnage they sunk each month would diminish. What marks this battle as particularly painful for the German Navy was that the convoy attacked was not even carrying war supplies. That type of convoy had already slipped past a line of U-boats. ONS 5 was heading back to the United States carrying nothing of true value to the war. Yet, as the U-boats would discover, it was protected just as fiercely by the British navy as if it were carrying the food and fuel an inbound convoy would carry.

Leaving Liverpool and sailing into heavy seas on April 21, ONS 5 included forty-two merchant ships and an all-British escort of destroyers and corvettes.

Long before ONS 5 came into sight of the U-boats, British aircraft found the U-boats, sinking two of them. At 9:00 a.m. on April 28, the convoy was spotted by one U-boat, which then called in five others with the intention of attacking at night.

Over the next week, ONS 5 was attacked by forty-three U-boats operating in two groups. Thirteen freighters of the forty-two ship convoys were sunk, but six U-boats were sunk and seven more damaged. The sinkings work out to a thirty percent loss for both sides. None of the escorting vessels were sunk. Six different escorts could claim credit for sinking a submarine by hedgehog or depth charge.

Forty-one U-boats were sunk in May 1943, the largest number in any single month; a loss so heavy Germany began to rethink its submarine strategy.

May was a decisive month for the Battle of the Atlantic, but the war continued on other fronts.

On July 26, the USS *Mayrant* (DD-402), a *Benham* class, was patrolling off Palermo, Italy, when it was attacked by German dive bombers. One near miss ruptured her side, sending water rushing into her compartments. The crew saved her by pushing mattresses into her holes. Her executive officer received a Silver Star for his role in saving the ship. His name was a familiar one—Franklin Delano Roosevelt, Jr., the son of the President of the United States, who had volunteered at the opening of the war.

While the war seemed to be going the Allies' way in the Atlantic, death and destruction could strike at any moment. The USS *Rowan* (DD-405), another *Benham*-class, had served as a convoy escort since 1941. On September 10, she was escorting empty invasion ships off Sicily when her radar picked up some rapidly moving ocean contacts advancing within 3,000 yards. The *Rowan* rushed forward and fired eight rounds of 5-inch shells, which seemed to drive the targets away as the range increased to 6,000 yards.

Within a few minutes, radar showed another contact at 2,800 yards and the 5-inch guns again fired under radar control. As the *Rowan* was turning, a torpedo hit her port side into the magazine. According to the after action report, she went down in forty seconds.

Her killer was the *S57*, a German E-boat, seen by only one crew member. "No one else seems to have seen or heard them."[1]

It was the only time in the war that an American destroyer was sunk by an E-boat, the original incarnation of the destroyer as envisioned in 1874 of a fast attack boat designed to fire torpedoes at much larger ships. At least three British destroyers were lost to them. The German E-boat, at 107 feet long, was roughly equivalent to the U.S. Navy's Patrol Torpedo (PT) boat at 80 feet long. It was capable of 43 knots, 10 knots faster than a destroyer. E-Boats only had four torpedoes, so they always maneuvered close to fire their 21-inch torpedoes before enemies had time to react to the torpedoes' 44 knot speeds.

By mid-1943, the United States was ready to implement a mode of combat against U-boats that the British had tried and rejected two years earlier.

Early in the war, Great Britain had used aircraft carriers to hunt U-boats, but early efforts had been disastrous. On September 14, 1939, the HMS *Ark Royal* (91), Britain's newest aircraft carrier, barely missed being torpedoed less than two weeks into the war. The U-boat that missed, *U-39*, was sunk by three accompanying destroyers, becoming the first German submarine lost during the war. That small victory did not last long. Three days later, the HMS *Courageous* (50), another carrier, was sunk, taking 519 sailors to their deaths. Great Britain immediately ended its experiment of hunting submarines from aircraft carriers.

In December of 1941, Great Britain tried a different tactic—using aircraft carriers as escort vessels. The HMS *Audacity* (D-10), a German merchant ship converted into the first escort carrier, was assigned to escort

Convoy HG76 back to the British Isles from Gibraltar. Grumman Wildcats (called "Martlets" by the British) flew air cover, spotted and strafed U-boats, and called in their positions for the accompanying destroyers and corvettes. Eventually five U-boats were sunk, but so was the HMS *Stanley* (I-73), a former *Clemson* destroyer, the USS *McCalla* (DD-253), and the *Audacity*. The *Stanley* had been the first of the former American four stackers to claim a German U-boat, but was the second to be sunk after being in British service for just one year.

Since most of the freighters made it home, the Allies considered the battle a victory for their side. The Germans agreed.

Germany's U-boat commander Admiral Donitz noted the *Audacity's* contribution in the battle in a report: "The worst feature was the presence of the aircraft carrier. Small, fast maneuverable aircraft circled the convoy continuously, so that when it was sighted, the boats were repeatedly forced to submerge or withdraw."[2]

By late 1942, the United States was launching escort aircraft carriers: quickly-produced ships built on freighter hulls. At just under 500 feet long and weighing 9,800 tons, a ship like the USS *Card* (CVE-11) usually carried around twenty-eight aircraft, divided between fighters and torpedo bombers. By comparison, the Atlantic Fleet's USS *Ranger* (CV-4), the first designed aircraft carrier commissioned in 1934, was 730 feet long, weighed 14,000 tons, and normally carried seventy-six aircraft.

Accompanying the escort carriers were several four stacker destroyers in 1943 that were replaced by new destroyer escorts right out of the shipyards starting in 1944.

A rejected British concept was using carriers to provide moving air cover for convoys. The American concept was the creation of a hunter-killer group unattached to convoys with the specific mission of finding and sinking submarines.

The two most successful groups in the Atlantic were built around escort carriers USS *Bogue* (CVE-9) and USS *Card* (CVE-11).

The *Bogue's* escorts included, over different patrols, the USS *Lea* (DD-118), USS *Du Pont* (DD-152), USS *George E. Badger* (DD-196),

USS *Clemson* (DD-186), USS *Belknap* (DD-251), USS *Osmond Ingram* (DD-255), and USS *Greene* (DD-266). The *Lea* and *Du Pont* were *Wickes* class while the others were *Clemsons*.

The *Bogue* did not sink any subs on her first three patrols, but an Avenger torpedo bomber sank a U-boat on her fourth, and two more on her fifth. On her seventh patrol, the *George E. Badger* succeeded when a Wildcat/Avenger team had been unable to sink a U-boat. It took four depth charge runs, but the *U-613*, a mine-laying submarine, was finally destroyed. The destroyer's sonar operator reported "a loud howling noise which increased in intensity."[3] That was the sound of a submarine's hull being breached.

In December of 1943, the *George E. Badger* participated in the sinking of another submarine by using her depth charges and deck guns. She would later be converted to an *APD*, becoming the mother ship for an Underwater Demolition Team in the Pacific.

The *Bogue*'s aircraft would sink seven German U-boats, one Japanese submarine delivering war material to Germany, and her escort destroyers would sink two submarines. The *Card*'s aircraft would sink eight U-boats and her escort destroyers would sink three.

USS *Borie* (DD-215), a *Clemson*, fought an hour-long battle with a U-Boat in October of 1943 before it sank from the heavy damage. *NHHC photo.*

It was one of the *Card*'s escorts that would be involved in one of the most dramatic destroyer versus U-boat fights of the war.

The USS *Borie* (DD-215) was a *Clemson* class commissioned in 1920, and one of the few of her class that had remained in continuous active service rather than being decommissioned after World War I. She had sailed in the Black Sea off Turkey, around the Philippine Islands and off China with the Asiatic Fleet, and then back to the United States where she joined the Neutrality Patrols in the Caribbean. In June. she was assigned to the *Card* as one of her escorts.

The *Borie* was on her fourth patrol with the *Card* on October 31, when she picked up a radar contact on what would later be confirmed as the *U-256*, a Type VIIC launched in 1941. The *Borie's* captain, Lieutenant Commander Charles H. Hutchins, thought he had sunk the *U-256* and continued searching for more. He had only damaged the *U-256*. It would go on three more patrols and would be surrendered.

After 2:00 a.m., the *Borie* picked up another radar contact, another Type VIIC, the *U-405*. The *Borie* dropped depth charges in the 15-foot seas and forced the U-boat to the surface just 400 yards away. The *Borie* maneuvered to 1,400 yards away, then "opened fire with all main battery guns and 20-millimeter machine guns as they came to bear during turn."[4]

The submarine's deck gun crew also opened fire with its six 20-millimeter guns, scoring hits in the *Borie's* forward engine room and near the bridge. The destroyer's gun crews retaliated for those hits.

"*Borie's* 20 battery was extremely effective and in a matter of seconds had wiped out every exposed member of the sub's crew topside... The submarine made continuous effort to man their deck guns, but as each man emerged from the conning tower hatch to the bridge, he was immediately met by a hail of 20-mm projectiles."[5]

The *Borie's* 4-inch gun crew then blew the submarine's deck gun entirely off the submarine.

Hutchins steered his destroyer to ram the *U-405*, but as he reached the submarine, a large wave picked up the *Borie* and slammed it down onto the submarine at a twenty-five to thirty degree angle from parallel.

Even at this close range, the *Borie's* guns continued to fire at the submarine.

The submarine's crew continued trying to man their 20-millimeter anti-aircraft guns, but the *Borie's* crew cut them down with Thompson submachine guns, shotguns, and pistols. The after action report detailed how two German sailors were knocked into the ocean by a thrown sheath knife and a brass shell casing from a 4-inch gun thrown by the apparently beefy American number two gun captain.

The destroyer and U-boat were locked together for many minutes before heavy wave action pulled them apart and the sub moved away by 500 yards. The *Borie* closed again and fired her depth charge projectors, which straddled the sub and shook the *Borie* since she was so close. The *Borie* then fired her own torpedoes at the submarine, but they missed. Finally, another 4-inch shell hit the sub's diesel exhaust and the submarine crew began abandoning ship.

As the *Borie* moved in to pull the Germans from the water, men still on the deck of the submarine began firing white star shells into the sky. Those shells were answered by another submarine which fired a torpedo at the *Borie*. The *Borie* stopped its efforts to rescue the men in rubber rafts.

"These evasive tactics forced the ship to run directly over group of survivors. They were not seen again as *Borie* cleared area, using radical zigzag."[6]

The battle from initial contact to the sub sinking was one hour and four minutes.

The *Borie's* captain described the effectiveness of the 20-millimeter battery as "murderous" at ranges from 1,200 yards down to 40 feet. He also complained about a problem with the *Clemson* class known for twenty years: it could not turn sharply. He said the wide turns known to be common with *Clemsons* "was a severe handicap, resulting in prolonging the action and making possible the sub's evasion of a direct blow in ramming tactics."[7]

Hutchins praised his executive officer who remained in the ship's Command Information Center: "except when the sub was alongside.

During that phase of the action he used a Tommy gun from the bridge with telling effectiveness."[8]

A combat artist recreated the *Borie* battle with the U-405. *NHHC photo.*

At daylight, the *Borie* was still afloat, but the pounding on top of the submarine had caused extensive damage with the forward engine room flooded, and the aft engine room taking on water. For the next several hours, the crew jettisoned everything that could be discarded, including the removable guns and most of the 4-inch ammo. All day the crew tried to save their ship, but by 4:30 p.m., the captain ordered abandon ship.

None of the crew had been killed in the gunfights with the Germans, but the 20-foot waves and the cold sea claimed twenty-seven crewmen as they tried to swim to the USS *Goff* (DD-247) and USS *Barry* (DD-248), two other *Clemsons* attached to the *Card*.

The *Borie*, with twenty-three years of continuous service at sea, had to be torpedoed by an Avenger from the *Card* before it would sink.

Just two weeks after one of the oldest destroyers in the U.S. surface Navy had to be sunk by an aircraft from the U.S. Navy, one of the newest destroyers almost made history by attacking the Commander-in-Chief of the entire Navy, President Roosevelt.

The USS *William D. Porter* (DD-579) was a brand-new *Fletcher,* having only finished its shakedown in September. Her first assignment was to escort the battleship USS *Iowa* (BB-61) to North Africa. The *Iowa* was carrying President Roosevelt to conferences with Winston Churchill in Cairo and Tehran.

On November 14, the destroyer was going through a torpedo drill, as any new ship with an inexperienced crew would do. The drill was supposed to be a dry run, but one inexperienced crewman fired a live torpedo in the direction of the *Iowa.* The captain of the *William D. Porter* broke radio silence and informed *Iowa* of the incoming torpedo. It exploded harmlessly in the *Iowa's* wake. The incident rated a single line in the war diary of the *William D. Porter.*

Navy wags used the incident to paint the *William D. Porter* as a hard luck ship. Stories persist, without reference to any after action reports or war diaries, that the *Iowa* trained its guns on the *William D. Porter,* that the crew was placed under arrest on suspicion of an assassination attempt, and the captain was released from service. In fact, the captain served through the Korean War and was promoted to rear admiral.

Still, there may have been some consequences of firing a torpedo at the President of the United States. Within a month, the *William D. Porter* was sailing in the Aleutians.

On December 13, aircraft from the USS *Bogue* spotted the *U-172,* a Type IXC U-boat. Four four stackers including the class namesake, the *Clemson, George E. Badger, DuPont,* and *Osmond Ingram,* all rushed toward the contact. For the next twenty-seven hours, the old destroyers dropped depth charges and kept the submarine within sonar contact. Finally, her batteries and air exhausted, and the submarine surfaced. She tried shelling her tormentors, but within a few minutes of trading cannon shots with the *Osmond Ingram,* she surrendered. The *Osmond Ingram,* the first destroyer named after a common seaman from World War I, was given credit for the kill. An old destroyer dating from 1920 had just sunk one of Germany's newest and best U-boats that was only two years old.

Through six patrols over the length of a year, the *U-172* had sunk twenty-five ships and 145,815 tons of shipping, ranking it the fifteenth most successful U-boat of World War II based on tonnage sunk. One of its victims had been a troop ship that had already offloaded its men and was on its way back to home port.

For the history of destroyers, 1943 ended on a poignant note. The USS *Leary* (DD-158), a *Wickes* class, was the first destroyer equipped with radar in April 1937. In 1940, she was one of the first destroyers to start escorting British-bound ships off Iceland. On November 9, 1941, she was the first American destroyer to make a solid U-boat contact, but she did not attack.

On December 24, 1943, she made another radar contact and was pursuing it when she was hit by two torpedoes on her starboard side. A few minutes later, a third torpedo struck. The last time anyone saw the ship's captain, Commander James E. Kyes, he was giving his own life-jacket to a mess attendant.

The *Leary*, a historic and old ship in the U.S. Navy, had been sunk by the *U-275*, an undistinguished submarine that had sunk nothing over seven patrols. The submarine had fired a Gnat, a new type of torpedo that homed in on the sound of an enemy's propellers. The torpedo had only been introduced in September, so even in its destruction, the *Leary* made history.

11

Pacific Theater 1943

"Our losses for this single battle were fantastic."

The USS *Nicholas* (DD-449) and USS *O'Bannon* (DD-450) under construction side by side at Bath Iron Works. The two *Fletchers* would win a combined thirty-three battle stars. *NHHC photo.*

The year 1942 had been terrible for American destroyers in the Pacific. Twenty-four had been lost, including five gallant, old *Clemsons* in the Asiatic fleet in the first three months. Seventeen destroyers had gone down in the Solomon Islands, contesting the Japanese, who had been reinforcing their troops on Guadalcanal in the last six months of the year. Of those seventeen, three were *Wickes APDs* that were combat veterans of World War I. The rest were relatively modern ships of *Bagley*,

Benson, Sims, Porter, and *Mahan* classes. All of the American tin cans had gone up against the best the Japanese forces had in the air, both on and under the sea.

The Japanese had also suffered, losing twelve destroyers in those same actions. They held the edge at the end of the year by sinking five more American destroyers than they had lost off Guadalcanal in 1942, but that number was deceiving. The United States could quickly replace its sunken destroyers. Japan could not.

The new year brought new hope in the form of more *Fletchers*: a heavier, faster class that had begun to show up at the end of 1942. *Fletchers* were rolling out of eleven shipyards on both coasts, taking fewer than two hundred days from keel laying to commissioning. By contrast, the USS *Gleaves* (DD-423) had taken more than two years to build and commission when it was first laid down in 1938.

That assembly line production was important. American shipyards were launching ten *Fletchers* every month. Meanwhile, the *Yugumo*-class destroyer, developed around the same time as the *Fletcher,* took eighteen months to construct. Only nineteen vessels were built of that entire class in four years.

Not every idea conceived for the new *Fletchers* worked out. Five *Fletchers* were modified while still under construction to carry the Kingfisher observation float plane, a standard feature on larger cruisers and battleships. Designers reasoned that having an observation aircraft on scouting destroyers would be helpful to the fleet. While the idea of radioing in effectiveness of naval fire was sound, finding space for an aircraft on the smaller hull of a destroyer proved to be problematic. A handful of launchings and recoveries took place, but all five *Fletchers* reverted to their original configurations.

Other experiments proved very valuable. On the night of January 23-24, several American cruisers and destroyers were assigned to destroy a Japanese airfield under construction on Kolombangara Island, about 230 miles northwest of Guadalcanal. Japanese Betty bombers approached the ships after midnight. They were spotted at 18,000 yards by the USS

Radford (DD-486), a *Fletcher* that just arrived from a brief Atlantic convoy patrol. The *Radford* fired its first 5-inch shells at 7,000 yards and its last at 5,000 yards just after 3:00 a.m. The ship commenced firing two minutes after tracking began, with the first hits noted twenty seconds later. It took just thirty seconds of firing of the 5-inch guns to bring down four of the bombers. It was never light enough for any of the airplanes to be seen by lookouts, and no ship turned on a searchlight to spotlight them. The *Radford* had the distinction of being the first American warship to find, track, and destroy enemy aircraft using radar installed on the ship while it was still under construction.

The Japanese tried a new tactic to illuminate American ships in this engagement by dropping white lights into the ocean to mark the known edges of the attacking ships followed by flares to illuminate those same ships.

As more American destroyers arrived in the Solomons, they began applying old tactics to slow down the nighttime resupply train of Japanese destroyers running down The Slot from Rabaul to their troops on Guadalcanal. On the night of January 31, three mine layers ventured into the western waters of Ironbottom Sound. They laid more than three hundred mines between Noma Reef at the mouth of the Tenanbo River north of Cape Esperance—right in the regular path of the approaching Japanese. The destroyers were old four pipers: the USS *Tracy* (DD-214/DM-19), USS *Preble* (DD-345/DM-20), two former *Clemsons* converted to mine layers, and USS *Montgomery* (DD-121/DM-17), a former *Wickes* converted to a mine layer.

The crews of the three destroyers had all been at Pearl Harbor on December 7, 1941, with two so defenseless while under repair that their crews boarded nearby warships to help those crews shoot at the attacking airplanes. To the crew's knowledge, none of the mines they had previously laid in the Pacific had sunk anything.

That was about to change.

What no one in the U.S. Army or Navy knew was that the Japanese were preparing for a mass evacuation of Guadalcanal. Weeks earlier,

Emperor Hirohito had ordered the evacuation after his generals complained that their troops were starving to death because the Imperial Japanese navy had failed to deliver food. American aircraft, cruisers, and destroyers had succeeded in disrupting the Imperial Japanese Navy's supply lines running down The Slot from Rabaul. The Americans had won the Battle for Guadalcanal but did not yet know it.

Not long after the mine layers had dropped their mines early on the morning of February 1, a convoy of twenty Japanese destroyers were spotted rushing down The Slot in the early afternoon. That puzzled the Americans. Usually, the Japanese sent their supply destroyers in the dead of night. A flight of American airplanes damaged the destroyer *Makinami*, a *Yugomo* class, but still the fleet surged forward at 30 knots, nearly top speed. What the Americans did not realize was that this was the beginning of Operation KE, the mission to rescue the garrison on Guadalcanal.

The rush to reach Guadalcanal meant the Japanese destroyers' lookouts had little time to spot danger such as a recently laid minefield. Within a few minutes of entering the minefield, *Makigumo*, another *Yugomo*, hit one. Most of its crew were saved, but the ship had to be scuttled by one of its sister ships. The *Makigumo* was one of the nineteen copies of the class, commissioned just a year earlier. Displacing 2,077 tons and stretching 390 feet, the Japanese destroyer was 27 tons heavier and 14 feet longer than the *Fletcher*, the largest American destroyer.

The rescue mission was not starting well. Already, two new *Yugumos* had been lost in this one rescue operation, one from aircraft and one from a mine.

The irony was palpable. One of the most modern destroyers in the Japanese fleet had just been disabled by three of the oldest destroyers in the American fleet. The weapon used was a floating mine: a cheap, passive weapon developed by a Confederate general during the American Civil War nearly eighty years before the Japanese destroyer was laid down, and ten years before the creation of the destroyer ship type.

Admiral Nimitz recognized what had happened. He called the successful mine laying a "splendidly conducted operation...carried out by old ships, inadequate in speed, and gun power."[1]

Not yet aware that the Japanese were trying to evacuate their forces, the U.S. Navy, with only three destroyers in the immediate area, did not attack the remaining eighteen Japanese destroyers. Some brave American PT boats did attack the destroyers, now loaded with evacuees, as they made their way back north early on the morning of February 2. Several of the PT boats were destroyed, with little damage done to the Japanese destroyers. Once again, the American torpedoes proved to be problematic.

The Japanese, however, did leave their mark on the Americans earlier on February 1.

The USS *DeHaven* (DD-469) was the twelfth *Fletcher* to be commissioned and one of the early models to reach the Solomons in December of 1942. Its first action was the bombardment of Kolombangara on January 23, 1943. Its next action would put it down in naval history with a sad triple distinction: it was the first *Fletcher* lost in the war, the shortest-lived destroyer (to that date) with only 133 days from commissioning to sinking, and the last of fifteen American destroyers lost during the Guadalcanal campaign.

The USS *Nicholas* (DD-449) displaying a camouflage-scheme paint job. *NHHC photo.*

On February 1, the *DeHaven* and USS *Nicholas* (DD-449), another *Fletcher*, were protecting three empty Landing Craft Transports (LCTs). With the troops safely ashore, the crews of both destroyers were expecting an uneventful trip back to base. Many of the crew of the *DeHaven* were not wearing long-sleeved shirts or lifejackets, habits more experienced crews adhered to in enemy waters since there was little time to prepare for an attack.

The pilot of an observation aircraft operated by the Japanese army had spotted the two *Fletchers* earlier in the day, but mistook them for cruisers because of his unfamiliarity with their larger size. Fearing the phantom cruisers were about to shell their retreating soldiers, the Japanese observer called for bombers to attack what really was an insignificant force posing no threat to the coming evacuation.

Just before 3:00 p.m., a flight of fourteen aircraft appeared to be heading for the *DeHaven* and the *LSTs*. The crews were not immediately concerned at the sight, particularly since the airplanes were coming from the direction of Henderson Field, now securely in American hands. The *DeHaven* did not open its antiaircraft batteries until the red meatball insignia on the wings of six approaching airplanes were seen by lookouts. Three bombs hit the destroyer, including one smashing into the bridge, killing all of the officers who had been waiting to positively identify the approaching bogies. It was a newcomer's mistake on which the Japanese capitalized. More than half of the crew were killed, including ten of the fourteen officers. A survivor estimated that the time from the first bomb hit to the time the ship sank in three pieces was no more than four minutes.

The Japanese would send two more columns of destroyers down The Slot over the coming week to rescue nearly 12,000 troops. Still, the Americans did not realize that the Guadalcanal Campaign was over until advancing ground forces could not find any Japanese soldiers on February 9. There would be no final climatic battle on Guadalcanal, either on land or sea. The Japanese ground forces did something they had rarely done before this battle and would rarely do after. They retreated; a strategic move that saved more than ten thousand men.

How many of those Japanese soldiers who actually survived is unknown. Admiral Yamamoto described them as "so undernourished that their beards, nails and hair had all stopped growing, their joints looked pitifully large."[2]

For more than six months, the Marines and soldiers on Guadalcanal bravely took their poundings from the Japanese naval artillery and withstood the banzai charges from the Japanese soldiers, losing an estimated 1,600 men.

But it was the U.S. Navy that finally strangled the Japanese food supply line to Guadalcanal, forcing the Japanese to abandon the island. The Navy paid for that victory in lives. More than five thousand American sailors on ships of all types were lost in Ironbottom Bay.

Of the fighting forces, the Japanese suffered the most, losing more than nineteen thousand men—a number that includes the more than nine thousand who starved to death because the U.S. Navy doggedly kept the Imperial Japanese Navy at bay.

The Japanese evacuation of Guadalcanal did not mean they were abandoning all of the Western Pacific, or even the Solomons. They still held Kolombangara, about 230 miles to the northwest of Guadalcanal, and their major stronghold on New Britain, Rabaul, about 665 miles further to the northwest.

The war of attrition in the South West Pacific had now begun in earnest. With the bitter memory of the losses suffered at the Battle of Coral Sea off the southwest coast of New Guinea in May 1942 still fresh, the United States was ready to move in that general direction again.

When the Americans did move, it proved to be a disaster for Japanese destroyers, but it was not the U.S. Navy giving the Japanese a plastering. It was land-based bombers and fighters from the American and Australian Air Forces.

On February 28, the Japanese launched a convoy of eight transports from Rabaul carrying nearly seven thousand troops bound for Lae, New Guinea. They were escorted by a formidable force of eight destroyers.

For three days, from March 2-4, the convoy was attacked by a wide variety of American and Australian aircraft in what would be called the Battle of the Bismarck Sea. No American carriers were involved. All of the aircraft were based from uncaptured regions of New Guinea, the same vast island that was the destination of the Japanese convoy.

The first destroyer to go down was the convoy's flagship, *Shirayuki,* a *Fubuki,* strafed by Australian Beaufighters and bombed by American B-25s. *Tokitsukaze*, a more modern *Kagero* class just two years commissioned, fared no better. Then it was the turn of the *Asashio,* launched in 1937 and the lead of its ten-ship class launched in 1937. The next day, the *Arashio,* another *Asahio* class, was hit by three bombs.

In the course of two days, all eight Japanese transports and four of the eight escorting destroyers were sunk by land-based Allied aircraft. The only involvement by the U.S. and Australian Navies was a second day torpedo attack on an already crippled transport by two PT boats. The Japanese lost one of its oldest and one of its newest destroyers, plus two that were only six years old—all destroyed by a variety of low, medium, and high-level bombing, plus the effects of strafing from heavy machine guns and 20-millimeter cannons. Even though the Japanese had air cover of more than one hundred airplanes, only two Allied bombers and four fighters were knocked down. The Allies had overwhelmed the Japanese both in the air and on the sea.

"Our losses for this single battle [Bismarck Sea] were fantastic. Not during the entire savage fighting at Guadalcanal did we suffer a comparable blow. We knew we could no longer run cargo ships, or even fast destroyer transports to any front on the north coast of New Guinea, east of Wewak," a Japanese staff officer wrote after the battle.[3]

On March 6, the Japanese sent two destroyers to reinforce its soldiers on Kolombangara, an almost round island in the New Georgia group of islands on the north end of The Slot. After an uneventful evening dropping off the supplies, the two destroyers began their journey back to Rabaul. What they did not know was they were under the watchful radar-assisted eyes of three American cruisers and three destroyers. The two Japanese destroyers—*Murasame*, a *Shiratsuyu* class, and the larger *Minegumo,* an *Asahio* class—were still not equipped with radar.

The radar installed on *Fletchers* proved to be a major advantage over the Japanese, who resisted its installation as it was not part of their attack at all costs naval culture. *NHHC photo.*

The two Japanese destroyers were spotted at 15,200 yards by the USS *Waller* (DD-466), a *Fletcher,* at 12:57 a.m. using its standard surface radar. Less than four minutes later, the cruisers fired their first salvo, and the *Waller* fired a spread of torpedoes at *Murasame*. Both cruiser shells and destroyer torpedoes hit home. It was the first time since the Battle of Balikpapan, one year prior, that an American destroyer's torpedoes had hit an enemy ship. By 1:06 a.m., the fire shifted to the second destroyer. Within thirty-six minutes, both Japanese destroyers were sinking. The firing was so swift and accurate that neither Japanese destroyer was able to get off rounds or torpedoes at any American ships. The action was close enough to the Japanese-held Kolombangara that most of the crews were able to row to shore.

The *Murasame* had been a very capable destroyer. During the naval battles off Guadalcanal, it was credited with hitting two American cruisers and one destroyer. Just hours before she was sunk, she sank an American submarine.

Just as Japan's most skilled air crews had been killed at the Battle of Midway in June 1942, now it was their experienced destroyer crews which were being picked off in the early spring of 1943. In the course of less than six weeks, the Japanese had lost seven destroyers in the Western Pacific, with just one American destroyer sunk in the same time period in the same region. All of the Japanese destroyers sunk were combat veterans of several sea battles.

The ruggedness of American destroyers was demonstrated on March 27 far from the hot, sticky climes of the South Pacific. It was in the freezing water of the North Pacific near the Komandorski Islands, 150 miles west of the furthest west island of Alaska. The USS *Bailey* (DD-492), a *Benson* class, was part of a cruiser-led task force that discovered the Japanese trying to reinforce their troops in the Aleutians. For three hours, the two opposing fleets hurled shells at each other, with the *Bailey* taking three direct hits from Japanese cruisers' 8-inch shells. Remarkably, only five men were killed aboard the *Bailey* while the two sides slugged it out without either suffering a sinking. The Japanese finally turned around.

When the *Bailey* was put into dry dock for repairs on Mare Island on April 8, more than a third of its underwater plates were found to be wrinkled or dented from near misses. The sailors were less upset by the near misses that had almost sunk them than they were by one direct hit from the Japanese. The otherwise inconsequential strike had hit their galley, leaving the crew with nothing but cold sandwiches to eat when the air temperature in Alaskan waters was barely above freezing.

Back in the southwest Pacific on April 5, 1943, the USS *O'Bannon* (DD-450), a *Fletcher,* was involved in a close contact incident that became a legend in U.S. Navy lore. As with many legends, the details part ways with the truth.

Commander Donald MacDonald, the captain of the *O'Bannon,* picked up a radar contact at 7,000 yards at 2:30 a.m. He cautiously approached what turned out to be the *RO-34,* a medium-sized Japanese submarine. Instead of attacking with his deck gun from a distance or ramming the submarine, MacDonald brought the destroyer close to the submarine before moving back off again so that he could fire his 5-inch guns. At least one shell pierced the conning tower. He later finished it off with depth charges.

At one point after the encounter, the ship's cook made an offhand remark to the captain that the submarine and destroyer were so close that the crew could have thrown potatoes at the Japanese.

That joke grew into a story that the O'Bannon's deck crew threw potatoes at the deck crew of the submarine who were sleeping on deck when the destroyer approached. According to the story, the Japanese thought the potatoes were hand grenades and ducked rather than man their deck gun to fight the destroyer. The story somehow made its way into the American press. Maine potato growers struck a plaque and presented it to the O'Bannon in June 1945. The plaque read: "A tribute to the officers and men of the USS O'Bannon for their ingenuity in using our now proud potato to sink a Japanese submarine in the spring of 1943."

The story is amusing, but any captain who brought his destroyer alongside a Japanese submarine close enough that his men could throw potatoes would have been court-martialed for endangering his ship. One other part of the story that does not make sense is why potatoes would have been stored on deck and more easily reached than machine guns. Decades after the war, MacDonald said in a newspaper interview: "I've been trying to drive a stake through this story for years."[4]

Three days later, a veteran of the months-long campaign to take and hold Guadalcanal was sunk. USS *Aaron Ward* (DD-483) was a *Gleaves* class operating in the region for nearly a year. During the November 12, 1942 Naval Battle of Guadalcanal, she had sunk one Japanese destroyer before being disabled by nine enemy shells. Thanks to the efforts of her crew to keep her moving out of Japanese range, she survived with fifteen dead and was towed to safety. After repairs at Pearl Harbor, she returned to the waters around Guadalcanal.

On April 7, 1943, a flight of Japanese dive bombers caught her escorting three LSTs (Landing Ship Tanks) near Savo Island. The concussion and shrapnel from several near misses tore holes in her hull. This time, she was unable to be saved. Twenty men died from the bombardment. In two battles, it had taken nine 8-inch shells from Japanese cruisers and five bombs to finally sink the *Aaron Ward*. Her captain, Lieutenant Commander Frederick J. Becton, would return to fight another day. One of the young officers on board the LSTs who watched the bombing of the destroyer was Lieutenant (j.g.) John Fitzgerald Kennedy, who was on his way to take command of *PT-109*.

On May 4, Admiral Halsey again turned to minelayers to surprise the Japanese, who still thought they could run down The Slot. Three old four stackers, including two *Wickes* classes, USS *Gamble* (DD-123/DM-15), USS *Breese* (DD-122/DM18), and USS *Preble* (DD-345/DM-20), a *Clemson,* drew the assignment to lay a minefield in Blackett Strait between Arundel Island and Kolombangara Island. *Preble* had been one of the four stackers that laid a minefield in March, claiming one Japanese destroyer off the northeastern coast of Guadalcanal. All three had been at Pearl Harbor, with *Gamble* claiming the downing of one Japanese aircraft.

Five minutes after midnight on May 7, the three destroyers started laying three strings of mines. In less than half an hour, 250 mines were laid.

It took less than six hours for the Japanese to find the mines with the hulls of three destroyers. Three *Kagero*-class destroyers—class leader *Kagero* herself, *Oyashio*, and *Kuroshio*—all hit mines. One sunk immediately and two were finished off by American air attacks. A fourth destroyer, *Michishio*, an *Asahio* class, was strafed by American fighters when it lingered too long trying to pick up survivors; but it survived. Out of nineteen copies of the *Kagero*—the pride of the destroyer fleet in the late 1930s—seven were now at the bottom of the sea within a year and a half of the war starting against the Americans. That was a thirty-seven percent loss of one destroyer class the Japanese had counted on for the entire war.

Never mind the fancy, new, giant *Fletchers*. Without firing a shot, three old four stackers with half the weight of a *Fletcher* had just sunk or damaged three of Japan's newest and most powerful destroyers using the eighty-year-old design of the mine.

The Japanese, now wise to what was happening, became more careful about looking for mines before sending their fleets forward. They swept up a field laid off of Kula Gulf two weeks later.

On the early morning of July 5, just after midnight, the USS *Strong* (DD-467), a *Fletcher* which had escorted the four mine layers two months earlier, participated in support shelling of the northwestern coast of New Georgia. For reasons still murky seventy-five years later, only one destroyer, the USS *Ralph Talbot* (DD-390), a *Bagley* class, noticed some blips on its radar at 12:31 a.m. coming from a direction in the Kula Gulf that should have been empty of American ships. Eighteen minutes later, a torpedo slammed into the *Strong*'s port side.

That strange radar contact, perhaps missed by the other destroyers and cruisers due to land interference, had been three Japanese destroyers. Two older destroyers, *Nagatsuki*, a *Mutsuki*-class from 1927, and *Yunagi*, a *Kamikaze* class from 1925, were led by the *Niizuki*, an *Akizuki*-class destroyer. The *Niizuki* was a newer, heavier design that entered service in the summer of 1942. At 2,700 tons and 440 feet long, it was larger than the *Fletcher* class by nearly 650 tons in displacement and 64 feet in length. This particular destroyer had only been put into service four months earlier.

The *Akizuki* class had four-gun houses of twin mounted 3.9-inch guns that were smaller than the 5-inch guns that had been standard on Japanese destroyers for decades. While the guns were smaller, there were more of them; eight guns per ship compared to six in older destroyers. To make room for more anti-aircraft guns, the *Akizuki* class had only one four-tube torpedo mount with reloads for a full complement of eight Type 93 torpedoes.

More importantly, these new destroyer models were equipped with radar. This was something Japanese naval designers had ignored in previous ship designs, thinking it was a defense they would never need considering Japanese naval culture dictated sailing directly into danger to attack the enemy no matter the odds. Apparently big naval losses to the radar-equipped Americans had changed Japanese minds about relying on searchlights and binoculars to spot their enemies.

In this first engagement for the *Niizuki*, her radar had proved its value. The *Niizuki* had seen the American destroyers at a range of 14 miles. Upon seeing the American ships, the taskforce commander realized his mission to reinforce the Japanese army troops had to be abandoned. The men he was supposed to supply were now being bombarded. With those ground forces under attack and without any orders to engage the Americans in a surface battle, the Japanese commander saw no reason to endanger his own new destroyer and his three companion destroyers. He turned his force around and headed north.

But before they left, all four destroyers fired a spread of fourteen Type 93 torpedoes. The range was 11 miles, a long distance, but well under the extreme range for that type of torpedo at 24 miles. The Japanese commander knew that if the torpedoes hit anything, they would be able to see the flashes in the dark sky. Any weapon with 1,000 pounds of explosives in its nose traveling at 48 knots was bound to leave a mark if it struck home.

Just before the single torpedo of all fourteen fired hit, a sonarman on the *Strong* picked up the sound of high-speed screws. The loudness of the sound puzzled him, perhaps indicating that he was one of the first U.S. Navy sailors to hear what a Type 93 torpedo sounded like as it approached from a long distance. The executive officer assumed the sound was a false reading caused by some underwater equipment being used in the landing. Seconds later, an officer on deck saw the ominous wake too late to issue a warning to the bridge.

The *Strong's* crippling was violent and sudden, but apparently without much visible fire. It wasn't until the American fleet commander's call for her to report was not answered that the other ships realized the *Strong* had been torpedoed.

The captain of the nearby USS *Chevalier* (DD-451), another *Fletcher*, rammed his ship into the *Strong's* damaged port side in an effort to get close enough to enable the *Strong's* crew to leave their stricken ship. Reports say it was both accidental and intentional. That maneuver, which caused only slight damage to the *Chevalier*, turned out to be just what was needed as many men just stepped from one ship to the other. More than 240 men were rescued by the *Chevalier* in the hour before she had to back away to get out of range of the Japanese coastal batteries beginning to zero in on the two ships.

Not all of the crew had time to make it to the *Chevalier* when it was alongside. Among them were Lieutenant Hugh Barr Miller and several others who jumped off the ship and were injured by concussion when the *Strong's* depth charges went off as the ship sank. Miller and other survivors made it to Japanese-held Arundel Island. Miller ordered the other men to leave him behind and search for a way off the island as he thought he was hopelessly injured. They did as ordered, but were never seen again.

Miller, however, did not die. He found the body of a Japanese soldier and ate his rations. He began exploring further and further from his hideaway. He ambushed a Japanese patrol and killed all five of them with a hand grenade he had taken from the dead soldier.

Over the next five weeks, Miller evaded Japanese patrols and even attacked some machine gun nests with captured grenades. On August 16, Miller ran onto the beach when he heard an American airplane's distinctive engine sound. He caught the eye of the pilot who reported that a man who looked like Rip Van Winkle could only be an American because he had a red beard. An amphibious airplane returned to pick up Miller and a cache of Japanese documents he had captured during his adventure. He would be awarded the Navy Cross.

From the first of July through the end of 1943, destroyers on both sides slammed into each other in the same general area around New Georgia, 250 miles northwest of where they had been fighting during the Guadalcanal Campaign starting in the second half of 1942.

On July 6, the night after the *Strong* went down, an American task-force of three light cruisers and four destroyers returned to the Kula Gulf, just to the east of Kolombangara Island and north of the northern tip of New Georgia. They lay in wait for a force of seven Japanese destroyer transports escorted by three more modern destroyers trying to land 2,600 troops at Vila on the southern end of Kolombangara.

The Americans had the advantage in gun power in what would be called the Battle of Kula Gulf. The three cruisers, with their 8-inch guns, would be able to reach out and touch the Japanese destroyers before they could target the Americans, but the Japanese had the advantage in torpedo power. All of the Japanese ships had the Type 93 torpedoes.

Two of the Japanese destroyers, *Niizuki* and *Nagatsuki,* had fired the torpedoes, killing the *Strong* the previous night. This night, the *Nagatsuki* was performing a transport role. Escorting the other seven transport destroyers were *Tanikaze,* a *Kagero* class commissioned in 1942; *Suzukaze,* a *Shiratsuyu* class commissioned in 1937; and *Niizuki,* an *Akizuki* class just commissioned in March 1943.

The seven transport destroyers were mostly old 1920s destroyers converted to fast attack transports with the curious exception of *Hamak-aze,* a *Kagero* class then two years old. The use of a new destroyer in a transport role may indicate that there were no other suitable transports to send on this mission. The war of attrition was being won by the Americans.

Just before 2:00 a.m. on July 6, each of the two forces sighted the other using radar. Unfortunately for *Niizuki,* she was in the lead and her radar blip was so large with her displacement at 2,700 tons that she appeared to be a cruiser. Therefore, the Americans concentrated their fire on her. Within seconds, she was sinking, perhaps without even firing her guns at an enemy in her first engagement. One of the newest and largest Japanese destroyers had been sunk just four months after its commissioning.

The two remaining Japanese destroyers fired a volley of Type 93 torpedoes. Three of those torpedoes hit the USS *Helena* (CL-50), a light cruiser damaged at Pearl Harbor and repaired. She had been heavily engaged during the Guadalcanal Campaign. Now, she was sinking. Before the sea battle was over, one of the older Japanese transport destroyers would be hopelessly grounded after disembarking its troops. It would be destroyed by American air attack the next day. Just a third of the 2,600 troops that the convoy was carrying would make it onshore.

The Battle of Kula Gulf was something of a draw in terms of tonnage lost by both sides, but the Americans realized that they should have performed better than they did with seven offensive ships against three escort destroyers.

Coincidentally, on July 7, 1943, the day after the Battle in the Kula Gulf, an interesting shipbuilding coincidence occurred. The day after the *Niizuki*—an *Akizuki*-class destroyer—was sunk, the Americans laid down their first *Allen M. Sumner* class, their biggest and most modern destroyer. At 2,200 tons, the *Allen M. Sumner*-class destroyer was about 150 tons heavier than the *Fletcher's* 2,050 tons, but the same length at 376 feet. The difference came at the beam as the *Sumner's* beam was 41 feet compared to the *Fletcher's* at 39.5 feet. The extra width gave the *Sumner* a two-foot shallower draft at 15 feet and 9 inches. The *Allen M. Sumner* would have six 5-inch guns in three twin enclosed gun mounts— one more gun than the *Fletcher* class.

The major improvement came in anti-aircraft protection. The *Allen M. Sumners* mounted twelve 40-millimeter Bofors guns and eleven 20-millimeter Oerlikon cannons compared to the early *Fletchers*, which had six 40-millimeter guns and seven 20-millimeter cannons. Even when the *Fletchers* were upgraded to add more anti-aircraft guns, the standard *Allen M. Sumners* still had more protection from aerial attack. The *Allen M. Sumners* gave up some top speed, rated at 34 knots compared to the *Fletchers'* 36.5 knots.

One other advantage the *Allen M. Sumners* had over all previous American destroyers seems simple enough, but represented a significant innovation. An interior passageway ran the entire length of the ship, allowing the crew to stay inside when making their way from one end to the other. Every other American destroyer design dating back to the 1890s required men to walk along the exposed deck in all kinds of weather if they wanted to go from aft to forward.

The *Allen M. Sumner* class was not perfect. Captain Frederick Julian Becton, future commander of the USS *Laffey* (DD-724), found two flaws when he traveled to Bath Iron Works in Maine to examine the *Laffey* while it was being built.

The opening into the pilothouse was extremely low, causing even men of medium height to duck to get through without banging their heads. Becton traced the origin of the design defect all the way back to the Navy's Destroyer Design Office in Washington, D.C. When the ship's designer contacted the office to ask what the Navy wanted the measurements to be for the doorway, a young woman secretary took the average height for everyone in the office during lunch and sent that information back to the designer. That measurement made it into the blueprints for all of the destroyers. Apparently, everyone in the office that day was short and it was too late to correct the design. There is no record of how many officers and seamen in a hurry reacting to an enemy threat bashed their heads on their own destroyer doorways.

Becton discovered another design flaw: the designer had not built a captain's sea cabin in the pilothouse. The sea cabin was a tiny room with a bunk and a head (toilet) where the captain could rest but still be immediately available. That amenity was able to be added after designers looked at how railroad passenger cars included tiny bathrooms.

The *Allen M. Sumner* class did not quite match up to the *Akizuki* class since the *Akizukis* had two more guns and weighed 500 more tons. Still, American industrial might was demonstrated with the *Allen M. Sumners* as only seven *Akizukis* were built during the war compared to fifty-eight *Allen M. Sumners*.

As they had at Guadalcanal, the Japanese doggedly stuck to their commitments to reinforce their ground troops on Kolombangara. Just one week after the inconclusive Battle of Kula Gulf, Japanese destroyers were back again on the night of July 12-13 to fight the Battle of

Kolombangara, or Second Kula Gulf. This time, the Japanese escorts included the 1920s era light cruiser *Jintsu*, an old *Mutsuki*-class destroyer from the 1920s, a *Hatsuharu*-class destroyer from the 1930s, and two *Kageros* from the late 1930s. Also present was a brand new *Yugumo*-class destroyer, the *Kiyonami*, which was just six months old. The four destroyer transports all dated back to the 1920s, with the newest being completed in 1927. They were loaded with 1,200 troops meant to land at Vila.

Facing this second reinforcement effort were two light American cruisers, one light New Zealand cruiser, and ten American destroyers. Most of the destroyers were *Fletchers*, with two *Gleaves*, a *Gridley*, and a *Benson* to round out the mix. On paper, the Americans outclassed the Japanese in total number of ships, number of new ships, and age of the involved ships.

American radar found the Japanese just before 1:00 a.m. on a moonlit night. Moments later, the *Jintsu* switched on its powerful searchlight, surprising the Americans who did not know that the Japanese ships had radar detectors. This move by the lead Japanese cruiser gave its following cruisers visible targets, but at the cost of her own safety. Within forty-five minutes, *Jintsu* was exploding from concentrated shell fire and a torpedo. Nearly five hundred Japanese seamen were killed, leaving few survivors.

Before the American destroyers fired their torpedoes, the Japanese had fired their own spread. One hit heavily damaged the New Zealand cruiser HMNZS *Leander*. The American fleet commander, Admiral W.L. Ainsworth, sent his cruisers in pursuit of the fleeing destroyers, which was what they wanted. The Japanese had unleashed a barrage of Type 93 torpedoes at the pursuing cruisers and destroyers. Cruisers USS *Honolulu* (CL-48) and USS *St. Louis* (CL-49) were both damaged, as was the USS *Gwin* (DD-433), a *Gleaves* class that had survived an encounter with a Japanese cruiser and two destroyers while fighting off Guadalcanal. This time, she was not so lucky. Just a week earlier, she had rescued many of the crew of the cruiser *Helena* as it went down in the first Battle of Kula Gulf. A single Type 93 torpedo broke the *Gwin's* back and sixty-nine men were killed. Still, she refused to sink until American torpedoes finally sent her to the bottom.

In two weeks, the American Navy's Task Force 18, commanded by Admiral Walden Ainsworth, had suffered through two costly and embarrassing engagements which they should have won handily. At the Battle of Kolombangara, he lost the services of three light cruisers, a destroyer was sunk, and more than 1,200 Japanese troops landed as reinforcements. His taskforce had been virtually crippled with little to show for the loss of ships and men, with the exception of the Japanese loss of an elderly cruiser and its 850-man crew.

American admirals had to come up with better strategies than simply winning the war of attrition. The Japanese were still coming down The Slot to resupply and reinforce their men at Vila so that more ships had to be found to fight them.

Arriving from Tulagi was Destroyer Division 12, led by Commander Frederick Moosbrugger. These destroyers included the USS *Dunlap* (DD-384), a *Mahan*, and *Gridleys* USS *Craven* (DD-382) and USS *Maury* (DD-401). Attached to this division were three *Benham*-class destroyers from Destroyer Division 15: USS *Lang* (DD-399), USS *Sterett* (DD-407), and USS *Stack* (DD-406).

On the night of August 7, 1943, Moosbrugger's destroyers would give the Japanese a dose of their own torpedo fire medicine. Up until this night, American destroyers had rarely hit anything with their 21-inch torpedoes. That would change during the Battle of Vella Gulf.

The Japanese successfully resupplied their troops on Kolombangara some nights, but had been stopped four times since May. The number of destroyers sent on these missions kept dwindling. This night, only four—two *Kageros* named *Hagikaze* and *Arashi,* and two *Shiratsuyus* named *Kawakaze* and *Shigure*—were making the run with nine hundred soldiers and fifty tons of supplies. While neither the Japanese nor Americans realized it, the *Arashi* was already a legendary destroyer in American eyes. She had led the Dauntless dive bombers to the cluster of four Japanese aircraft carriers attacking Midway Island in June 1942 by leaving a wide "V" wake in the ocean that pointed to the carriers like a giant arrow.

All of these destroyers were normally escort destroyers, but for this night, had been forced into the role of transports. This use of newer, faster destroyers may indicate that the Japanese admirals were running out of ships best suited to supply their ground troops.

It was a twelve-hour trip for the Americans from Tulagi to the north side of Kolombangara. The Americans saw four pips on their radar screens at 11:33 p.m. Even though some available Japanese destroyers were now equipped with radar, none of these seemed to be. It was a moonless night, and the Japanese lookouts were hampered in detecting trouble. They made no moves to avoid the onrushing Americans. Several minutes later, the American destroyers unleashed a spread of twenty-four 21-inch torpedoes at a range of 6,300 yards, expecting hits at 4,000 yards. It would take four and a half minutes for the American torpedoes to reach their targets traveling at 26.5 knots.

The Americans did not miss.

Three of the four Japanese destroyers were hit almost simultaneously. At ten minutes after midnight on August 17, the *Arashi* blew up, with one observer vividly describing it as "a bed of hot coals thrown a thousand feet into the air."[5] The only surviving destroyer was *Shigure,* and her rudder was hit by a dud torpedo. None of the American destroyers were hit by anything from the Japanese side. The battle had lasted no more than forty minutes with no damage done to any of the American destroyers. More than 1,500 Japanese sailors and soldiers were killed. All of the Japanese in the water refused American attempts to pull them aboard.

One Japanese officer acknowledged their defeat in particularly descriptive terms: "The enemy [Americans] took the initiative from us and we drank the bitter dregs of defeat."[6]

After the failures of the Mark 15 torpedo through 1942, the American victory at the Battle of Vella Gulf demonstrated that the torpedo still had value as an offensive weapon carried by destroyers. Seven of the twenty-four American torpedoes fired by Moosbrugger's division had hit Japanese destroyers. The changes that had been made to the torpedoes were disarming the magnetic exploder, replacing the original firing pin springs with stronger ones, and resetting the standard running depth from 10 feet to 6 feet.

The Japanese failure to land more supplies at Kolombangara led to increasingly desperate measures. They now tried ferrying the surviving troops to nearby bases by barges rather than risk evacuation by destroyers. That did not work either. For the next several months, American destroyers patrolled the waters, sinking the undefended barges at will. On two nights in October, forty barges were sunk.

As impressive as the Battle of Vella Gulf in August had been for the U.S. Navy, the Battle of Vella Lavella, fought just to the northwest on the night of October 6, was nothing short of disappointing.

Just six hundred Japanese soldiers remained on the island of Vella Lavella, a number small enough to be loaded onto one or two destroyers. Curiously, the Japanese sent an overwhelming force, nine destroyers, to escort twenty barges. The plan was to run those barges onto the shore, load up with men, and then move out to the destroyers as quickly as possible. Once the soldiers were on board, the three destroyer transports and six escort destroyers would be ready for combat. While previous engagements had been about resupplying ground troops, this time, the Japanese wanted a surface battle as well.

The Americans were caught understrength when they learned of the approaching Japanese force. Only three American destroyers—the USS *Selfridge* (DD-357), a *Porter*, USS *Chevalier* (DD-451), the *Fletcher* which had rescued most of the crew of the *Strong*, and USS *O'Bannon* (DD-450), another *Fletcher*—were immediately handy to face the Japanese. Three other destroyers were diverted from convoy duty to rush to the area: the USS *Ralph Talbot* (DD-390), a *Bagley*, and two *Fletchers*, USS *Taylor* (DD-468), and USS *La Vallette* (DD-448). Though underway toward the coming fight, those three destroyers were still 20 miles, or nearly an hour, away from linking up with the first three destroyers.

The leader of the first three destroyers, Captain Frank R. Walker, had a decision to make: maneuver for an hour and wait for his reinforcements or engage the numerically superior forces with just his three destroyers. He chose to engage.

The Japanese commander hesitated to rush into the fight, buying time for Walker and causing some confusion in the Japanese column. One of his destroyers, the *Yugumo*, broke ranks and charged on her own, launching torpedoes that hit the *Chevalier,* which slowed so quickly that it was rammed by the *O'Bannon.* Another Type 93 torpedo hit the *Selfridge.* All three destroyers of the advance force were now damaged early in the engagement.

Luckily for Walker's force, a Japanese scout plane commander excitedly identified the advancing three destroyers of Captain Harold Larsen as a force of "cruisers." This pilot had never seen a destroyer as large as a *Fletcher.* Startled, the Japanese fleet commander turned and began a retreat, though he had accomplished part of his mission as most of the Japanese soldiers were rescued.

The Battle of Vella Lavella was a Japanese victory: sinking one American destroyer, damaging another, and causing the third to ram the second. About the only thing the Americans accomplished was they had sunk the lead vessel of the *Yugumo* class.

Just three weeks later on November 1, the United States and Australia began landing nearly 180,000 troops on Bougainville. The Japanese responded by sending two heavy cruisers, two light cruisers, six destroyers, and five transport destroyers to land troops to oppose the Americans. When the Japanese believed American submarines were stalking them, they sent the troop transports back in anticipation of a major engagement.

For months, the naval engagements in the Solomons had been American taskforces attacking Japanese attempts to reinforce their troops around Kolombangara. Now the roles were reversed. The approaching Japanese force was planning to attack American transport ships still unloading soldiers on Bougainville. That was a mistaken report from Japanese spotter aircraft peering into the darkness. The American transports had already left the beachhead. What was waiting for the Japanese attack force was an American attack force of four light cruisers and eight destroyers, two more destroyers than the Japanese were bringing.

Commander Arleigh Burke developed a destroyer attack philosophy of arriving silently, firing a torpedo spread, then following up with shelling. *NHHC photo*.

Among the destroyers the Japanese would meet were Destroyer Squadron 23, all *Fletchers,* commanded by Captain Arleigh Burke, USS *Charles Ausburne* (DD-570), USS *Dyson* (DD-572), USS *Stanly* (DD-478), USS *Claxton* (DD-571), USS *Foote* (DD-511), USS *Converse* (DD-509), USS *Spence* (DD-512), and USS *Thatcher* (DD-514). At some point during the preceding months, the squadron had adopted the nickname the "Little Beavers" after the sidekick of the Western comic strip hero Red Ryder. The squadron showed its pride of comradeship by painting a logo of Little Beaver, a little Indian boy aiming a bow and arrow, on the bridges of their ships.

Like Moosbrugger, Burke had quietly chafed at the way destroyers were thought of by higherups; subservient to the heavier gunned cruisers and often used to screen battleships, aircraft carriers, and troop transports. While the destroyer was suited for those jobs, Burke imagined an additional use as a fast attack force operating in tight groups that could fly with torpedoes, follow up with 5-inch shells, and then move out of harm's way. He believed in quick decisions and quick firing. He once mentioned the difference between a good officer and a bad one was "ten seconds," meaning a good officer would fire ten seconds sooner than a bad officer. Those ten seconds may mean the difference between sinking an enemy ship and being sunk yourself.

The Battle of Empress Augusta Bay opened at 2:46 a.m. on November 2, 1943, with the aggressive Burke launching torpedoes, all of which missed because the Japanese lookouts had sighted the cruisers and changed course suddenly. Before the Japanese could launch their own torpedoes, the American cruisers opened fire and hit the *Sendai,* a 1920s cruiser. The next two and a half hours were a melee, with both Japanese and American destroyers colliding with each other in the darkness. The *USS Spence* was straddled by shells that could only have come from other American destroyers.

"We've just had another close miss. Hope you are not shooting at us!" cried the *Spence's* captain over the radio.

"Sorry. But you will have to excuse the next four salvos. They're already on their way," replied Burke, speaking for his division.[7]

The naval battle lasted nearly three hours, with the Japanese losing a light cruiser and destroyer in addition to damage to another cruiser and destroyer. One American destroyer, the USS *Foote,* was heavily damaged. Near the end of the battle, the American cruisers and destroyers formed in a circle, much like a Western movie wagon train, to concentrate their antiaircraft fire, bringing down at least twenty of the seventy Japanese aircraft attacking them.

The Battle of Empress Augusta Bay was an American victory, but an unsatisfying one as confusion had kept the Americans from coordinating their attacks.

Two weeks later, and more than 1,100 miles to the northeast of the Solomons, fifty destroyers played a major role in preparing the Gilbert Islands for invasion by the U.S. Marines. USS *Ringgold* (DD-500) and USS *Dashiell* (DD-659), both *Fletchers*, cruised into the lagoon in front of the beaches of Tarawa, close enough that Japanese shore batteries could reach them. One Japanese shell put a 2.5-foot hole in the *Ringgold's* hull below the waterline. Lieutenant Commander Wayne A. Parker, the engineering officer, couldn't find a large emergency plug, so he climbed into the hole himself like the mythical Dutch boy who plugged the hole in the leaking dike to save his town.

"That jagged hole was mighty uncomfortable. It cost me five minutes of anxiety and a new pair of trousers," Parker said.[8]

On November 25, the USS *Radford* (DD-446) made its second submarine kill of the year by sinking the *I-19*. The *Radford's* crew did not know it at the time, but they had scored a major revenge kill. The *I-19* had sunk the carrier USS *Wasp* (CV-7), and severely damaged the USS *O'Brien* (DD-415) and the battleship USS *North Carolina* (BB-55) in September 1942 with a single spread of six torpedoes. The *O'Brien*, a *Sims* class, sank more than a month later after steaming 3,000 miles. Its crew could never stop the leaking caused by the Type 93 torpedo hit. The *I-19* was one of Japan's most successful submarines in terms of sinking American warships, but because of the hunting skills of a *Fletcher*-class destroyer, it was no longer a threat.

Burke still wanted his chance to prove the value of destroyers as offensive ships when they were unencumbered by the need to screen cruisers from attack. He would soon get the opportunity at the Battle of Cape St. George.

On November 24, the Japanese sent five destroyers loaded with 950 soldiers from Rabaul to Burka, an island just across from Bougainville. These men were meant to replace some seven hundred sick Japanese soldiers. As usual, the two escort destroyers were newer, heavier *Yugumos* while the three transport destroyers were two *Fubukis* and one *Mutsuki*, all 1920s designs.

It was after 1:41 a.m. when Destroyer Squadron 23 (*Charles Ausburne, Dyson, Claxton, Converse,* and *Spence*) detected the Japanese formation at 22,000 yards. The escort ships had already landed the replacements and loaded up the sick and injured. Burke had missed the chance to sink the transports dropping off the fresh troops because one of his destroyers had boiler problems and could make no more than 31 knots. That was fast, but slower than Burke had wanted to make, which was top speed of 34 knots. When he sheepishly reported to his commanders that he couldn't make top speed, his nickname for the rest of the war became "31-Knot Burke."

Burke closed to 5,500 yards and his destroyers launched fifteen torpedoes at the Japanese, who had still not sighted the Americans. The two *Yugumos* were new enough that they should have had radar, but no Japanese ship raised a warning. Without ever seeing what hit them, both of the escorting *Yugumo* destroyers, one just ten months old, were hit. One blew up. The other was crippled.

With the major threat gone, Burke started pursuit of the three destroyer transports, which were now seven miles ahead of him. The three transports wisely split up and ran in three different directions. Burke chose one unlucky Japanese ship to which he led all his destroyers. That was *Yugiri,* which was sunk by gunfire. The other two transports fled into the dark of the night. The battle had lasted two hours. No American destroyer had been touched by any Japanese torpedo or shell. No one was hurt. At least six hundred Japanese sailors and soldiers died during the encounter with the Little Beavers.

Burke had just scored one of the most lopsided victories in the Pacific war with the Battle of Cape St. George, just northwest of the northern tip of Bougainville. His tactics of arriving quickly and silently, then launching a torpedo attack before opening gun fire had proven devastating to the Japanese.

This would be the last of the naval battles around the Solomons, stretching from Guadalcanal to Bougainville. Counting the Battle of Savo Island in August 1942 and ending with Cape St. George, there had been fifteen naval battles, with twelve of them being night engagements. Early in the war, the Japanese, better trained at night fighting, had won—or fought to a perceived draw—ten of these battles. But they could not afford many more such victories. They were losing too many ships.

CHAPTER
12
Atlantic Theater 1944

*"Man on deck of sub attempting to man gun
disintegrates."*

I n the Atlantic, 1944 began with a destroyer victory over pirates and a
still unsolved tragedy.

As the war progressed, Germany not only continued to send U-boats
across the Atlantic, but also its own freighters to buy war material to
take back to Germany. By this time, Allied freighters crossing the Atlantic
were formed into convoys, so any freighters traveling alone aroused
suspicions.

On January 1, 1944, an American bomber buzzed a freighter off
Brazil that was flying a Union Jack. The bomber was surprised to receive
anti-aircraft fire from a supposed Ally. Another bomber was shot down
by the same freighter, but not before the USS *Somers* (DD-381) plotted
its position. The *Somers* was the lead ship for its class of 1,850-ton ships
built in the mid-1930s.

This was not the first time the *Somers* had encountered a mysterious
ship. She had boarded another disguised ship in November 1941 that
turned out to be smuggling rubber to Germany. Its boarding crew would
eventually share prize money awarded by a court when the rubber was
sold. In effect, the Destroyer Men had played the role of arresting pirates

and were financially compensated like eighteenth century privateers. It was the last time a U.S. Navy crew would be awarded prize money.

Now, since the United States was officially at war with Germany, there would be no monetary reward, just satisfaction in sinking German ships. Within several days, the *Somers* and the USS *Jouett* (DD-396), a *Somers* class, tracked down and sank three blockade runners. Expressing their victories in the same terms used by U-boats, the two destroyers had sunk three German merchant ships totaling 21,000 tons. On board the freighters was raw rubber that Germany desperately needed and which the U.S. could also use.

The mysterious and tragic incidents that started the year occurred off the port of New York around the same time that the *Somers* and *Jouett* were scoring victories at sea.

The USS *Turner* (DD-648), a *Fletcher*, was returning from convoy duty and had dropped anchor near the Ambrose Light in order to prepare the ship for returning to its New York City berth. Around 6:15 a.m. on January 3, an explosion shook the ship and started fires. Another larger explosion at 7:42 a.m. sank the *Turner*. About half of the crew, including the captain, was killed. Although the initial speculation was a U-boat attack, no other ship recorded a contact. The mystery remains unsolved, but current speculation proposes that there was an accident stowing the ammunition kept handy during convoy duty.

One positive development came of the tragedy. This was the first time in American history that helicopters were used in a medical emergency. Plasma was flown to the ships treating the injured sailors.

The year 1944 brought new German technology to the ocean battlefield.

At this point in the war, German aircraft were flying low on the water to avoid ship radar. As they approached their targets, the Germans would pop up to altitude to deploy a new weapon: radio-controlled glide bombs.

The Germans tried two types on ships: the Fritz X and the Henschel Hx293. The Fritz X looked much like the winged V-1 buzz bombs that would drop into London later in 1944. Once released by twin-engine bombers, the bomb's liquid-fuel engine would start and propel it to a speed of more than 350 miles per hour. After the bomb's motor cut out, a bomber crewman, now sitting out of range of anti-aircraft guns, guided the bomb to its target using radio signals.

A Canadian destroyer, HMCS *Athabaskan* (G-07), a *Tribal* class, had been the first ship to encounter this new kind of weapon in August 1943, when a glider bomb passed entirely through the ship, exploding outside of it. The German controller had made a mistake: making his glide path too shallow. That allowed the bomb to pass through the hull of the ship above the waterline rather than dropping the bomb down into the body of the ship.

This new type of bomb was deadly for a destroyer assisting in the bombardment of the Anzio, Italy beaches.

Commissioned just three weeks before the war started in 1939, the HMS *Janus* (F-53) was a J class, a 1,690-ton destroyer measuring 356 feet long. By the start of 1944, her crew consisted of combat veterans of more than three years, having participated in two sea battles and more than twenty convoy escorts. She was operating off the Anzio beachhead, providing shore bombardment on January 23, when she was struck by a guided bomb. She sank in twenty minutes, taking nearly half of her crew with her.

While radio-controlled bombs guided to their targets seemed like a better idea than dropping normal bombs from height, it did not work as well as the Germans had hoped. Within a few weeks of learning about the new weapons, American radio engineers figured out how to jam the radio signals.

The guided bombs never became something the U.S. Navy feared thanks to field research conducted by engineers on two destroyer escorts.

The USS *Frederick C. Davis* (DE-136) and USS *Herbert C. Jones* (DE-137), *Edsall* class sister ships, laid down within a few weeks of each other at the same yard, were equipped with early versions of the glider bomb radio jamming devices. The devices were so secret that even the ships' captains were not told what they were. The jamming devices were tested during the Anzio landings in late January through early February. Twenty-six glide bombs were dropped by German bombers, but the two American destroyer escorts were able to send all of them into the ocean. Another thirteen glide bombs were launched toward ships at sea that month, but did little damage. According to a convoy after action report, "The efficiency with which the *F.C. Davis* and *H.C. Jones* jammed radio-controlled bombs is an outstanding achievement on the part of these vessels."[1]

While the Germans were experimenting with their new glide bombs during the first months of 1944, the hunter-killer concept was paying off for the Americans. U-boats were being detected and sunk on a regular basis. By this time, the old four stackers had been mostly relieved of convoy duty by newer, smaller, but slower destroyer escorts.

On March 9, USS *Leopold* (DE-319), an *Edsall* class on her second patrol, was sunk by two torpedoes in the North Atlantic. She was the first of twelve destroyer escorts that would be lost in the war in the Atlantic and the Pacific.

The brand-new destroyer escorts being commissioned in late 1943 and 1944 may have had fresh paint, but there was still a place in the U.S. Navy for the old tin cans from the 1920s. One complement of three four stackers showed the German Luftwaffe that despite their age, they were no joke on April 1, 1944.

The USS *Whipple* (DD-217), USS *Alden* (DD-211), and USS *John D. Edwards* (DD-216), all *Clemsons,* were true sister ships laid down within a month of each other at William Cramp & Sons shipyard in Philadelphia in 1918. The *Whipple* and *John D. Edwards* had been continuously at sea since their commissioning in 1919, but the *Alden* had spent most of the 1920s decommissioned. The *Whipple* may have been the most traveled ship in the U.S. Navy, having served in all of the navigable seas. All three were survivors of the distant battles fought by the Asiatic Fleet in the spring of 1942 and were assigned to follow the rear of UGS-36, a seventy-two ship convoy heading from the United States to Tunisia. The convoy made it all the way across the Atlantic before it found trouble in the Mediterranean between Oran and Algiers. On the night of April 1, a flight of German two-engine bombers tried a new convoy attack tactic. Advance planes dropped flares on all four sides of the convoy to illuminate the ships. In response, the convoy escorts, including some British and American destroyer escorts, filled the sky with anti-aircraft bursts. At least three Germans were shot down, with only one freighter damaged. The attack had been a failure, but it did result in convoy escorts being warned not to shoot at the lights in the sky because they were flares, not attacking aircraft.

It was too dark for any ship to claim individual shoot downs of the Germans, but the attack came from the rear, which the three old sisters were protecting. All three would survive the Germans, but not the scrapping yards after the war.

The old saying that "necessity is the mother of invention" was proven when the USS *Donnel* (DE-56), a *Buckley*-class destroyer escort, lost its stern from a U-boat attack on May 3. She was repaired, but deemed too fragile to return to sea duty. Instead, she sailed for Cherbourg, France, and was used as a floating power station for six months. The idea worked so well that several other destroyer escorts were pressed into the same service of being seagoing electric power stations.

The USS *Buckley* (DE-51) was the only ship in the U.S. Navy in World War II that repelled enemy boarders. *NHHC photo.*

On the night of May 5-6, 1944, the crew of the USS *Buckley* (DE-51) discovered that there was still a need for sailors to know hand-to-hand combat techniques developed centuries earlier.

The *Buckley*, the lead ship of its destroyer escort class, was part of the USS *Block Island* (CVE-21) escort carrier hunter-killer group patrolling about 500 miles west of the African coast. When a night-flying Avenger spotted a surfaced U-boat about seven miles from the carrier, the *Buckley* rushed to the coordinates. The U-boat mistook the approaching destroyer escort for a much-needed milch cow refueling submarine, and even fired flares to help guide the approaching ship.

At 2,100 yards, the *Buckley* opened up with its 3-inch guns and scored a direct hit just forward of the conning tower. The *U-66* returned fire with its deck gun, but missed, as did a torpedo.

The *Buckley* rammed the submarine, a normal tactic that often resulted in a submarine quickly sinking. To the *Buckley's* crew's surprise, some of the Germans boiled out of the hatches of their submarine brandishing small arms. The Americans responded with submachine guns, pistols, and even hurled coffee cups. One German was killed by a .45 pistol round. Another *Buckley* crewman slugged a German as he climbed over the *Buckley's* gunwales, resulting in the only injury to the crew—a bruised hand. After a minute-long brawl, the *Buckley* backed away, leaving five bewildered Germans on deck. They were guarded by a sailor armed with a hammer who took them below. Under interrogation of the prisoners, the *Buckley's* crew learned they were not trying to take over the destroyer escort, just board a ship that would not be sinking.

Now, the *U-66* tried to ram the *Buckley,* but the submarine slid under the destroyer's keel. As the submarine passed under the destroyer, one of *Buckley's* sailors tossed a hand grenade down the open hatch.

One German sailor died a particularly gruesome death.

"Man on deck of sub attempting to man gun disintegrates when hit [with] 40-millimeter shells," reported the captain in his after action report.[2]

The submarine emerged on the other side of the *Buckley* and began sinking. Sailors reported hearing sizzling sounds as the water reached the fires now burning inside the submarine. It took just sixteen minutes from the first shot fired to the sub sinking. The *Buckley* expended 105 rounds of 3-inch shells, three thousand rounds of 20-millimeter rounds, and 360 .45 caliber bullets; some from Thompson submarine guns and some from Model 1911 pistols. Thirty rounds of 00 buckshot were also fired. The captain did not give an accurate count of how many coffee cups were thrown other than "several."[3]

Thirty-six Germans, about two-thirds of the crew, were rescued. The crew had run out of fresh food and most were suffering from vitamin deficiencies. They probably deemed themselves lucky to be captured as the *U-66* may not have made it back to port with low fuel supply and a diminished crew.

Note the crewman with the bandaged hand on the right in the back row. He slugged a German sailor trying to board the USS Buckley and suffered the only American casualty in the battle—a bruised hand. *Photo found at www.Usmilitariaforum.com.*

The *Buckley* had spent its first nine months as a training ship along the Atlantic coast and had just joined the hunter-killer group on April 22. Just two weeks later, she did battle with *U-66*, which was the seventh most successful U-boat in World War II. In ten patrols over three years, the *U-66* had sunk thirty-three merchant ships for 200,000 gross tons, damaged two others, and had damaged two small British torpedo boats.

Whether it was luck or good training on the part of the *Buckley,* or the grinding down of the war on the crew of *U-66,* the result was obvious. The inexperienced American destroyer escort crew had sunk the experienced, but perhaps war-weary, German U-boat crew.

The Germans got their revenge on the USS *Block Island* hunter-killer group just three weeks later when the *U-549* fired three torpedoes into the escort carrier. Then minutes later, the USS *Barr* (DE-576) took a torpedo in its stern from the same U-boat. The *Block Island* would sink, but most of its crew would be rescued. The *Barr* would survive to be repaired and sent to the Pacific. The *U-549* would be hunted down and sunk with all hands by the USS *Ahrens* (DE-575) just thirty minutes later. The roles of hunter-killer had reversed. The *U-549* was on just its second patrol while the *Block Island* and its escorts had been at sea more than a year with several submarine kills over four anti-submarine patrols to their credit.

Sinking the *U-549* was personal for the crew of the *Ahrens.* She and the *Barr* were sister ships, laid down on successive days in the Bethlehem Hingham Shipyard in Hingham, Massachusetts in November 1943.

When Captain D.V. Gallery, captain of the escort carrier USS *Guadalcanal* (CVE-60), captured the bulk of the crew of the *U-515* in April, he thought of another bold idea: capture an entire submarine. He may not have known that the British had captured the *U-110* in 1940, recovering an Enigma machine and codebooks, but the submarine had sunk while under tow.

Now, four years later, the Allies knew the submarine designs had changed and assumed new technology was being installed, but they had no real sense of what was under the sea. Captain Gallery pitched the idea to his superiors. He had just captured the crew of one of the best U-boats in service. Why not complete the mission and capture a boat as well? He had the assets: his escort carrier's twenty-seven aircraft and five destroyer escorts.

The *Guadalcanal* and its destroyer escorts were cruising off North Africa on June 4 at just after 11:00 a.m. when the USS *Chatelain* (DE-149), an *Edsall* class, made a sound contact less than a mile away. A Wildcat pilot confirmed that he could see a submarine under the water. He began firing his machine guns into the water over the sub so that the approaching destroyer escorts could easily find it.

The *Chatelain* launched its depth charges before the other escorts could arrive, and in less than fifteen minutes from detection, the *U-505*, a Type IXC built in 1941, had surfaced. The USS *Pillsbury* (DE-133), an *Edsall* class, and USS *Jenks* (DE-665), a *Buckley* class, surrounded the submarine and started pelting it with machine fire—a tactic intended to frighten the crew inside when they heard the bullets hitting the hull.

The tactic worked too well. The *U-505's* crew abandoned the submarine so fast that they left the screws turning. The boarding crew from the *Pillsbury* had a hard time catching up to the submarine still moving through the water. When they did, Lieutenant A.L. David, who had served on submarines, led the way down the hatch. He shut down the engines and closed the seacocks that had been opened to sink the submarine. The boarding crew started pumping the water out.

Captain Galley's idea had worked. He captured the crew and the U-boat itself. Only one German was killed. The *U-505* was towed to the Bahamas where a team of Navy investigators examined it, but only after repainting it in the colors of an American submarine. If there were any German agents around the harbor, they hadn't noticed the extra interest in the submarine. She was not a brand-new model as Gallery had hoped to capture, but he had still done something no other American captain had accomplished since the War of 1812: capture an intact enemy vessel on the high seas. The *U-505* is now on display at the Museum of Science and Industry in Chicago, Illinois.

Two days later, the invasion of France began on the Normandy beaches. Destroyers would play a key role in providing support bombardment, but three destroyers and a destroyer escort would be lost as a result of the invasion.

Thirty-three American and three British destroyers plus six American destroyer escorts were assigned for close in bombardment support. The destroyers cruised toward the beach, drawing as close as 800 to 1,000 yards to the shore. Some destroyers reported touching the sandy bottom as they shelled everything from shore batteries to machine gun nests to columns of marching German soldiers.

The USS *Corry* (DD-463) was one of the early casualties on D-Day before any of the soldiers had even landed on Utah Beach. The *Corry* was a three-year-old *Gleaves* that had sunk the *U-801* in March as part of the *USS Block Island* hunter-killer group. The *Corry* and USS *Fitch* (DD-462) started firing around 5:35 a.m., cruising parallel to the beach.

Though minesweepers had silently moved into the area during the early morning to pull up German mines, they did not get them all.

At 6:33 a.m., just minutes before the first landing craft dropped its ramp, the *Corry* was shaken by an explosion. The after action report claims it hit a mine, but some sailors thought an artillery round came in at the water line. She soon lost all steam and several other destroyers, and one PT boat rushed to her aid. As the destroyers shelled the German emplacements on one side of their ships, they were lowering boats on the other side to pick up the *Corry's* crew. The destroyers had put themselves even closer to the beach in order to shield the rescue operation.

For more than eight hours, destroyers stayed close to shore to bombard German positions. When the war was over, German Army Field Marshal Gerd von Rundstedt told an interrogator that their defeat was due to "the power of the Allies' naval guns, which reached deep inland...making impossible the bringing up of reserves needed to hurl the Allied invasion forces into the Channel." He added that the "naval artillery was terrific."[4]

The USS *Meredith* (DD-726) was an *Allen M. Sumner* class that struck a mine off the Normandy beachhead and sank just thirty-one days after it was commissioned as a warship. *NHHC photo.*

It was just before 2:00 a.m. on June 8 that the USS *Meredith* (DD-726), an *Allen M. Sumner* class, became the shortest-lived destroyer of World War II. She sailed from Boston on May 8 with a convoy, and then escorted the invasion force across the English Channel on June 6. After laying down shore bombardment fire on June 6, she was assigned normal patrolling duty. That night, she struck a mine. A tow line was attached, but while being towed to a port, her seams began opening up. She broke in half and sank, taking thirty-five dead officers and sailors with her. She had been a warship for just thirty-one days.

Like the USS *Jacob Jones* lost in World War I and its successor lost in World War II, the *Meredith* was an unlucky name for a destroyer. The USS *Meredith* (DD-434), the predecessor to this ship, was a *Gleaves* that was sunk in the Pacific while escorting a supply convoy to Guadalcanal in October of 1942.

Several hours after the *Meredith* was hit, the USS *Glennon* (DD-620), another *Gleaves*, also struck a mine. The USS *Rich* (DE-695), a *Buckley* class, rushed in to help. As she screened a minelayer trying to get a towline to the *Glennon,* the *Rich* struck her own mine. As the *Rich* wallowed from the explosion, she struck a second and then a third mine. All of this explosive activity attracted the attention of surviving German shore batteries. Ninety-one men were killed when the *Rich* sank. The same German gun crews now zeroed in on the struggling *Glennon* and found her range. For all the punishment she took, only twenty-eight men were killed. She finally sank around 9:45 p.m.

The destroyer losses continued for a full week after D-Day. The USS *Nelson* (DD-623), a *Gleaves,* was torpedoed by a German E-boat at 1:05 a.m. on June 12. The *Nelson* was severely damaged and towed to Ireland where repairs were made.

There was some controversy about the E-boat attack. The E-boats had been spotted on radar by several ships, but those picket ships did not issue an immediate challenge, thinking the approaching ships must be Allied. The *Nelson* was torpedoed fourteen minutes after the unknown blips appeared on radar.

"Challenging imposes too great a penalty on the screening vessels. If this ship could have opened fire as soon as control reported on target without challenge, she probably would not have been hit," wrote the *Nelson's* captain in his after action report.[5]

It took a couple of months, but the USS *Somers* (DD-381), the same destroyer that had started the year capturing blockade runners, took revenge for the *Nelson* on August 12. The *Somers* was patrolling off Port Cros, France, when her radar picked up two ships moving toward the invasion fleet after midnight. The *Somers* challenged the two ships but received no answer. The *Somers* even signaled with her searchlight to make sure the two ships knew they were being challenged.

The two ships turned out to be German—a corvette, and a sloop. They were no match for a real warship like the *Somers*. She sank the smaller ship with a single salvo of 5-inch shells—a testament to how accurate radar-directed salvos had become. The larger corvette was hit at least forty times. The corvette was boarded and a number of documents were recovered that proved useful, such as a map showing where the Germans had laid mines.

By the second half of 1944, hunting submarines was difficult because many were being kept in port. The schnorkel that U-boat designers had hoped would give them an edge by allowing the boats to stay underwater while recharging their batteries proved to be of little true value.

The USS *Fiske* (DE-143), an *Edsall* class, was the last destroyer escort sunk in the Atlantic on August 2, 1944. She found the *U-804*, an undistinguished submarine on the surface near the Azores, but was herself torpedoed. She broke apart in less than ten minutes. Thirty-three men were killed.

The last destroyer escort damaged in the Atlantic by a U-boat was the USS *Fogg* (DE-57), a *Buckley* class that had made several successful convoys before December 20, 1944. She was torpedoed by the *U-870*, a submarine that made only two patrols. The *Fogg* made it back to port, but four men were lost.

The last American destroyer lost in the Atlantic theater was not sunk by the Germans, but by Mother Nature.

The USS *Warrington* (DD-383) was a *Somers* class that had been continuously at sea since 1938. She had been part of the Neutrality Patrols in the Caribbean, then shifted to the Pacific in January 1942.

Assigned to escort the USS *Hyades* (AF-28), a refrigerator ship loaded with food, to Trinidad, the *Warrington* was off the Bahamas on September 12 when the two ships sailed into an unpredicted hurricane. All afternoon, the two ships fought high winds and waves. By midnight on September 13, the two ships had lost sight of each other. By 4:30 in the morning, the *Warrington* sent out a distress call that her engineering spaces were flooding, and she was in danger of losing all power. By 2:00 p.m. that same day, she sent out one last call: "WE NEED ASSISTANCE."[6]

Assistance never arrived. One final wave pushed the *Warrington's* stern down and then the rest of the ship simply slipped beneath the waves. On September 13, sixty-eight survivors were rescued. A total 253 officers and sailors drowned. Not one of them qualified for a Purple Heart because the sinking did not result from combat.

The sea had claimed the USS *Warrington*, one of five destroyers lost to weather during the war. It was the last destroyer lost in the Atlantic. The first destroyer lost in the Atlantic (and the first in the war) was the USS *Truxtun*, which had run aground and sunk on February 18, 1942 off of Newfoundland during a storm. Ironically, the first and last destroyers lost in the Atlantic were both lost to nature rather than combat.

CHAPTER

13

Pacific Theater 1944

"A fight against overwhelming odds from which survival can't be expected."

After the Gilbert Islands invasion in the fall of 1943, the next target for the United States was the Marshall Islands, about 500 miles to the northwest. Held by the Japanese since the end of World War I after transfer from the defeated Germans, the Marshalls were twenty-four atolls on which Japan had built bases. Japan considered the Marshalls to be part of Japan's outlying defenses for the home islands 2,400 miles to the northwest.

The difference in naval combat in the Pacific in just two years' time was dramatic. While the last half of 1942 had been slugfests between Japanese and American cruisers and destroyers around Guadalcanal, the remainder of the Japanese surface fleet in 1944 was nowhere near the Marshall Islands. American destroyer duty was looking for scattered submarines and shelling Japanese land emplacements.

While that sounds safe, it was not.

The *USS Anderson* (DD-411) was one of the first of the *Sims* class to put to sea in 1939. She had been at sea ever since, serving in both the Atlantic and Pacific. She had been engaged in several combats with Japanese airplanes, shooting down some as they attacked carriers, but she had missed all of the engagements with Japanese surface ships that had damaged or sunk so many other American destroyers. On January 30, the *Anderson* moved in close to shell Wotje, a neighboring island to Kwajalein and the main American target that had been shelled for two days by American battleships. Wotje had not received such attention. As the destroyer drew close to shore, Japanese artillery hit the *Anderson's* Combat Information Center, killing the ship's captain and five others. She was repaired at Pearl and continued her service through the end of the war.

Some destroyer victories in the Marshalls came easily.

The *USS Burns* (DD-588), a *Fletcher,* had just recovered some downed fliers when she picked up an unknown contact at 12:23 a.m. on January 30. The contact at 21,000 yards could have been anything, even American ships, so the *Burns* sailed on alone to investigate. It was a dark, moonless night with rain squalls, so lookout identification of friendly ship silhouettes would not be possible. At 1:07 a.m., the captain hailed the contacts and asked them to identify themselves if they were American. No answer was returned.

The *Burns* sailed on until opening fire at 9,000 yards using radar control of its 5-inch guns. Supposedly, the first salvo hit a Japanese oil tanker as the sky suddenly lit up. At 6,000 yards, the destroyer shifted to another target. That too caught on fire. As she closed to 2,000 yards, she used her 20-millimeter and 40-millimeter guns to hit two other targets that were now visible thanks to the two burning ships. In just thirty-four minutes, the *Burns* had fired 494 rounds of 5-inch shells, 928 rounds of 40-millimeter shells, and 845 rounds of 20-millimeter shells to sink one tanker and three cargo ships. She had not taken a single round in response. The radar had penetrated through the darkness.

Captain D.T. Eller wrote in his after action report: "This action is considered an indication of the potentialities and fire power of modern destroyers...Destroyers are perfectly suited now for such attacks and should be able to completely disrupt Japanese convoys far in advance of present fleet operations."[1]

Eller, though not part of Arleigh Burke's Little Beavers, was echoing what Burke had been arguing for some time: destroyers should be turned loose to fight on their own when not needed to screen larger cruisers and aircraft carriers.

In the same report, Eller wrote something that would be proven incorrect before the end of the year: "Japanese aircraft have not so far had great success against 2100-ton destroyers [*Fletchers*] and it is not believed that they will."[2]

HMS *Petard* (G-56) captured Enigma machine codebooks, and sank three enemy submarines in three different oceans. *Royal Navy photo.*

The HMS *Petard* (G-56), a P-class launched in 1941, was already a destroyer that had contributed tremendously to the war effort by capturing Enigma machine codebooks from an Atlantic U-boat in October 1942. She had sunk the *U-559*, and then sunk an Italian submarine a few months later. For the next year, she was on convoy duty in the Mediterranean and Aegean seas before being sent to escort Convoy KR8 in the Indian Ocean. The largest ship in the convoy was the SS *Khedive Ismail*, a troop ship loaded with more than 1,500 passengers and crew, including more than seventy women serving as nurses in the British Army.

Lying in wait was a behemoth, the Japanese submarine *I-27*. At 356 feet long and weighing 2,631 tons (compared to the common U-boat Type IIC's length of 219 feet and 871 tons), she was large enough to carry her own float plane.

At 2:30 p.m. on February 12, the *I-27* fired a spread of four torpedoes at the troop ship. Two struck and the ship went down in minutes, carrying nearly 1,300 people to their deaths. It was the third largest loss of life from a troop ship sinking in the war.

Petard rushed in and dropped three patterns of depth charges. The concussion from the charges killed some of the men and women in the water, but the destroyer captain had no choice if he wanted to kill the *I-27*. The submarine finally surfaced, and *Petard* continued its attack with its guns. It finally finished off the submarine by launching its own surface torpedoes. It took seven torpedo hits before the giant *I-27* would finally sink. The *Petard* once again recovered important papers, including the submarine's logbook that an alert crewman saw floating in the water. The logbook gave details about the Japanese navy's operations in the area. Only one man from the submarine's 100-man crew, more than twice the complement of American and German submarines, survived.

The *Petard* was the only destroyer in the war to sink three enemy submarines serving in three different enemy navies in three different oceans.

By mid-spring, there were still no large Japanese surface fleets challenging large American fleets, but Japanese submarines remained a threat. The destroyer escort USS *England* (DE-635) was particularly good at finding and sinking them. Twelve days later in May, the *England* dispatched six Japanese submarines—a record that none of its larger sisters, the destroyers, ever matched during the war.

The *England* was a *Buckley*, armed with three 3-inch guns, two 40-millimeter Bofors guns, and eight 20-millimeter Oerlikon cannons. Each ship was armed with a hedgehog thrower, up to two hundred depth charges, and a K-gun depth charge thrower. Finally, there was one triple-mount of 21-inch torpedoes.

All the *England* needed to sink Japanese submarines was its hedgehog thrower. Each 65-pound shell contained 33 pounds of TNT explosives. Twenty-four could be thrown at once 200 yards in front of the ship.

When the *England* sailed from San Francisco at the end of December 1943, it was with a new crew. Its executive officer said of the fourteen officers, only five had ever been to sea. Of the two hundred enlisted men, only forty had been to sea.

On May 19, Naval Intelligence, which was routinely reading coded Japanese messages, passed along word that the supply submarine I-16 would be making its way to Bougainville. The *England* and two other destroyer escorts went out to meet it. The *I-16* was another huge submarine, 358 feet long, and 52 feet longer than the *England*. While the crew of the *England* did not know it at the time, it was also a historic submarine. It had launched one of the midget submarines that had penetrated Pearl Harbor on December 7, 1941. She had sunk three freighters earlier in the war but was now reduced to carrying rice to a starving garrison still on Bougainville.

In its first ever combat situation, the *England* scored five or six hits with its fifth hedgehog attack. The hits were enough to rupture the hull of the submarine and lift the stern of the destroyer escort completely out of the water when the submarine exploded underwater. None of the Japanese crew of ninety-five survived.

The next day, intelligence passed word that seven Japanese submarines would be heading into the operational area. To maintain secrecy, the destroyer escorts were ordered not to report on anything until they returned to port. Reporting kills over the radio might tip off the Japanese that the Americans had figured out where the subs would be.

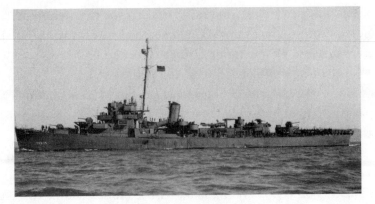

USS *England* (DE-635) sank six Japanese submarines in twelve days in the Pacific. *NHHC photo.*

Curiously, the standing orders to the destroyer escorts were to pursue only the five submarines in the part of the ocean that was under Admiral Halsey's command, but to ignore the two submarines that would be in General MacArthur's command. A bureaucratic dispute between an admiral and a general over an imaginary line in the Pacific Ocean was dictating where, when, and how destroyer escorts would pursue enemy submarines.

On May 22, the *England* claimed the *RO-106*, a medium-sized submarine that had only sunk an LST in its career. This time, the sub was sunk with a single salvo of hedgehogs.

On May 23, two other destroyer escorts could not pin down a contact. When the squadron commander ordered them away to allow the *England* to try, she immediately found the *RO-104*. Ten or twelve of the twenty-four hedgehogs hit at 300 feet deep. Once again, the resulting underwater explosion rocked the *England*. Though it was obvious that the submarine was dead, orders were to drop depth charges on the chance that the sub-marine had somehow faked its own death by exploding its own torpedoes outside of the submarine. It was a ridiculous theory, but one coming from higherups, so the *England* followed orders. The collection of fractured wood with Japanese writing proved that the submarine was dead.

With three kills in a few days, the crew was no longer jubilant. One asked the executive officer, Captain John Williamson, how he should feel about killing other sailors.

Williamson replied: "The more of the enemy we can kill, and the more of his ships we can sink, the sooner it will be over. This is our duty. Sinking these submarines may save untold numbers of our troops or ships. We can't get into it deeper than that. We cannot sit in judgment of our actions now. We are in a war that we must win, for to lose it would be far worse."[3]

On May 24, the *England* got its fourth kill, the *RO-116*, but its crew was puzzled by the lack of a huge explosion like the ones that had rocked the ship during the previous three kills. Still, pieces of the sextant box belonging to the submarine's captain floated to the surface, proving the destruction.

On May 26, the *England* fired a single hedgehog pattern of twenty-four rounds and sunk the *RO-108* when four to six of the charges hit the submarine. It had taken less than twenty minutes from the first surface radar contact with the submarine to its sinking. There was just one full charge of twenty-four hedgehog rounds left in the ammo locker. She had to return to port for more ammunition and fuel after sinking her fifth submarine since May 18.

By this time, the two other destroyer escorts operating with *England* were frustrated. When *England* radioed another destroyer escort asking its position, the reply was terse: "We're not telling you where we are. We have a damaged sub, and we're going to sink him. Don't come near us!"[4]

The two other ships tried and failed, but the *England* dropped a hedgehog pattern and claimed the *RO-105*. At least half of the charges hit. On board this submarine had been one of Japan's most experienced submariners and commander of a submarine division.

The *England* had sunk six submarines in twelve days. In eleven firing runs of twenty-four rounds of 65-pound hedgehog charges, Williamson estimated hits in seven of those eleven runs over a contact. Williamson had no explanation for how the *England* had been so successful. Three different sonar operators were on duty during the six attacks so that success could not be attributed to one skillful sonar operator.

There were some curious facts associated with her victims. Four of the submarines were constructed in the same shipyard within four months of each other. Two of her victims started construction the same day in the same yard.

The *England* would not sink any more submarines and would survive a kamikaze attack on May 9, 1945, just under a year from when she began her twelve day stretch of victories.

Destroyers, originally designed to fire torpedoes at larger ships, took on all kinds of roles when there were no Japanese ships to fight.

USS *Robinson* (DD-562) demonstrates how close destroyers could get to a beach while shelling enemy positions. *NHHC photo.*

On July 7, the USS *Heywood L. Edwards* (DD-663), a *Fletcher,* saw swimmers in the water off of a beach on Saipan. Moving in to investigate, she was hailed by the men who turned out to be American soldiers who had swum from the beach to avoid advancing Japanese. The captain's gig and a whaleboat were lowered to retrieve forty-four soldiers and a prisoner.

The USS *Robinson* (DD-562), a *Fletcher,* discovered on her first assignment that she did not have to fight Japanese ships to be effective. In her first salvo of fire support for the invasion of Saipan, her 5-inch guns hit an ammo dump. A few minutes later, she shifted fire to artillery batteries that had been hitting Marines on the beaches. In September when she was part of the invasion fleet of the Carolina Islands, she sailed close to the beach in order to protect Underwater Demolition Teams that were clearing the beach of obstacles. When Japanese tanks crawled down to the beach to machine gun the frogmen, the *Robinson* blew them apart. When the naval destroyer was first developed in the 1870s, its designers never thought it would be dueling with army tanks—a weapon that would not be invented for another forty years during World War I.

By the early fall of 1944, both the United States and Japan were eyeing the next obvious battleground: the Philippines. Destroyers and destroyer escorts would play key roles in what would become the last and largest surface naval battles of the war.

On October 20, U.S. troops began landing on Leyte Island. The Imperial Japanese Fleet that had avoided major combat for more than a year was not going to let General Douglas McArthur return to the Philippines unopposed. The Battle of Leyte Gulf would last four days, October 23-26, 1944. Though historians use the encompassing term "Battle of Leyte Gulf," there were several distinct naval engagements fought in the area of Leyte Gulf.

The Imperial Japanese Navy divided itself into three fleets: the Northern Force, Center Force, and Southern Force.

The Northern Force was something of a paper tiger consisting of two battleships, four cruisers, and four aircraft carriers, but with very few aircraft on board. Most had already been shot down by American airplanes. The Japanese intended to lure the American fleet away from the landing sites by making sure the carriers were seen and judged to be the primary targets.

The Center Force was built around five battleships, twelve cruisers, and fifteen destroyers. The Southern force had two battleships, four cruisers and eleven destroyers.

The Japanese plan was relatively simple: lure the American Seventh and Third Fleets into chasing the Northern Force. Once away from the American beachheads, now clogged with troop transports and supply ships, the Center and Southern Forces would sweep in to destroy the mostly defenseless supply ships.

The first action, the Battle of Palawan Passage on October 23, involved only two American submarines spotting the Center Force and sinking two heavy cruisers. On October 24, the Battle of Sibuyan Sea involved American aircraft finding and bombing still more ships from the Center Force including sinking one Japanese battleship.

Land-based Japanese aircraft took off during this phase of the battle and found the USS *Princeton* (CVL 23), an escort carrier, which had been covering the troop landings with its fighters. At 9:38 a.m. on October 24, a single Japanese dive bomber dropped a single bomb on the carrier's flight deck, setting off secondary explosions when it hit a loaded airplane. The USS *Irwin* (DD-794), a *Fletcher*, closed on the stricken carrier to fight fires and take off 645 crewmen.

As the *Irwin* pulled away, the USS *Morrison* (DD-560) came alongside to rescue more men. As the *Princeton* rolled in the rough seas, she snagged the *Morrison's* masts in her own stacks. The fire on the carrier was so intense that the *Morrison's* paint was scorched. The *Morrison* finally broke free, making room for the light cruiser USS *Birmingham* (CL-62) to try towing the *Princeton*. A huge internal explosion blew flaming wreckage onto the cruiser, injuring many of her crew. Once the rest of the crew was rescued, the *Princeton* was sunk by torpedoes fired from American destroyers.

By the late afternoon on October 24, Admiral Halsey, believing the Center Force was virtually destroyed, ordered his Third Fleet north to attack the Northern Fleet's carriers. A task force was supposed to have been left behind to cover the entrance of the San Bernardino Strait, but a mistaken message from Halsey to the rest of his admirals left the Strait open and empty of all defending American ships as the American Third Fleet headed north to destroy the Japanese Northern Force.

On October 25, the Southern Force attacked at what would become known as the Battle of Surigao Strait, the second and last battleship-to-battleship action in the Pacific. Destroyers would also play an important role.

The Southern Force was led into the Surigao Strait between Dinagat Island and Leyte Island by two old battleships, *Fuso* and *Yamashiro*. The battleships were accompanied by a single heavy cruiser and four destroyers.

The two old battleships were considered obsolete by the Japanese, but they were available and put into service. Spotted and harassed by PT boats earlier in the night, the Japanese fleet came under torpedo attack at 2:58 a.m. on October 25 by Destroyer Squadron 54, consisting of nine *Fletchers*. The squadron was experienced in finding submarines and shelling shore batteries, but none of them had ever encountered Japanese surface ships.

It was a complete reversal of roles for the Japanese and Americans. Early in the war, the Japanese, reputed masters of night fighting, would fire torpedoes on the unsuspecting Americans. This time, Destroyer Squadron 54 fired twenty-seven torpedoes from three destroyers. *Fuso* was hit by torpedoes from the USS *Melvin* (DD-680). At 3:38 a.m., she exploded and broke into two halves.

Less than twenty minutes later, torpedoes from the USS *McDermut* (DD-677) hit three Japanese destroyers—*Yamagumo, Michishio*, and *Asagumo*—all from the *Asahio* class built in the 1930s.

Not long after that, torpedoes from the USS *Killen* (DD-593) from Destroyer Squadron 24 hit the *Yamashiro*. At 4:11 a.m., torpedoes launched from a third division, Destroyer Squadron 56, hit the battleship again with USS *Newcomb* (DD-586), and the USS *Bennion* (DD-662) likely firing the torpedoes. It was not until decades later that the *Bennion's* torpedo hit was credited to it.

A general melee broke out with the USS *Albert Grant* (DD-649), taking several 6-inch shells from American cruisers. Most of the thirty-nine Americans killed during the battle were on the *Albert Grant*. Several thousand Japanese sailors died when the two battleships sank.

When morning came, it was found that the Japanese had lost two battleships and three destroyers, while for Americans, only the *Albert Grant* was damaged, mostly from friendly fire. The Japanese were no longer masters of the night ocean.

Admiral Jesse Oldendorf made an interesting observation after the battle in describing how close the American destroyers were to each other during the battle: "[American] destroyers appeared as one blip on the enemy screen and they fired at the center of the blip, which made their shells fall exactly between the attacking destroyers so that none of the destroyers in this attack were hit."[5]

Just when the Americans were basking in the glow of their tremendous victory at the Battle of Surigao Strait, disaster struck just hours later during the Battle off Samar in the Philippine Sea off Samar Island some 300 miles away.

Having seen the destruction of the Southern Force and assuming that the Center Force was retreating, Admiral Halsey launched his Third Fleet northward after the Northern Force. Ten American carriers, six battleships, eight cruisers, and forty destroyers all left the Leyete landing area in a hunt for Japanese carriers. The landing areas were left to the protection of the Seventh Fleet.

What Halsey had not counted on was the supposedly retreating, battered Center Force turning around and advancing on the northernmost part of the Seventh Fleet through the undefended San Bernardino Strait. While the Seventh Fleet was strong, it was also scattered.

The Center Force had been battered by American submarines and aircraft, but it was not scattered and not defeated. It still had four battleships, eight cruisers, and eleven destroyers in a tight formation capable of roaring down at 30 knots on anything in front of it.

The first person to realize an attack was imminent on the northern-most portions of the Seventh Fleet was a U.S. Navy pilot who accurately described the oncoming ships as battleships, cruisers, and uncountable destroyers. When Admiral Clifton Sprague heard the excited radio report, he angrily demanded that the pilot take another look and report again. Sprague could not believe there was any viable Japanese fleet in his area.

When the pilot repeated what he saw, Sprague, on board one of the escort carriers, realized that all of the American ships in the area were in danger of being sunk—all of them.

The first American ships in the path of the Center Force was Task Force TG77.4.3, which went by the nickname Taffy 3. Taffy 3 was made up of six escort carriers screened by three destroyers and four destroyer escorts. Escape by running was not an option. While the destroyer escorts could make 24 knots and the destroyers could make 34 knots, the escort carriers could only make 19 knots. Japanese cruisers and destroyers could make up to 35 knots.

The approximately 180 aircraft on the escort carriers could not protect their own carriers on such short notice. The airplanes were all loaded with ammunition and bombs meant to attack Japanese land forces, not heavy, armored cruisers and battleships. Still, the airplanes launched to do what they could. The advancing Japanese were so close before they were discovered that the American pilots anxiously watched near miss splashes around their carriers as they waited their turn to launch.

Even worse, the Americans could not hide in and fight from darkness as they had in so many previous sea battles. When the Japanese force came over the horizon, it was 6:45 a.m. A few minutes later, the Japanese started firing from 17 miles away. Sprague did the only thing he could do; he radioed Halsey for help without even attempting to encode the message. He also asked the destroyers and destroyer escorts of Taffy 3 to do what they could.

The Battle off Samar on October 25, 1944 would go down in history on account of the bravery of Destroyer Men.

USS *Johnston* (DD-557) was one of the members of Taffy 3 that rushed into battle against a superior Japanese force at the Battle off Samar in October of 1944. *NHHC photo.*

Leading the Japanese formation was the battleship *Yamato,* a 65,000-ton monster battleship armed with nine 18-inch guns. Each gun could fire a 3,200-pound shell 26 miles. The next eleven ships in the Center Force all had 16-inch, 14-inch, or 6-inch guns. The eleven Japanese destroyers all had 5-inch guns, the same caliber guns carried by American destroyers, though the Japanese guns could fire more than a mile further than the American 5-inch guns.

The destroyers and destroyer escorts in Taffy 3 could fire 5-inch shells weighing 55 pounds 10 miles. Each of the 2,050-ton destroyers had ten torpedo tubes, but once they were gone, they would have to rely on their guns.

The American destroyers, all *Fletchers,* were the USS *Hoel* (DD-533), USS *Johnston* (DD-557), and USS *Heermann* (DD-532). All were combat veterans of shore bombardments, but none had been in a surface engagement.

The destroyer escorts were USS *Samuel B. Roberts* (DE-413), USS *John E. Butler* (DE-439), USS *Raymond* (DE-341), and USS *Dennis*

(DE-406). All of the escorts were *John E. Butler* class, the newest class of destroyer escorts. All were 306 feet long, weighed 1,350 tons, and were armed with two 5-inch guns, twin 40-millimeter Bofors guns, ten 20-millimeter Oerlikon cannons, hedgehog throwers, and depth charges. Each had three 21-inch torpedo tubes. None of the DEs had gone up against a surface Japanese ship.

The only defense that the destroyers and the destroyer escorts had were their torpedoes and 5-inch guns—if they could get close enough to use them.

The realization of what Taffy 3 was facing sank in on the bridge of each ship. Captain Robert Copeland of the *Samuel B. Roberts* voiced it in a cool, calm message he sent over the intercom.

"A large Japanese fleet has been contacted. They are 15 miles away and headed in our direction. They are believed to have four battleships, eight cruisers, and a number of destroyers. This will be a fight against overwhelming odds from which survival cannot be expected. We will do what damage we can."[6]

The closest destroyer to the advancing Japanese was the USS *Johnston* (DD-557), commanded by Commander Ernest E. Evans, an American Indian with Cherokee and Creek ancestry, who was naturally nicknamed "Chief" when attending the Naval Academy. Post-war accounts describe him as a man "who had great faith in all of us [his crew]...a true, instinctive fighter."[7]

Evans had forewarned his crew about future fighting when the *Johnston* was commissioned: "This is going to be a fighting ship. I intend to go in harm's way, and anyone who doesn't want to go along had better get off right now. Now that I have a fighting ship, I will never retreat from an enemy force."[8] With the line "I intend to go in harm's way," Evans was invoking the famous words of Captain John Paul Jones, American Revolutionary hero and father of the U.S. Navy.

His crew believed him. None of them left the ship.

At 7:20 a.m., just thirty-five minutes after the Japanese force was sighted by the observation aircraft, the *Johnston* was rushing toward the incoming Japanese fleet, laying down a smokescreen to help hide the escort carriers that were running as fast as they could in the opposite direction. The *Kumano*, a light cruiser that had survived American aerial attacks on several occasions, was the closest. With its first salvos, *Johnston* hit the cruiser. A few minutes later, *Johnston* fired her torpedoes, which blew off the bow of the cruiser. With its lead cruiser now suddenly slowing and American torpedoes in the water, the following Japanese cruisers had to swing to either side. The attack of a lone American destroyer had thrown the Japanese column into disarray.

Despite running at flank speed, the *Johnston* was hit by three 14-inch shells from the battleship *Kongo*, an old, veteran battleship launched in 1911. Ironically, she had been built in Great Britain back when Japan had been an Ally. In this war, the *Kongo* had been in battles against other British ships built in the same Vickers-Armstrong yard.

All of the *Kongo's* shells hit the *Johnston* but did not explode as they were armor-piercing and the 5/16-inch skin of the *Johnston* did not qualify as armor. Moments later, more shells hit the destroyer's bridge, but still she continued moving. At 8:20 a.m., the *Johnston* found itself cruising near the *Kongo*. At least forty 5-inch shells landed on the battleship, but the *Johnston's* gunnery chief later described their ineffectiveness saying that "it was like bouncing paper wads off of a steel helmet."[9]

Within a few minutes, a line of Japanese destroyers came into view. *Johnston* brought all of her guns to bear on them. The lead ship was hit a dozen times and the second ship was also hit. Remarkably, the column of Japanese ships veered off rather than take more fire from the heavily damaged *Johnston*.

At 10:10 a.m., the *Johnston* sank with 186 crew lost. The destroyer had been the first into the fight and the last out of it. Captain Evans did not survive. Survivors in the water watched as a Japanese destroyer slowly cruised past the sinking ship. On her deck was the crew standing at attention. A man that the *Johnston's* survivors supposed was the Japanese captain came out on the bridge and saluted.

It was a remarkable gesture: Japanese sailors saluting their enemies.

The *Hoel* too laid smoke as it rushed forward after the *Johnston* had charged ahead. Following were the *Heermann* and the *Samuel B. Roberts*. It was one of the *Yamato's* smaller 6.1-inch guns that first hit the *Hoel's* bridge at 7:25 a.m. Still, the *Hoel* pressed on, firing her torpedoes. The Japanese ships took no torpedo hits from the *Hoel*, but they did turn away from them, buying more time for the escort carriers to continue running. By 8:30 a.m., the *Hoel* was virtually surrounded by the approaching Japanese ships. At 8:55 a.m., the *Hoel* sank, fifteen minutes before the *Johnston*. Only eighty-six men survived. More than 250 went down with the ship.

The *Heerman*, with the *Samuel B. Roberts* fast at her stern, attacked the cruiser *Haguro* at 7:50 a.m., then fired torpedoes at the battleships *Haruna* and *Yamato*. Both battleships turned away from a destroyer a fraction of their size.

Still operating at full speed at a few minutes after 8:00 a.m., *Heermann* engaged the cruiser *Chikuma*. At the same time, three different battleships now directed their fire at the single destroyer. Though taking hits, she still fought the *Chikuma*, which later sank.

The *Samuel B. Roberts* was so small that it might not have been seen by the Japanese cruisers early in the battle. At less than 4,000 yards, she fired her torpedoes at the cruiser *Chokai*, hitting her and forcing her out of the attacking line. At 8:10 a.m., the destroyer escort started firing on the *Chikuma* at the same time as the *Heerman* was targeting the same ship. The *Samuel B. Roberts* fired almost its entire supply of 5-inch shells at the cruiser since she was the closest Japanese ship, and also the closest enemy to the escort carriers. By 9:00 a.m., the other Japanese ships were sighting in on the destroyer escort. There was no way a destroyer escort would survive the shelling of battleships and cruisers.

Despite their gallant defense, the destroyers and destroyer escorts could not keep all of the Japanese ships out of range of the escort carriers. The USS *Gambier Bay* (CVE-73) was sunk by cruiser gunfire. The USS

St. Lo (CVE-63) was sunk by the first Japanese aircraft intentionally flown into American ships. Inspired by typhoons sent by the gods to sink invading Mongolian fleets in the thirteenth century, the Japanese would call their new tactic "divine wind," or kamikaze. The USS *Kalinin Bay* (CVE-68) was heavily damaged when she was hit by two kamikazes.

With three of the escort carriers sinking or burning and their protective escorts also sinking, the fleet of American transports Taffy 3 had been protecting was within Japanese reach.

Then, a miracle happened.

A few minutes after the *Samuel B. Roberts* had been destroyed, the Japanese commander, Admiral Kurita, ordered all of his ships to reassemble. Kurita, on board the *Yamato*, began pondering how many other warships lay ahead of him in Leyte Gulf, and whether Admiral Halsey had turned around the Third Fleet and was coming up in his rear. Kurita looked at his attacking fleet and saw his ships fighting scattered, individual battles with what he thought were large aircraft carriers and cruisers. In reality, they were fighting slow escort carriers, destroyers and destroyer escorts. His own battleship had turned away from a salvo of torpedoes he assumed had come from a cruiser, but which had come from a single *Fletcher*-class destroyer.

Kurita, who had been bloodied the day before and now today, decided that the forces ahead of him were too large and the forces behind him were on their way. Rather than be caught in a pincer, Kurita turned his fleet around and retreated. With the rest of the escort carriers in easy range and nothing to stop him but more destroyers and destroyer escorts, Kurita turned away, believing his force was about to be destroyed.

By nothing more than hard fighting, a tiny American force had turned around a mighty Japanese fleet.

The battle had started around 7:00 a.m. when the Japanese battleships had started firing. The *Hoel* sunk at 8:55. The *Samuel B. Roberts* sank around 10:00 a.m. The *Johnston* sank ten minutes later. The length of the battle was remarkable. Most of the earlier sea battles in the Pacific were over in a short time, sometimes in minutes as one side or the other targeted and sank its opponent quickly. This battle lasted well over three hours when the vastly superior Japanese force should have rolled right over the destroyers and destroyer escorts of Taffy 3 within a matter of minutes. It was the audacious acts of the American captains who sailed at full speed into the path of far larger and more heavily armed ships that threw off the Japanese battle plans.

Two escort carriers were sunk, one to shellfire and one to a kamikaze. A third was heavily damaged. Had the Japanese not turned around when they did, the other three escort carriers would have been within their gun ranges in a matter of minutes.

Though it was one of the most dramatic battles in U.S. Naval history, only one Medal of Honor was awarded.

Part of the citation for Commander Ernest Evans of the *Johnston* reads: "Undaunted by damage sustained under the terrific volume of fire, he unhesitatingly joined others of his group to provide fire support during subsequent torpedo attacks against the Japanese and, outshooting and outmaneuvering the enemy as he consistently interposed his vessel between the hostile fleet units and our carriers despite the crippling loss of engine power and communications with steering aft, shifted command to the fantail, shouted steering orders through an open hatch to men turning the rudder by hand and battled furiously until the *Johnston,* burning and shuddering from a mortal blow, lay dead in the water after 3 hours of fierce combat. Seriously wounded early in the engagement, Comdr. Evans, by his indomitable courage and brilliant professional skill, aided materially in turning back the enemy during a critical phase of the action. His valiant fighting spirit throughout this historic battle will venture as an inspiration to all who served with him."

Though its large surface fleet had just been turned back, the Japanese were not going to allow the Americans to land troops in the Philippines without some form of resistance.

The use of the kamikaze against the escort carriers on October 25 was just the beginning of this new Japanese tactic. On November 1, four different destroyers were stuck with the *Abner Read* claiming the unfortunate distinction of being the first destroyer sunk by suicide airplanes. The previous year, she had struck a mine in the Aleutians and had lost her stern and seventy crewmen. This time, she lost another twenty-two.

Another destroyer that was struck by a kamikaze off the Philippines was the USS *Ward* (DD-139/APD-6). The *Wickes*-class destroyer, one of the oldest ships in service, had become famous in the Navy for having found and sunk a midget submarine lurking off Pearl Harbor ninety minutes before the airplane attack on December 7, 1941. She had been converted to a fast attack transport and served a relatively peaceful life for the last three years. She had not come under enemy fire until that day when a kamikaze hit her and started fires that could not be extinguished. A nearby destroyer, the USS *O'Brien* (DD-725), was ordered to sink her rather than allow her to become a floating hazard to other American ships.

It was December 7, 1944, three years to the day when the *Ward* had actually opened the war against Japan. The captain of the *O'Brien* was Commander William Outerbridge, who had commanded the *Ward* on December 7, 1941. He stoically reported that he felt nothing emotionally at having to sink a destroyer he had once commanded.

Admiral Halsey was roundly criticized after the Battle off Samar for not recognizing the trap that the Japanese sprung which resulted in the deaths of more than one thousand sailors and the loss of five ships in the Seventh Fleet.

Admiral William Halsey was sometimes criticized for his handling of his fleets. *NHHC photo.*

Six weeks later, he would face more criticism and a court of inquiry for a natural disaster that would claim almost as many lives as were lost off Samar.

On December 17, the Third Fleet, the same one that had been lured away from Samar, was refueling in the Philippine Sea some 500 miles east of Luzon when the weather began to deteriorate. Before the destroyers could refuel, the storm worsened. By mid-morning on December 18, Typhoon Cobra was upon the fleet with winds over 100 miles per hour. Three destroyers, USS *Hull* (DD-350), USS *Monaghan* (DD-354), two *Farraguts*, and USS *Spence* (DD-512), *a Fletcher,* simply disappeared beneath the ocean. *Spence* had not yet taken on any fuel but had pumped out her water tanks in anticipation of taking on the fuel, so she was extremely light.

The *Farragut* design of the *Monaghan* and *Hull* had always been problematically top-heavy, but the ships had remained in service with the captains expected to compensate for that defect when they encountered heavy seas.

If there was one bright spot after Typhoon Cobra passed, it shown on the heavily damaged destroyer escort USS *Tabberer* (DE-418). Ignoring orders from Admiral Halsey that the ships rendezvous in calmer waters, her captain cruised a box search pattern in the still heaving seas looking for survivors. The *Tabberer* picked up fifty-five men who would have certainly died if the search had been delayed until calmer seas as Halsey had ordered.

Some 790 men were lost on the three destroyers. Nearly two hundred aircraft were destroyed when they broke their chains below decks on the carriers and crashed into the bulkheads.

At a court of inquiry in the last week of December, the presiding officers gingerly blamed Halsey for "errors of judgement" in not recognizing that the Third Fleet was steering into a typhoon. The court ignored the fact that Halsey had been warned several times that the storm was becoming deadly. The court was harsher with the captains of the lost destroyers, two of which were now dead, for not breaking station and maneuvering on their own to save their ships. Halsey had not issued specific orders to break station. The court ruled that orders or not, the captains should have followed their instincts to save their ships.

The captain of the *Hull*, who did survive, was not disciplined by the Navy, but his fictional image was created by an officer who transferred off the *Hull* before the typhoon. Novelist Herman Wouk wrote the novel *The Caine Mutiny* about a tyrannical destroyer captain hated by officers and crew. In the movie version, Humphrey Bogart played Captain Philip Queeg, an officer whose mental illness is revealed during a court of inquiry called to question the captain's performance during a typhoon.

Nature was not through with the Third Fleet or Halsey. Another typhoon rocked the ships in 1945, but the loss of life did not come close to what happened to end the U.S. Navy's war in the Pacific in 1944.

14

Atlantic Theater 1945

"I think that is the end of the sub."

The Allied war against the Germans from 1940-1943 had focused on the Battle of the Atlantic. The land invasions of Sicily, Italy, and France came in 1944. By the turn of 1945 and the defeat of the German Army in its last gasp at The Battle of the Bulge, the war's end seemed inevitable. Germany's ability to sink ships had been greatly reduced, so the Atlantic was relatively quiet compared to what was happening in the Pacific.

With the war winding down, the Allies, particularly the Americans, began planning for a post-war world. It was a battle-scarred American *Benson*-class destroyer that played a major role in creating a friendly relationship with Saudi Arabia and the United States that has lasted into the twenty-first century. That relationship began when a curious but respectful crew of Destroyer Men encountered a foreign culture in February 1945.

The destroyer that played that huge role in international relations could have been considered a hard-luck ship.

The USS *Murphy* (DD-603) was one of the first Atlantic destroyers to prepare for the inevitable invasion of Europe when it provided shore bombardment during Operation Torch, the invasion of North Africa in October 1942. Getting too close to shore, however, resulted in a German shore battery round going into the *Murphy's* engine room. It killed three men. In July 1943, the *Murphy* provided the same kind of duty during Operation Husky, the invasion of Sicily. She experienced several near misses from German bombers that wounded more men. Her gunners downed two German aircraft.

Escorting a convoy out of New York in October 1943, the *Murphy's* bow was severed in a collision with an oil tanker just seventy-five miles out of port. This time, thirty-six men were killed. She was towed back to New York and underwent seven months of repairs, including having a new bow section welded into place.

She returned to combat in time to help in the D-Day landings, throwing shells onto German defenses behind Omaha Beach. She then left to provide bombardment for Cherbourg and finally returned to New York for overhaul in early September.

While waiting for a convoy, the *Murphy* received orders to escort the cruiser USS *Quincy* (CA-71) across the Atlantic. On board the *Quincy* was President Roosevelt, who would meet with other Allied leaders in Malta.

Most of the destroyers were deployed as protection against a submarine attack as the Mediterranean was still a hunting ground for U-Boats. The *Murphy* was given a secret mission to proceed to Jidda, Saudi Arabia to pick up King Ibn Saud for a separate meeting with Roosevelt.

Conscious that the Muslim culture was like nothing he had ever encountered, Commander Bernard A. Smith, captain of the *Murphy*, found an encyclopedia entry on Islam and used it to instruct his officers and crew not to smoke or drink in the king's presence. Helping to smooth the way was a U.S. Marine, Colonel William A. Eddy, an advisor to the king, who had also helped plan the Allied landings in North Africa.

Problems arose before the *Murphy* could pick up the king.

The king's foreign minister was appalled at the small size of Commander Smith's cabin, the natural place to house the king on his short voyage to meet President Roosevelt. The foreign minister settled on setting up a tent on the deck. Yards of canvas were sewn into a huge tent erected on the deck as if the king were traveling in the desert. A nervous captain had to disregard regulations banning canvas on deck as a fire hazard.

Next, the foreign minister objected to the ship's steel decks. He had servants spread dozens of rugs to cover the deck on which the king might step. He also sent an ornate throne on which the king could sit while inside the tent; a mere chair was too common for a king.

The personal staff of Saudi King Ibn Saud onboard the USS *Murphy* (DD-603). Note the rugs covering the destroyer's deck. *NHHC photo.*

Water from Mecca was also brought on board as the fresh water served to American sailors and officers was not good enough for a king.

When Commander Smith casually asked how many people would be traveling with the king, the casual answer was "perhaps two hundred."

Commander Smith gasped and replied, "Every cabin and bunk on the ship is occupied. The maximum we can take is ten!"[1]

With Colonel Eddy's help, forty-eight of the king's entourage were approved to travel, including the king's cook, doctor, fortune teller, and official coffee pourer.

On the day of sailing, the captain's headaches grew worse. A barge pulled up loaded with eighty-five sheep. The king's cook intended on slaughtering the sheep one by one for the entourage's meals.

"This was just too much – the proverbial straw that might break the *Murphy's* back," wrote Commodore John S. Keating, the commander of the destroyer squadron to which the *Murphy* belonged. More negotiations occurred and the number of sheep to be kept in a pen on the fantail was reduced to the number that would be consumed during the trip.

During the three-day trip, customs clashes took place. An Arab was found with a lighted charcoal burner over an ammunition handling area. When a Lucille Ball comedy was shown below decks for the crew, one of the king's sons demanded to see it. The captain elicited a promise from the son not to tell the king that he had watched a movie showing an American red-haired actress in her underwear. The son readily agreed. An international crisis was averted over a movie comedy.

By all accounts, the crew and the Arabs warmed to each other over the short voyage, even with a language barrier. The crew even cleaned the king's bodyguards' guns and swords—a feat that Colonel Eddy did not think was possible as it was Arabic custom not to draw swords unless in combat.

One thing that puzzled the Saudis was the black mess stewards on board the *Murphy*. The Arabs assumed they were Africans and did not understand why the stewards did not answer when addressed in Arabic.

When it came time to leave the *Murphy*, the officers gave the king two Thompson submachine guns and ammo. The king returned the gesture with gifts of swords and watches to the officers. Every member of the 265-man crew received a gift.

The meeting between Roosevelt and the king went well, with understandings reached about the U.S. helping develop the nation's oil interest. Roosevelt's main goal, getting the Saudis' approval to relocate the European Jews to Israel, was not achieved. Still, the two leaders got along, and the president later pledged in an April 5, 1945 letter: "I would take no action, in my capacity as Chief of the Executive Branch of this Government, which might prove hostile to the Arab people."[2]

Roosevelt died the next week on April 12, but the February meeting between him and the king of Saudi Arabia established the relations between the two countries that continue today.

After the *Murphy* delivered her passengers to the meeting without major protocol breaches, the sheep pen was taken down, the rugs removed, and the tent stowed away. She went in for refit and was sent to Japan for occupation duty.

During the five months left of the war in the Atlantic, destroyer escorts fought most of the action against the remaining U-boats.

The *U-248* was a totally undistinguished Type VIIC that had spent 103 days at sea on two patrols without attacking anything. Apparently her main mission on the ocean was to send weather reports so that other submarines could put to sea. All those intercepted radio reports back to Germany allowed several destroyers escorts prowling the Atlantic northeast of the Azores to home in on her. Operating on their own, without the help of an escort carrier, were the USS *Otter* (DE-210), USS *Hubbard* (DE-211), USS *Hayter* (DE-212), and the USS *Varian* (DE-798). All were *Buckley* class. The first three were true sister ships, all laid down in July and August 1943 and built in Charleston, South Carolina. The *Varian* was also laid down in August 1943 in Orange, Texas, but was given a much higher hull number when many destroyer escorts were cancelled as the war was winding down.

The mission took several days to find the weather-reporting submarine, but it took only two hours for the team of destroyer escorts to sink it at a loss of all hands. For reasons not given in the reports, the kill came from depth charges, not from the proven, more efficient hedgehogs that were standard on all destroyer escorts. The kill also demonstrated how sophisticated submarine hunting had become. It had not been unusual early in the war for teams of destroyers to spend days stalking U-boats.

On February 11, the *U-869*, another undistinguished submarine, was sunk off the New Jersey coast. Just how it was destroyed is still a matter of controversy. Some suggest it was killed by a hedgehog attack by the USS *Howard D. Crow* (DE-252). Others think it might have killed itself when an acoustic torpedo it may have fired at the *Crow* homed in on its own screws. The submarine was on its first mission.

On February 11, 1945, a hunter-killer group comprised of four destroyer escorts all crewed by members of the United States Coast Guard was formed. The USS *Menges* (DE-320), USS *Mosley* (DE-321), USS *Pride* (DE-323), and USS *Lowe* (DE-325) were all *Edsall* class sister ships built by Consolidated Steel Corporation in Orange, Texas, in the spring and summer of 1943.

The crews of each of these destroyer escorts all had a score to settle with the Germans.

The *Menges* had been torpedoed by the *U-371*, a deadly killer with twenty ships to her credit, on May 3, 1944. The stern of the *Menges* had been blown off, but the ship was saved, towed to a port, and a new stern welded in its place. Thirty-one men were killed.

The *Mosley* and the *Pride* had escorted Convoy UGS 38 to Algeria without incident until April 20, 1944, when three waves of German bombers attacked at 9:00 p.m. One troop ship disintegrated when a German aerial torpedo hit a storage hold carrying bombs. All but one of the 580 men on board the ship disappeared in a massive explosion.

The *Lowe* had narrowly avoided being torpedoed by a U-boat on the same night of April 20 when it was escorting Convoy UGS 32.

On March 18, the group discovered the *U-866*, another undistinguished submarine on only its second patrol. When the *U-866* came under attack, its captain settled to the bottom, hoping that he would be lost in underwater clutter, but that only outlined him for the destroyer escorts' sonar. After six hours of attacks, but only sixty-five depth charges expended, a large underwater explosion was heard. Quantities of wood and German papers floated to the surface—evidence that the *U-866* would not be surfacing.

In the early spring of 1945, finding and killing U-boats off the U.S. coast became a priority for the United States because of a poorly conceived, last-ditch German propaganda effort to frighten the United States into pulling its resources back across the Atlantic. The American government believed in late 1944 that Germany was planning to attack American cities with the same V-1 buzz bombs and V-2 rockets that had rained down on Great Britain. Germany claimed it would deliver those weapons by submarines.

The American government took Germany at its word and announced at a press conference that U.S. cities might soon come under rocket attacks from submarines. The Navy created Operation Teardrop to find and kill these submarines threatening to attack American civilian populations.

On April 15, contact was made north of the Azores Islands with the first of six U-Boats operating under the wolf pack name of "Seewolf." These were the submarines that Americans suspected were carrying the rockets. Sinking them became a priority.

USS *Frost* (DE-144) and USS *Stanton* (DE-247), both *Edsall*-classes commissioned in 1943, moved in for an attack after radar picked up a surface contact just 3,500 yards away. *Frost* had sunk four U-boats in 1944. *Stanton* was a veteran of convoy duty. Their crews knew how to find U-boats. Within a few minutes, hedgehogs from both ships had exploded under water, indicating a hit on a hull. Within a few minutes, a tremendous explosion shook the ships, confirming that the *U-1235*, an undistinguished Type IXC/40, had been lost with all hands.

"That is the end of the attack. I think that is the end of the sub. The explosions jarred us completely off the deck," said one ship captain who was more than 12 miles away from the action.[3]

Forty minutes later, the *Frost* found the *U-880* on the surface. Through thick fog, the *Frost* illuminated the sub with its searchlight just 650 yards away. The *U-880* dived, but hedgehog shells from the *Frost* and the *Stanton* found her below. Like the other submarine, she was undistinguished. All of the U-boat aces who had roamed the Atlantic early in the war had been killed or captured.

The efficiency of the destroyer escorts at this point in the war was impressive. In less than four hours, late at night in heavy seas shrouded with fog, two U-boats had been sunk. No effort had been made to bring them to the surface to see if they really were armed with rockets.

On April 19, the USS *Buckley* (DE-51), the destroyer escort that had beaten off a boarding by U-boat crewmen almost a year earlier by throwing coffee cups and punches, teamed up with USS *Reuben James* (DE-153) to sink another U-boat off Nova Scotia. It took just twenty-four hedgehog shells to sink the *U-548*, which had sunk a Canadian frigate a year earlier. That was its only successful patrol.

The namesake of this modern *Buckley*-class destroyer escort was the USS *Reuben James* (DD-245), the *Clemson* class that had been sunk by a U-boat nearly 2,000 miles away off Iceland in October 1941. That old four stacker had no radar, sonar, huff-duff, hedgehogs, K-gun depth charge thrower, or even 20-millimeter guns. All those weapons were standard on the modern destroyer escort named after her. In less than four years, the necessity of war had accelerated the Navy's ability to find and readily sink the type of U-boats that had sunk the original *Reuben James*.

Just two days later, the USS *Neal Scott* (DE-769) and USS *Carter* (DE-112), both *Cannon* classes commissioned in July 1944, found the *U-518* in the same area in "mountainous" seas, but only 150 feet down. It took just one pattern of hedgehogs to sink the submarine. While its captain was only on his second patrol, the submarine itself had sunk or damaged twelve ships during its career.

Despite all technology now being standard on destroyer escorts to protect them from U-boats, death was still a threat for the Americans.

The USS *Frederick C. Davis* (DE-136), an *Edsall* class, was a hardened veteran by April 24, 1945. Commissioned in July 1943, she had escorted convoys, fought off air attacks, and helped sink the *U-73* in December 1943. The *U-73* had been a skilled killer with twelve Allied ships to her credit, including a British aircraft carrier. In 1944, the *Frederick C. Davis* provided weeks of shore bombardment service for the troops trying to fight their way off the Anzio beachhead. She had also been one of the ships equipped with radio jamming devices to stop

German-guided bomb attacks. Her gunners were also good, with thirteen claimed downed German airplanes to their credit.

On April 24, a pilot from the escort carrier *Bogue* saw the *U-546* running on the surface some 275 miles southwest of Newfoundland. This was the first time any aircraft from Operation Teardrop had contributed to the mission. All of the other contacts had been made by the destroyer escorts. At 8:29 a.m., the "Fighting Freddie" made a sound contact only 2,000 yards from it. That was too close for comfort. Before the destroyer escort had time to mount an attack, she was hit by a torpedo fired from just 650 yards away.

The ship broke up within five minutes, killing 115 out of 209 of her crew.

Eight destroyer escorts rushed to the scene, both to rescue the men from the cold water and to exact revenge. It took more than ten hours of depth charging and hedgehog attack to bring the wounded submarine to the surface, where it was finished off with surface gunfire. Thirty-three U-boat crewmen were rescued. They were taken to Fort Hunt, Virginia, where under intense and perhaps cruel interrogation, they insisted that no U-boats were carrying any rockets.

The controversy continues today whether the U.S. committed war crimes during the crews' interrogation, but the fear of rocket attacks on U.S. cities in 1945 was real. While no German submarine was large enough to carry rockets, tests had been conducted by the Germans to determine if V-1s could be launched from submarines.

Within five years after the war, the United States was experimenting with launching its own rockets from submarines.

One other submarine, *U-881*, would be sunk by Operation Teardrop on May 6, 1945. The USS *Farquhar* (DE-139), an *Edsall* class, made her first and only kill within five minutes of making the sound contact. Germany would surrender two days later. This would be considered the last U-boat sunk during the war.

On the same day and a little earlier than when the *U-881* was sunk, there was a sea battle much closer to American shores. Just as the war was ending in 1945, there was a savage reminder how the U-boat war started off American shores in 1942.

At 5:40 p.m., the collier *Black Point* was sunk near Narragansett Bay off the northern coast of Rhode Island with the loss of more than a dozen men. The attacking submarine was the *U-853*, an undistinguished submarine that had only sunk a small sub chaser a few weeks earlier.

Within two hours, the frigate USS *Moberly* (PF-63) and sister ship destroyer escorts USS *Amick* (DE-168) and USS *Atherton* (DE-169) were on the scene of the sinking.

Both destroyer escorts were *Cannon* classes commissioned in July 1943. Both had convoy experience, but had not sunk a U-boat. Just five miles east of Grove Point on Block Island, Rhode Island, the destroyer escorts made a sound contact. For almost a day, the target was attacked with hedgehogs and depth charges. Other ships came in to help. Two blimps even flew over to get in on the action. It was not until the U-boat captain's hat floated to the surface that the destroyer escorts' captains finally believed that they had killed their quarry.

The sub chaser that the *U-853* had sunk on April 23, 1945, off the coast of Maine was the *Eagle 56*. Before sinking, five survivors claimed to have seen a submarine surface. Painted on the conning tower was an emblem, a red horse on a yellow shield, the same emblem carried on the *U-853*. Even though these eyewitnesses saw the submarine surface after the *Eagle 56* exploded, a Navy board of inquiry did not accept their stories and blamed the sinking on a boiler explosion. That made little sense considering the boilers had been regularly inspected.

That finding of the board of inquiry kept all of the crew, including the dead, from being awarded the Purple Heart, a medal given to combat wounded. It was not until 2001 that the Navy reversed its decision and agreed that the *Eagle 56* had been sunk by the *U-853*, which was known to be operating off the coast of Maine on the day the USS *Eagle 56* (PE-56) exploded. The few survivors were finally given their Purple Hearts.

The *Eagle 56* was one of sixty steel-hulled submarine chasers that had been built by the Ford Motor Company on a Detroit,

Michigan-assembly line in 1918 and 1919. The finished boats were sailed through the Great Lakes to the Atlantic. By the time World War II came around, only eight were still in service because they had a design flaw that made them ill-handling in the open ocean. Designed to be submarine chasers in 1918, an early idea that would later result in the destroyer escort in 1943, the 221-foot-long *Eagle* boats were abject failures at what they had been commissioned to do.

Still, just as the World War I era *Wickes* and *Clemsons* were pressed into service in World War II, the remaining *Eagle* boats were also used as coastal patrol boats during the war.

The *Eagle 56* was on constant patrol off the American coast during the war, but was in only one action during all of World War II—the day it was sunk.

It was what happened one day earlier in the war that made the *Eagle 56*'s last days so interesting. On February 27, 1942, the *Eagle 56* was dispatched to pick up survivors of the USS *Jacob Jones* (DD-130) 30 miles east of Cape May, New Jersey.

The coincidences surrounding the *Eagle 56* and the *Jacob Jones* are striking. Both were commissioned in October 1919 within a week of each other. Both were obsolete by 1942 but still serving their countries. Both were sunk in their only combat engagements with a U-boat. Both were sunk less than 30 miles off the continental United States, the only American warships lost that close to the shore. The *Eagle 56* picked up thirteen survivors of the *Jacob Jones* and the *Eagle 56* had only thirteen survivors.

The *Eagle 56* met its death just 475 miles north of where she rescued the crew of the *Jacob Jones* three years earlier.

CHAPTER

15

Pacific Theater 1945

"The gates of hell awaited us."

The year 1945 in the Pacific started just as 1944 had ended: with Japanese aircraft attacking American ships—the same action that had precipitated the United States' entry into the war on December 7, 1941.

The four naval battles fought over four days, called the Battle of Leyte Gulf, on October 23-26, 1944, were the best chance that the Imperial Japanese Navy had to destroy the American troops landing on Leyte Island. But by the end of October, the bulk of the Imperial Japanese Navy was now resting on the bottom of the Pacific off the Philippines. The kamikazes, which first showed up in the Leyte Gulf battles, could not sink enough American ships to stop the invasion, so General MacArthur kept his promise to "return" on October 20, 1944, when he waded ashore on Leyte.

Now, in January 1945, the invasion of Luzon, home of the Philippine Islands' capital of Manila, was imminent. The American ships that launched the invasion of Leyte were now steaming 500 miles to the north to the Lingayen Gulf. The Japanese had one more chance to stop the retaking of the Philippines. With no more battleships, cruisers, or destroyers, they had only land-based aircraft left to stop the Americans.

Three years earlier, as they dived on the battleships in Pearl Harbor, the Japanese pilots were interested in their own survival. Now, as they dived on everything from aircraft carriers to Landing Ship Tanks (LSTs) off Luzon, they were interested in riding the divine wind of kamikazes to their glorious deaths.

The Japanese did little on the first three days of the year, but on January 4, kamikazes attacked the USS *Ommaney Bay* (CVE-79) in the Sulu Sea. The next day, another wave was seen with sixteen Japanese aircraft scoring hits or near-misses on two other escort carriers and destroyer USS *Helm* (DD-388).

The USS *Walke* (DD-723) was an *Allen M. Sumner* class that took the place of the USS *Walke* (DD-416), a *Sims* that had been sunk in August 1942 off Guadalcanal. This *Walke* was a veteran of Normandy beach bombardments and had transferred to the Pacific in late September. In late November, her new skipper, Commander George Fleming Davis, thirty-three years old, took command after a varied career on destroyers, battleships, and cruisers. On January 6, the *Walke* was escorting minesweepers in Lingayen Gulf when a number of Japanese aircraft arrived over the landing areas just before noon. Four Zeroes targeted the *Walke*. Two were shot down a distance from the ship. A third crashed into the bridge.

According to Davis' Medal of Honor citation, "[Davis] remained steadfast in the path of the third plane plunging swiftly to crash the after end of the bridge structure. Seriously wounded when the plane struck, drenched with gasoline and immediately enveloped in flames, he conned the *Walke* in the midst of the wreckage; he rallied his command to heroic efforts; he exhorted his officers and men to save the ship and, still on his feet, saw the barrage from his guns destroy the fourth suicide bomber. With the fires under control and the safety of the ship assured, he consented to be carried below. Succumbing several hours later, Commander Davis, by his example of valor and unhesitating self-sacrifice, steeled the fighting spirit of his command into unyielding purpose in completing a vital mission. He gallantly gave his life in the service of his country."[1]

Thanks to Davis's actions, the *Walke* survived to fight right through the Vietnam War.

That same day, the USS *Allen M. Sumner* (DD-692), the namesake of the class, was hit, losing fourteen men.

The Japanese suicide pilots must have targeted whatever ship they saw first rather than trying to target specific types of ships. With a bay full of aircraft carriers, battleships, cruisers, and troop transports—all ships that were larger and seemingly more important than destroyers—the kamikazes still targeted several World War I era four stackers. These veteran ships would have been among the smallest ships in the bay (314 feet long for a *Wickes* destroyer compared to the escort carrier at 512 feet long, a light cruiser at 600 feet long, or a battleship at 624 feet long).

On January 6, the USS *Long* (DD-209/DMS-12), a *Clemson,* was hit. The *Long* had been in and out of commission several times since first launched in 1919. She had served in the Aleutians, New Guinea, Marshalls, Solomons, and had never been directly attacked until the Zero hit her below the waterline. Still, only one sailor was killed. The USS *Hovey* (DD-208/DMS-11), another *Clemson* laid down just a month earlier in the same William Cramp & Sons yard, would pick up many of the *Long*'s crew. The *Long* was hit a second time later that same day and sank beneath the waves with a broken keel.

Tragically, the next day, the *Hovey* herself would be hit by a Japanese aerial torpedo, and would sink, carrying twenty-four of the *Long* survivors to their deaths. The *Long* and the *Hovey,* sister ships with consecutive hull numbers, went down within twenty-four hours of each other. They were two hard-fighting ships with nine and eight battle stars. The same day the *Hovey* went down, the USS *Palmer* (DD-161/DMS-5), a *Wickes* converted to a minesweeper in 1940, was sunk in six minutes by two bombs.

On January 7, the four destroyers of Destroyer Squadron 23 participated in the last surface engagement between the American Navy and the Imperial Japanese Navy. It was a pitiful performance by the once-mighty and once-feared Japanese.

The USS *Charles Ausburne* (DD-570), USS *Braine* (DD-630), USS *Shaw* (DD-373), and USS *Russell* (DD-414), two *Fletchers*, a *Mahan*, and a *Sims*, were screening a transport column just after 10:00 p.m. when they all saw a single radar contact at 15,000 yards. When they closed to 10,000 yards, star shells were fired, exposing the single destroyer *Hinoki*, a *Matsu* destroyer class of 1,260 tons commissioned in September 1944. The *Matsu* class had been rushed into production with increased anti-aircraft capabilities and radar, intended to be a destroyer better prepared to ward off American aircraft.

The *Hinoki* had escaped being sunk just a few days earlier when she split from another destroyer, the *Momi,* which had been caught by American torpedo airplanes. The *Momi* sank with all hands while the *Hinoki* was damaged but limped back to port.

Despite firing torpedoes in her wake to scatter the chasing destroyers, the four American tin cans closed to just 1,100 yards before smashing the *Hinoki* with their 5-inch guns. The American shells were so destructive that a search could not find a single surviving Japanese among the 211-man crew.

The Americans discovered that the Japanese suicide attacks came on the surface of the ocean as well as from the sky.

The USS *Phillip* (DD-498), and the USS *Robinson* (DD-562), both *Fletchers,* were among the first ships to encounter the *Shinyo* class of suicide boats on January 10. Driven by a single man, the *Shinyo* was a small motorboat capable of speeds almost as fast as a destroyer. It was packed with 660 pounds of explosives, making it the equivalent of a single large airplane bomb. Some boat models had rockets mounted on both sides.

The inescapable problem of the *Shinyo* was it was also visible to the increasingly sensitive radar carried by all American ships. As it cruised off Luzon in the Philippines on January 10, the *Phillip* picked up a small craft heading toward it. The boat was moving too fast and was too low in the water for the *Phillip* to target it with its 5-inch guns, but the ship's alert 20-millimeter Oerlikon gunners blew up the small boat's bow-mounted explosives just 20 yards before it could smash into the destroyer's hull. Another destroyer, the *Robinson*, was attacked at night while at anchor, but the explosion did no structural damage to the hull. That same day two Landing Craft Infantry (LCI) boats were sunk by *Shinyos* and a transport was hit.

The threat of the Philippines' invasion fleet being attacked by these suicide motorboats was real, but the Japanese war planners kept most of the 6,000 they built in reserve on the home islands for a last ditch defense by civilians that never materialized. Only seven American ships, most of them smaller landing craft, were sunk by the suicide boats. The only destroyer damaged by a *Shinyo* was the USS *Hutchins* (DD-476) on April 27 off Okinawa, but there were no casualties.

On January 10, the same day the *Phillip* was attacked, the USS *Clemson* (DD-186/APD-31), the venerable namesake for 156 following four stackers, had a minor collision with the USS *Pennsylvania* (BB-38). Still she pressed on with her duties of transferring troops. With service in both major theaters, the *Clemson* was awarded nine battle stars.

At the end of January, the Americans began to focus their attention on Corregidor, the island in Manila Bay that had been their last stronghold in the Philippines until it was surrendered on May 6, 1942, after a four-month siege. Naval bombardment began on January 22, 1945, with paratroopers landing on February 16.

Destroyers cruised close to shore to shell the same tunnels built and surrendered by Americans, now occupied by Japanese. It was because of that dangerous proximity to Japanese shore batteries that a water tender second class was awarded the Medal of Honor.

Twenty-four-year-old Elmer Charles Bigelow was on board the USS *Fletcher* (DD-445) on February 14 when fragments from a Japanese artillery shell fired from Corregidor penetrated the number one gun magazine. According to his posthumous Medal of Honor citation: "BIGELOW, acting instantly as the deadly projectile exploded into fragments which penetrated the number one gun magazine and set fire to several powder cases, picked up a pair of fire extinguishers and rushed below in a resolute attempt to quell the raging flames. Refusing to waste the precious time required to don rescue-breathing apparatus, he plunged through the blinding smoke billowing out of the magazine hatch and dropped into the blazing compartment. Despite the acrid, burning powder smoke which seared his lungs with every agonizing breath, he worked rapidly and with instinctive sureness and succeeded in quickly extinguishing the fires and in cooling the cases and bulkheads, thereby preventing further damage to the stricken ship."[2]

Bigelow may have been off-duty at the time as he was on deck rather than below in the engine room when the shell hit. He did not wait for orders, did not ask for other volunteers, and did not run from the danger. He ran into it. One Destroyer Man, who likely would not have known his ship was in danger had he happened to be at his station below deck, saved the USS Fletcher from potential destruction.

On February 23, shelling from the USS Converse (DD-509) sealed an unknown number of Japanese soldiers inside the Malinta Tunnel, which had been the core of the Corregidor defenses for the Americans. Rather than simply die of suffocation or starvation, the Japanese blew themselves up in some of the branch tunnels. The powerful explosions also killed some American paratroopers who were on the sides of the mountain above the tunnel.

While the fighting for the Philippines was not over, the sealing of the American-built Malinta tunnel with Japanese defenders inside it by well-aimed 5-inch American destroyer shells seemed symbolic of the end of the fighting for the islands early in 1945. After ten days of hard fighting by ground soldiers, Corregidor was taken. MacArthur himself "returned" to the island on March 2.

The attack on Iwo Jima in February 1945 was necessary to give American aircraft a base from which to attack the Japanese home islands and provide an emergency runway for any damaged B-29s returning to their bases in Tinian. The Battle for Iwo Jima gave the Navy something of a break as the island was too far away from Japanese airstrips to mount kamikaze attacks.

That break would not last long as the next big target was Okinawa, considered by the Japanese to be one of their home islands. It was well within flying range from scores of Japanese air bases.

Now knowing how desperate the Japanese were, the Navy suspected the fight for Okinawa, an island 60 miles long and 18 miles wide, would be the toughest of the war.

Destroyer Men would agree.

On March 19, the Essex-class carrier USS *Franklin* (CV-13) was operating about 600 miles north of Okinawa, part of a force attacking the southernmost home island of Kyushu to divert attention and resources away from the coming attacks on Okinawa. The *Franklin* had already been hit by one kamikaze at Leyte Gulf, losing fifty men, but repairs put her back into action to launch aircraft about 50 miles off the coast of Kyushu. Slightly larger than the still-on-duty *Enterprise*, the *Franklin* was laid down one year to the day after Pearl Harbor. At 7:00 a.m., just as she was launching her planes, an apparently low-flying Japanese bomber popped out of the clouds and dropped two 500-pound bombs. One bomb was enough to set off explosions of loaded aircraft and rupture the ship's gasoline lines. Within minutes, it was clear that the *Franklin* was doomed.

Several destroyers moved alongside. Commander J.H. Wesson, the captain of the USS *Hickox* (DD-673), a *Fletcher,* lowered his whale boat to rescue men in the water. He then boldly nudged his destroyer closer to the *Franklin*.

The captain's after action report detailed the danger in very calm terms: "Put bow under after 40 mm gun sponson to allow men to jump from *Franklin* to *Hickox*...Observed numerous explosions on *Franklin* which appeared to be ammunition exploding."[3]

The *Hickox* rescued eighteen men from the carrier's fantail and another three were pulled from the water. As the destroyer was maneuvering to stay close to the carrier, its gunners knocked down two Japanese planes trying to make another run at the carrier.

For the rest of the day, destroyers pulled more than 850 *Franklin* crewmen from the sea, but more than 800 perished. The *Franklin* did not sink. She was repaired and eventually made her way back to the United States.

March 26, 1945 was a date Destroyer Men remember as the start of four months of Hell raining down from the sky around Okinawa.

The USS *Kimberly* (DD-521), a *Fletcher*, had already downed four kamikazes in action around the Philippines, but on this day, the pilot of one of the Japanese Aichi D3A dive bombers, commonly called "Vals" by the Americans, must have been experienced in combat. He showed great skill in avoiding all of the ship's anti-aircraft guns.

"The fire control problem was one of an extremely high deflection rate which the Japanese pilot further complicated by resorting to radical maneuvers including zooming, climbing, slipping, skidding, accelerating, decelerating, and even slow rolling...The target seemed to be completely surrounded by 5-inch bursts and 40 mm tracers...At about 1,500 yards range on relative bearing 170 degrees he leveled off and came straight in at an altitude of about 150 feet, performing right and left skids...Now only the after guns could bear and each 5-inch salvo blasted the 20 mm crews off their feet."[4]

The Val, armed with a 200-pound bomb, exploded on impact and crashed directly into the aft 40-millimeter gun mount. Just four men were killed.

The next day, March 27, the USS *O'Brien* (DD-725) was crashed by a bomber. The *O'Brien* was still captained by Commander W.W. Outerbridge, who had opened the war by sinking a Japanese midget submarine in Pearl Harbor an hour before the air attack while commanding the USS *Ward*. The *O'Brien* and *Kimberly* teamed up to return to Ulithi for repairs.

Being thin-skinned could have its advantages. The USS *Murray* (DD-576), a *Fletcher*, could not maneuver out of the way of an aerial torpedo on the same day the *O'Brien* was bombed. The torpedo was dropped just 200 yards from the destroyer. It punched a hole completely through the ship and exploded outside of the hull. Only one man was killed. The holes were patched over and the *Murray* continued on station until she could be relieved.

April 1, both April Fool's Day and Easter Sunday, was the day chosen for the ground assault against Okinawa. To give early warning to the transports about the numbers and types of approaching Japanese aircraft, ninety-six destroyers and fifty-one destroyer escorts were deployed around the island between March 26 and June 21. The outermost defensive ring of tin cans were in sixteen radar picket stations 40 to 70 miles away from the transport area to give early warning of Japanese aircraft approaching from the Japanese islands, China, or Formosa. An inner ring of destroyers were deployed 20 to 25 miles from the transports.

Assisting each destroyer on picket would be four support ships, usually Landing Craft Support (LCS) or Landing Ship Medium–Rocket (LSM-R) ships. This choice of escorts to the destroyers puzzled the captains of both ship types since the LCSs and LSMs had no radar and only a few 40-millimeter and 20-millimeter cannons as armament. The LSM-Rs were equipped with 75 ship-to-ground rockets which were useless against approaching fighters and sparked more curiosity among the captains.

The support ships soon gained the grim nickname "pall bearers" because their main duty was not knocking down kamikazes, but rescuing Destroyer Men if they had to abandon ship.

Flying above the picket ships were American fighter planes waiting for the Japanese to show up. Three years earlier, the Navy had only F4F Wildcats, a tough aircraft, but inferior to the Zero in most comparisons. Now, the Navy had F4U Corsairs and F6F Hellcats, fighters that the Zero could not match. The job of those pilots was to protect both the Destroyer Men below them and the unarmed sailors in the transports surrounding Okinawa.

All this firepower on the ocean and in the air would not be enough to stop all of the kamikazes. No surface action that the U.S. Navy had faced in the previous three years would be as bad as it would suffer coming from the air in the next few months.

On April 6, eleven destroyers were hit by kamikazes. Two would sink.

The USS *Bush* (DD-529), a *Fletcher,* was already hit and sinking when the USS *Colhoun* (DD-801), another *Fletcher,* rushed in to take off survivors.

Just as the *Colhoun* arrived to help, another wave of thirteen airplanes swarmed toward the two ships. *Colhoun,* named after USS *Colhoun* (DD-85/APD-2), *a Wickes* class which had been sunk off Guadalcanal in 1942, was captained by Commander George Rees Wilson. Wilson was no stranger to combat. He had sunk the Japanese destroyer *Yugumo* with a torpedo just after his own destroyer, the USS *Chevalier* (DD-451), was hit by a Japanese torpedo at the Battle of Vella LaVella in October 1943. The *Chevalier* had to be sunk by another American destroyer.

Colhoun knocked down five Japanese planes, but four crashed into the destroyer. For five hours, the crew tried to save her until she finally slid beneath the waves near midnight. Remarkably, only thirty-five men had been killed during the attack. She had only been in action since mid-February and had arrived off Okinawa just six days earlier. The Japanese had sunk two *Colhouns* in three years.

On April 12, more than two hundred kamikazes were launched, including a type the Americans had not yet seen, a manned bomb.

The USS *Mannert L. Abele* (DD-733), an *Allen M. Sumner* class, was equipped with extra radios as part of her specialty duty as a fighter director and radar picket ship. Though her first action was Iwo Jima in February, her inexperienced crew acquitted themselves well, participating in accurate ground support shelling. They learned quickly at Okinawa, shooting down several Japanese airplanes. She remained untouched until April 12.

The *Mannert L. Abele* was standing picket about 81 miles north of Okinawa. A regular aircraft hit the starboard side of the destroyer and then less than a minute later, something strange barreled into sight and hit further aft on the starboard side. Lieutenant James M. Stewart, the commander of *LSM (R)189* watched as the destroyer tried to engage the second Japanese aircraft: "It is difficult to say what it was that hit the DD-733...what appeared to be one plane, accelerated at a terrific rate, too fast for us to fire at. This plane dove at an angle of approximately 30 degrees, starting at about four miles away."[5]

A young ensign, George L. Way, was blown overboard by the kamikaze, but he clambered back on board and ordered the hands he could find to launch life rafts. He opened all of the closed hatches. At least ten men scrambled through now-open passageways.

Within three minutes, the 2,200-ton destroyer, the largest class the United States had ever designed, and bristling with dual 5-inch guns and 40-millimeter and 20-millimeter cannons, slipped beneath the ocean. She had been sunk by an aircraft incapable of climbing or landing and not armed with any machine guns or droppable bombs. All it was designed to do was crash into ships like the destroyer. More than seventy of her crew perished with the ship.

The *Mannert L. Abele* had been sunk by a new Japanese weapon: the rocket-powered, guided-bomb Ohka (meaning cherry blossom), but which waggish Americans nicknamed the Baka (fool). Designed in late 1944, the 19-foot-long craft with a 16-foot wing span was carried to combat under a twin-engine bomber, and then released once American ships were sighted. Once a target had been selected, the pilot powered on his rocket engines to boost his speed in a dive to nearly 500 miles per hour, a speed almost too fast for American gunners to track.

The same day the *Mannert L. Abele* was hit by an Ohka, so too was the USS *Stanly* (DD-478), a *Fletcher* on radar picket duty. She was busy directing fighters to fend off Japanese airplanes when a single Ohka crashed completely through the ship without detonating. Within seconds another Ohka, perhaps with a dead pilot, missed the ship completely but came close enough to cut the ship's flag loose before it too crashed into the sea. A third airplane tried to both bomb and crash into the *Stanly,* but failed at both. Within the course of a few minutes, the *Stanly* had evaded four attacks. Only four of her crew were wounded in the action.

More than six hundred Ohkas were manufactured, but only scores were ever launched, probably because the nation was running low on the skilled twin-engine pilots needed to fly the Ohkas out to the American ships. It was easy enough to quickly train someone to aim the Ohka since they didn't have to take off or land. But learning to fly the Mitsubishi GM-4, a twin-engine bomber nicknamed "Betty" by American intelligence officers, the typical craft carrying the Ohka, took training time that Japan no longer had. American aircraft were now dropping bombs on the home island airfields. The experienced pilots who bombed Pearl Harbor in 1941, the American carriers at Midway in 1942, and the invading fleets attacking Japan's island bases in 1943 were mostly dead. The Philippines Islands invasion in October 1944 cost more pilots. By the spring of 1945, Japan was pressing into service men and teenagers who had only the barest knowledge of steering an aircraft.

The USS *Laffey* (DD-724) was an Allen M. Sumner class that acquired the nickname the "Ship That Wouldn't Die" after multiple kamikaze hits off Okinawa. *NHHC photo.*

The Japanese knew the outlying American destroyers radioed their positions and numbers back to the main fleet so destroying the picket line ships became a priority for the kamikazes. Few observers could believe that any destroyer could survive such swarming tactics, but some famously did.

One, the USS *Laffey* (DD-724), an *Allen M. Sumner* class, became known as the "Ship That Would Not Die."

On April 12, the *Laffey* received orders to pick up a fighter director team from another destroyer. When the *Laffey's* captain, Commander Frederick Julian Becton, read the orders he thought: "The gates of hell awaited us."[6] Becton already had experience with what the Japanese could do to American destroyers. He was commanding the USS *Aaron Ward* (DD-483), a *Gleaves,* in November 1942 during the Naval Battle of Guadalcanal, when she was hit nine times by Japanese shells, but still survived. Less than a year later with Becton still in command, the

Aaron Ward was sunk in April 1943 by bombs from three Japanese aircraft.

On April 16, 1945, the *Laffey* came under constant attack starting at 8:30 a.m. Within fifteen minutes, her gunners had knocked down eight Japanese aircraft with only shrapnel hits from near misses wounding some men. The ninth plane finally hit on the port side, wiping out two 20-millimeter guns and their crews. A gasoline fire erupted. The heat from the fire caused off some 40-millimeter rounds to fire, blowing holes in the deck. That allowed more burning gasoline to flow down into a magazine. A team of men started hosing down the magazine to keep the stored rounds from exploding.

Then, a tenth kamikaze hit near the fantail, wiping out another 20-millimeter position and the rear 5-inch gun mount. Within seconds, an eleventh plane hit at almost the same position. A twelfth attacker dropped a bomb that jammed the rudder. The thirteenth attacker crashed into the afterdeck house. Another Japanese aircraft passed so close to the ship that it sheared off the lanyard holding the American flag. A sailor grabbed another flag and put it back above the ship. Yet another Japanese airplane dropped a bomb so close it showered the forward deck with shrapnel.

When an officer asked Becton if it was time to abandon ship, Becton replied: "Hell, No! We still have guns that can shoot. I'll never abandon ship as long as I have a gun that will fire!"[7]

The Laffey's captain, Commander Frederick Becton, refused to abandon ship "as long as we have a gun that will fire." *National Archives photo.*

This *Laffey*, named after the first USS *Laffey* (DD-459) sunk in November 1942 off Savo Island, would not be sunk by the Japanese.

More than twenty Japanese aircraft attacked the *Laffey*, with six crashing into the ship or dropping bombs close enough to damage it. Remarkably, only thirty-two men were killed and more than seventy were wounded—about a third of her crew of 338. The *Laffey* would be towed to safety and never again come under Japanese attack. She would be the last *Allen M. Sumner* in active service when she was retired in 1975. She is now a ship museum in Charleston, South Carolina's harbor.

Within three weeks, thirty destroyers or destroyer-escorts had been hit, with four being sunk by kamikazes. The losses were so shocking that the Navy's admirals ordered all-out assaults on known Japanese airfields in order to destroy potential kamikaze aircraft on the ground. While a good idea in theory, the home islands were dotted with airfields and the Americans did not have enough aircraft to hit all of the bases.

At various times during the later years of the war, the U.S. Navy would get reports of an American destroyer flying a Japanese flag. The sightings were dismissed as ridiculous misidentification until April 28, 1945, when American bombers bombed and strafed what looked like an American destroyer in a Korean port. Several months later, the mystery was solved when American occupation forces found the ship in Hiro, a port in Japan.

The Americans were seeing a ghost, a ship assumed destroyed by her own crew.

Tied up at the dock was the USS *Stewart* (DD-224), a *Clemson* from the ABDA command that had been abandoned in a scuttled dry dock at Surabaya, Java, on February 22, 1942. Desperate for any fighting ships, the Japanese had raised her in February 1943, a year after being under water in the damaged dry dock. The Japanese made her into *Patrol Boat 102*. Not long after the war, she was recommissioned as an American destroyer and sent to San Francisco. She was sunk off the city during gunnery practice.

Sometimes the war threw together ships in bizarre coincidences.

The USS *Little* (DD-803), a *Fletcher*, was on radar station off Okinawa on May 3 with the USS *Aaron Ward* (DD-773/DM-34), an *Allen*

M. Sumner-class destroyer converted to a mine layer. Radar picked up approaching aircraft and by 6:43 p.m., a swarm was attacking the picket ships. The *Little's* gunners shot down two, but four different aircraft slammed into the ship within two minutes. Within another few minutes, the ship sank with thirty crewmen dead.

The *Aaron Ward* arrived off Okinawa in March, having only been commissioned in January. She was hit by three kamikazes, but still managed to stay afloat. Towed to a port for repair, officials decided she was too badly damaged to save. Within five months of her commissioning, the destroyer was removed from service.

The original USS *Little* (DD-79/APD-4), a *Wickes* converted to a fast attack transport, had been sunk off Guadalcanal in September 1942. The original *Aaron Ward* (DD-48), a *Gleaves,* had been sunk off Guadalcanal in April 1943. In one kamikaze attack in May 1945, the Japanese had now put out of commission the namesakes of two earlier ships they had sunk in previous years.

On May 4, 1945, the USS *Morrison* (DD-560), a *Fletcher,* experienced a strange kamikaze attack from both Japan's most familiar fighter aircraft and its oldest, most obsolete aircraft. The *Morrison* was a favorite destroyer among aircraft carrier sailors. In October 1944, she received a Navy Unit Commendation for rescuing more than four hundred men from the stricken escort carrier USS *Princeton* (CVL-23).

At 8:25 a.m., the *Morrison* was attacked by three Zero fighters. One missed, but two others hit, causing both engineering spaces to flood. The *Morrison* was already doomed from that damage, but the Japanese were not finished. A flight of seven slow-flying, fabric and wood-covered float biplanes approached the ship. One crashed into one of the rear 5-inch gun mounts. Inexplicably, a second biplane landed in the *Morrison's* wake. The pilot was either assessing the situation to see if the *Morrison* was sinking or was taking his time to get his courage up. The *Morrison's* crew watched him take off, and fired their 20-millimeter guns to no effect. The second float plane then intentionally flew into the remaining 5-inch gun mount, igniting an ammunition storage area. Out of a crew of 331 men and officers, 179 were recovered from the ocean. Of those, only seventy-one were not wounded.

The sinking brought the *Morrison* her second Navy Unit Commendation, the only destroyer so recognized during the war. The Commendation concluded: "Her sturdy and valiant service under a prolonged suicide bombing attack contributed to the effective defense of our ships and reflects the highest credit upon the *Morrison*, her courageous officers and the men, and the United States Naval Service."[8]

The USS *Hugh W. Hadley* (DD-774) teamed with the USS *Robley D. Evans* (DD-552) to knock down kamikazes off Okinawa. *NHHC photo.*

Just a week later, on May 11, 1945, two destroyers would suffer through an even worse attack from Japanese aircraft.

The USS *Hugh W. Hadley* (DD-774), an *Allen M. Sumner,* proved that even rookie crews could accomplish remarkable things. The crew of the *Hadley* had not even seen a Japanese aircraft until shooting one down on March 31, the first day it arrived off Okinawa.

On May 11, four days after Germany surrendered, the crew would shoot down many more.

The USS *Robley Evans* (DD-552) was separated from the *Hugh Hadley* during much of their team effort in shooting down forty-six Japanese aircraft off Okinawa. *NHHC photo.*

Commander B.J. Mullaney of the *Hadley* would write in his after action report that his crew's skill in knocking down enemy aircraft came by everyone following a simple maxim printed on signs all over the ship: "Lead That Plane!" The sign reminded the 40-millimeter and 20-millimeter gunners they should fire in front of enemy aircraft so that the pilots would fly into the shells.[9]

Teamed with the veteran USS *Robley D. Evans* (DD-552), a *Fletcher* in the Pacific for a year, both ships would turn in a remarkable performance of shooting down kamikazes.

The *Evans* may have given everyone a false sense of security at 7:30 p.m. on May 10, when her 5-inch guns knocked down a torpedo plane before more than half the crew had even reached their battle stations.

The main attacks started the next day at nearly 8:00 a.m. when the ship's radar spotted large numbers of blips 55 miles out. While American aircraft were flying cover, their numbers were overwhelmed by an estimated 156 Japanese coming from three different formations.

The *Evans* opened the fight at 8:30 a.m. by splashing three Nakajima B5Ns, torpedo airplanes, called "Kates" by American intelligence. The Kates were flying one behind the other, separated by 1,500 yards. All of the kills came from the 5-inch guns using shells with Variable Time (VT) fuses. These fuses, also called proximity fuses, would explode when a sensor in the nose of the shell sensed it was near metal.

The *Hadley* shot down four airplanes flying just above the ocean trying to slip past the picket destroyers to reach the fleet. Within half an hour, the destroyer shot down twelve more aircraft.

Normally, the two destroyers would have operated close to each other for mutual protection, but rapid maneuvering kept them between two and three miles apart. By 9:00 a.m., the *Evans* was still afloat, but unable to provide effective fire. The *Hadley* and her four support ships were on their own.

"CIC [Command Information Center] reported that the Sugar George [or SG, a Navy term for surface] radar scope was filled with enemy planes...For 20 minutes the *Hadley* fought off the enemy single-handled, being separated from the *Evans*, which was out of action, by three miles and the four small support ships by two miles. Finally, at 09:20, ten enemy planes which had surrounded the *Hadley*, four on the starboard bow under fire by the main battery and machine guns, four on the port bow under fire by the forward machine guns, and two astern under fire by the aft machine guns, attacked the ship simultaneously. All ten planes were destroyed in a remarkable fight."[10]

The two tin cans destroyed a total of forty-six Japanese aircraft—though the total included three suicide hits for the *Hadley* and four for the *Evans*. All of those kills came in an air battle lasting just ninety minutes. One of the aircraft hitting the *Hadley* was an Ohka.

Mullaney in his after action report made it a point to credit his crew.

"Our mission was accomplished. The transports at the Okinawa anchorage were saved from attack by one hundred and fifty six enemy planes by the action of our ships. We bore the brunt of the enemy action and absorbed what they threw at us. It was a proud day for Destroyer Men…No captain of a man of war ever had a crew who fought more valiantly against such overwhelming odds. Who can measure the degree of courage of men, who stand up to their guns in the face of diving planes that destroy them? Who can measure the loyalty of a crew who risked death to save the ship from sinking when all seemed lost? I am proud to record that I know no record of a Destroyer's crews fighting for one hour and thirty five minutes against overwhelming enemy aircraft attacks and destroying twenty-three planes."[11]

Mullaney suggested destroyers placed on picket lines needed even more anti-aircraft guns. He suggested removing the torpedo tubes then expanding the Combat Information Center and adding radar and more 40-millimeter guns into deck space now freed up. The torpedo as a weapon—the original idea for the development of the destroyer in the 1870s was no longer needed when the major surface threat came from the air.

Remarkably, the total number of men killed on both ships was under sixty. Both ships survived their attacks and were towed back to the United

States. Neither would be deemed worthy of repair and would be scrapped within two years.

The USS Callaghan (DD-792), the last American destroyer sunk in World War II, was hit by a Japanese biplane trainer flying at less than 80 miles per hour. *National Archives photo.*

Twelve destroyers and a destroyer escort would be sunk by kamikazes off Okinawa. One destroyer captain, Commander C.J. Van Arsdall, Jr., captain of the USS *Anthony* (DD-515), a *Fletcher* that had won eight battle stars, described the sense of his men when he wrote in an after action report: "We found we could take it, but we didn't like it. Everyone knew that the duty was a nasty job, but a necessary one, and was well aware that every plane which managed to get in was a separate case of 'either you or us.' To the great credit of the men, nobody minded admitting that he was afraid, because nobody was fool enough to pretend he wasn't, and make fun of fear. And the fear was not expressed by hysteria, but by a growing tension which seemed to relax only when the guns were shooting. All hands felt much better at battle stations than at any other place."[12]

The last American destroyer sunk in World War II was the USS *Callaghan* (DD-792), a *Fletcher* scheduled to be relieved of picket duty on the morning of July 29 and ordered home to California. She was a veteran of more than fifteen months in the Pacific with experience shelling Japanese shore positions, sinking submarines and patrol craft, and downing kamikazes. She had won seven battle stars, and was named after Admiral Daniel Callaghan, who was awarded the Medal of Honor after dying in the Naval Battle of Guadalcanal in 1942.

Just like the *Morrison,* the *Callaghan* was sunk by a biplane that her gunners thought they had driven off. Lookouts and radar did not see her make a slow turn and come back around just feet off the ocean.

The determined Japanese pilot in the Kamikaze Special Attack Corps 3rd Ryūko Squadron who flew into the side of the *Callaghan* could make no more than 80 miles per hour. That slow speed may have thrown off the gunners who were used to tracking airplanes attacking them at 300 miles per hour. The 5-inch guns, firing shells designed to explode in the proximity of metal, would not explode against the wood and fabric of a biplane. The Japanese aircraft was a red-painted Type 93 intermediate trainer nicknamed "Red Dragonfly" by the Japanese. It was a basic trainer in which all Japanese pilots started their training,

As the *Callaghan's* crew watched their 20-millimeter shells chew through the fabric wings, the Red Dragonfly flew slowly into the ship's starboard side. The single bomb it carried exploded, flooding the ship and killing forty-seven of her crew.

Near to the *Callaghan* was the USS *Prichett* (DD-561), which suffered heavy damage when another biplane from the same kamikaze unit crashed just six feet off her stern. The next day, July 30, the USS *Cassin Young* (DD-793), was crashed by yet another member of the same kamikaze unit also flying the Red Dragonfly.

The annihilation of the 3rd Ryūko Squadron was complete, but remarkable. Of the seven members of the squadron flying the old biplanes that took off on July 29, three successfully crashed into American destroyers, sinking one and damaging the other two.

It was a strange coincidence that Japan's most effective and feared destroyer weapon, the 24-inch torpedo, bore the same official name as the last antiquated airplanes to inflict damage on the U.S. Navy off Okinawa. The Japanese designated both the torpedo and the trainer biplanes as Type 93s.

Nine days later, Hiroshima would be bombed, followed three days later by Nagasaki.

Destroyers had borne the brunt of warship losses by naval type for all of the major belligerents. The British suffered the most losses with 153 destroyers sunk. The Japanese lost 134. The Germans lost twenty-five—virtually their entire fleet sunk or scuttled. The Americans lost seventy-one destroyers and eleven destroyer escorts.

Of course, it was the crewmen of the destroyers who won the battles. Chief Frank S. Wright, Jr., the chief signalman on the USS *Charles Ausburne* (DD-570), was asked in a post-war interview to describe the morale of Destroyer Men.

"It was amazing to me to find the common American boy, the guy that delivered newspapers at home; shined our shoes; the butcher boy. Out here he just seemed to reverse his attitude toward life. Out here he had to work, he had to fight, and by golly, he enjoyed it out here. The harder they worked him the more he liked it," said Wright.[13]

The men learned how to do everything they needed to stay alive at sea while steaming toward an enemy.

"I didn't know a thing about cooking, but evidently I was a fast learner," said Billy Gene Conatser, an eighteen-year-old draftee cook on the USS *Murray* (DD-576), who manned a 40-millimeter battery during general quarters. "We were all there together. We were all new and we all had to learn together. We were all young men and made friends easily. We were close knit. We looked out for each other. It was boring and exciting. We had lots of bad weather, thinking we might sink, but there was no place to go. We tolerated it as a job we had to do to win the war."[14]

On August 23, 1945, Admiral Halsey selected three destroyers from Destroyer Squadron 21 to escort the USS *Missouri* (BB-63) and USS *Iowa* (BB-61) into Tokyo Harbor on August 29, 1945 to prepare for the surrender ceremony on September 2. They were the USS *Nicholas* (DD-449), USS *O'Bannon* (DD-450), and USS *Taylor* (DD-468). Between the three of them, the three *Fletchers* had won forty-eight battle stars.

The reason Halsey gave for selecting three little destroyers to lead the way over the aircraft carriers, battleships, and cruisers that had also fought the war was simple: "because of their valorous fight up the long road from the South Pacific to the very end."[15]

It was a fitting, simple statement that applied to all of the Destroyer Men who had gone to war in the Tin Can Navy aboard the Greyhounds of the Sea.

Ship Museums

The USS *Kidd* (DD-661) is docked on the Mississippi River in Baton Rouge, Louisiana. Visiting hours are found at: WWW.USSKidd.com. The phone number is: (225) 342-1942. The *Kidd* is the only remaining *Fletcher*-class destroyer in original World War II configuration. Launched in 1943, she received eight battle stars while fighting in the Pacific. She was hit by a kamikaze in April 1945, resulting in the deaths of thirty-eight men and the wounding of fifty-five.

The USS *The Sullivans* (DD-537), another *Fletcher*, is docked at the Buffalo and Erie County Military Park in downtown Buffalo, New York. Named after the five Sullivan brothers who died on a cruiser off Guadalcanal in 1942, she was launched in 1943 and received nine battle stars during her World War II service. Find hours at https://buffalonavalpark. org/ and call (716) 847-1773 for more information.

The USS *Cassin Young* (DD-793), another *Fletcher*, is docked at Boston's National Historical Park on Boston's Harbor. Visiting hours can be found at: https://www.nps.gov/bost/learn/historyculture/uss-cassinyoung.htm. The phone number is: (617) 242-5601. Commissioned on the last day of 1943, she was hit by a kamikaze on July 30, 1945, killing twenty-two men and wounding forty-five.

The USS *Laffey* (DD-724) is the only preserved *Allen M. Sumner*-class of destroyer, the successor to the *Fletcher* class. She is docked at the Patriot's Point Museum in Point Pleasant, South Carolina, across the river from Charleston. Visiting hours can be found at: https://www.patriotspoint.org/. The phone number is: (843) 884-2727. The Laffey is known as the "Ship That Would Not Die" after being attacked by multiple kamikazes off Okinawa.

The USS *Slater* (DE-766) is a *Cannon*-class destroyer escort preserved on the Hudson River in downtown Albany, New York. Visiting hours can be found at http://www.ussslater.org/. The phone number is: (518) 431-1943. She is open from April through November.

The USS *Stewart* (DE-238) is an *Edsall*-class destroyer escort at Seawolf Park on Galveston Island, Texas. Hours can be found at: https://www.galveston.com/seawolfpark/.

Bibliography

Books

Adcock, Al, *U.S. Flush Deck Destroyers in Action,* Squadron/Signal Publications, Carrollton, Texas, 2003.

Abbazia, Patrick, *Mr. Roosevelt's Navy: The Private War of the U.S. Atlantic Fleet, 1939-1942,* Naval Institute Press, Annapolis, Md., 1975.

Alden, John D., *Flush Decks & Four Pipes,* Naval Institute Press, Annapolis, Md., 1965.

Alford, Lodwick H., *Playing for Time: War on an Asiatic Fleet Destroyer,* Merriam Press, Bennington, VT., 2006.

Ballard, Robert, *The Lost Ships of Guadalcanal: Exploring the Ghost Fleet of the South Pacific,* Warner/Madison Press, New York, NY, 1993.

Becton, F. Julian with Joseph Morschauser III, *The Ship That Would Not Die,* Prentice Hall, Englewood Cliffs, NJ., 1980.

Bell, Frederick, Condition Red: *Destroyer Action in The South Pacific,* Longmans, Green, New York, NY, 1943.

Blackford, Charles, *Torpedoboat Sailor,* Naval Institute Press, Annapolis, Md., 1968.

Borneman, Walter R., *The Admirals: Nimitz, Halsey, Leahy and King, the Five-Star Admirals Who Won the War at Sea,* Little Brown, New York, NY, 2012.

Boyd, Carl and Akihiko Yoshida, *The Japanese Submarine Force and World War II,* Naval Institute Press, Annapolis, Md., 1995.

Brady, Tim, *Twelve Desperate Miles: The Epic Voyage of the SS Contessa,* Crown Publishers, New York, NY, 2012.

Branfill-Cook, Roger, *Torpedo: The Complete History of the World's Most Revolutionary Naval Weapon,* Seaforth Publishing, South Yorkshire, UK, 2014.

Brown, David, *Warship Losses of World War II,* Arms and Armor Press, London, UK, 1990.

Buell, Thomas B., *The Quiet Warrior: A Biography of Admiral Raymond A. Spruance,* Naval Institute Press, Annapolis, Md., 1987.

Bunch, Jim, *U-85: A Shadow in The Sea:* Deep Sea Press, Nags Head, N.C. 2003.

Burn, Alan, *The Fighting Captain: The Story of Frederick Walker and the Battle of the Atlantic,* Leo Cooper, London, UK, 1993.

Campbell, John, *Naval Weapons of World War II,* Naval Institute Press, Annapolis, Md., 1985.

Chesneau, Roger, Editor, *Conway's All the World's Fighting Ships, 1922-1946,* Conway Maritime Press, London, UK, 1997.

Clark Curet, *The Famed Green Dragons: The 4-Stack APDs in World War II,* Turner Publishing Paducah, KY, 1998.

Keegan, John, editor, *Collins Atlas of the Second World War,* Borders Press, NY 1989.

Connell, G.G., *Fighting Destroyer: The Story of the HMS Petard,* Crecy Books, Bodmin, UK, 1976.

Cooksey, Jon, *Operation Chariot: The Raid on St. Nazaire,* Pen & Sword Military, Barnsley, UK, 2005.

Cox, Jeffrey R., *Rising Sun, Falling Skies: The Disasterous Java Sea Campaign of World War II,* Osprey Publishing, Oxford, UK, 2014.

Cremer, Peter, *U-Boat Commander: A Periscope View of the Battle of the Atlantic,* Naval Institute Press, Annapolis, Md., 1982.

Crenshaw, Russel, *South Pacific Destroyer: The Battle for the Solomons from Savo Island to Vella Gulf,* Naval Institute Press, Annapolis, Md., 1998.

Crenshaw, Russell, *The Battle of Tassafaronga,* Nautical & Aviation Publishing Company, Baltimore, Md., 1995.

Cressman, Robert J., *The Official Chronology of the U.S. Navy in World War II,* Naval Institute Press, Annapolis, Md., 2000.

Crocker, Mel, *Black Cats and Dumbos: WW II's Fighting PBYs,* Crocker Media Expressions, Huntington Beach, Calif., 1987.

Cross, Robert F. *Shepherds of the Sea: Destroyer Escorts in World War II,* Naval Institute Press, Annapolis, Md., 2010.

Dailey, Jr., Franklyn E., *Joining the War at Sea 1939-1945,* Dailey International Publishers, Wilbraham, Mass., 1998.

Dallies-Labourdette, Jean-Philippe, *S-Boote German E-boats in action (1939-1945),* Histoirie & Collections, Paris, 2003.

Darlow, Michael and Barbara Bray, *Ibn Saud: The Desert Warrior Who Created the Kingdom of Saudi Arabia,* Skyhorse Publishing, New York, 2010.

Dorling, Taprell, *Endless Story: Destroyer Operations in The Great War,* Seaforth Publishing, 1931.

Dickens, Peter, *Narvik: Battles in the Fjords,* Naval Institute Press, Annapolis, Md., 1974.

Dickey, II, John L., *A Family Saga: Flush-Deck Destroyers 1917-1955 (Revised edition* edited by David W. McComb), Destroyer History Foundation, Boston Landing, N.Y., 2013.

Dorrian, James, *Saint-Nazaire: Operation Chariot-1942,* Pen & Sword Military, Barnsley, UK, 2006.

Dorrian, James G., *Storming St. Nazaire: The Dock Busting Raid of 1942,* Pen & Sword Military, Barnsley, UK, 1998.

Dorny, Louis B., *U.S. Navy PBY Catalina Units of the Pacific War,* Osprey Publishing, Oxford, UK, 2007.

Drury, Bob and Tom Clavin, *Halsey's Typhoon: The True Story of a Fighting Admiral, an Epic Storm and an Untold Rescue,* Grove Press, New York, NY. 2007.

DuBois, David, *The Last Stand of the Asiatic Fleet: MacArthur's Debacle in the Pacific,* Timber Ridge Press, Blanchard, Mich., 2017.

Duffus, Kevin P., *War Zone: World War II Off The North Carolina Coast,* Looking Glass Productions, Raleigh, N.C. 2012.

Dull, Paul S., *A Battle History of The Imperial Japanese Navy 1941-1945,* Naval Institute Press, Annapolis, Md., 1978.

Dunnigan, James F. & Albert A. Nofi, *The Pacific War Encyclopedia Vol. 1 & 2,* Facts on File, New York, NY, 1998.

Evans, Arthur S., Destroyer Down: *An Account of HM Destroyer Losses 1939-1945,* Pen & Sword Military, Barnsley, UK, 2010.

Evans, David C., and Mark R. Peattie, *Kaigun: Strategy, Tactics, and Technology in the Imperial Japanese Navy 1887-1941,* Naval Institute Press, Annapolis, Md., 1997.

Frank, Hans, *German S-Boats in Action in the Second World War,* Naval Institute Press, Annapolis, Md., 2006.

Frank, Richard B., *Guadalcanal: The Definitive Account of the Landmark Battle,* Random House, New York City, NY., 1990.

Friedman, Barry with Robert Robinson, *The Short Life of a Valiant Ship: USS Meredith DD-434,* self-published, 2012.

Friedman, Norman, British *Destroyers: From Earliest Days to the Second World War,* Naval Institute Press, Annapolis, Md., 2009.

Friedman, Norman, *U.S. Destroyers: An Illustrated Design History,* Naval Institute Press, Annapolis, Md., 2004.

Friedman, Norman, *British Destroyers & Frigates: The Second World War and After,* Seaforth Publishing, Barnsley, UK, 2006.

Gallery, Daniel V., *Twenty Million Tons Under the Sea: The Daring Capture of the U-505,* Naval Institute Press, Annapolis, Md., 1956.

Gannon, Michael, *Black May: The Epic Story of the Allies' Defeat of The German U-Boats in May 1943,* HarperCollins, New York, NY, 1989.

Gannon, Michael, *Operation Drumbeat: The Dramatic True Story of Germany's First U-Boat Attacks Along the American Coast in World War II,* Harper Row, New York, NY., 1990.

Garfield, Brian, *The Thousand Mile War: World War II in Alaska and the Aleutians,* Ballantine Books, New York, 1969.

Goebler, Hans with John Vanzo, *Steel Boats, Iron Hearts: A U-Boat Crewman's Life Aboard the U-505,* Savas Beatie, El Dorado Hills, Calif., 2008.

Gray, Edwyn A., *The Killing Time: The German U-Boats 1914-1918,* Charles Scribner's & Sons, New York, NY, 1972.

Hague, Arnold, *Destroyers for Great Britain: A History of the 50 Town Class Ships Transferred from the United States to Great Britain in 1940,* Naval Institute Press, Annapolis, Md., 1988.

Hara, Tameichi, *Japanese Destroyer Captain: Pearl Harbor, Guadalcanal, Midway-The Great Naval Battles as Seen Through Japanese Eyes,* Naval Institute Press, Annapolis, Md., 1967.

Harding, Stephen, *The Castaway's War: One Man's Battle Against Imperial Japan,* Da Capo Press, New York, NY., 2016.

Harper, Stephen, *Capturing Enigma: How HMS Petard Seized the German Naval Codes,* Sutton Publishing, Gloucestershire, UK, 1999.

Hawkins, Ian, *Destroyer: An Anthology of First-Hand Accounts of the War at Sa 1939-1945,* Conway, London, UK, 2003.

Henderson, Bruce, *Down to The Sea: An Epic Story of Naval Disaster and Heroism in World War II,* Smithsonian Books, Washington, D.C., 2007.

Henry, Chris, *Depth Charge: Royal Navy Mines, Depth Charges & Underwater Weapons 1914-1945,* Pen & Sword Military, South Yorkshire, UK, 2005.

Hidkham, Jr., Homer H., *Torpedo Junction,* Naval Institute Press, Annapolis, Md., 1989.

Hodges, Peter and Norman Friedman, *Destroyer Weapons of World War II,* Conway Maritime Press, Greenwich, UK, 1979.

Hone, Thomas C., *The Battle of Midway: The Naval Institute Guide to the U.S. Navy's Greatest Victory*, Naval Institute Press, Annapolis, Md., 2013.

Hornfischer, James D., *The Fleet at Flood Tide: America At Total War in the Pacific 1944-1945*, Bantam Books, New York, NY, 2016.

Hornfischer, James D., *The Last Stand of the Tin Can Sailors: The Extraordinary World War II Story of the U.S. Navy's Finest Hour*, Bantam, New York, NY, 2004.

Hornfischer, James D., *Neptune's Inferno: The U.S. Navy at Guadalcanal*, Bantam Books, New York, NY, 2011.

Hoyt, Edwin P., *The Lonely Ships: The Life and Death of the U.S. Asiatic Fleet*, Jove Books, New York, 1976.

Hughes, Thomas Alexander, *Admiral Bill Halsey: A Navy Life*, Harvard University, Cambridge, Mass., 2016.

Ireland, Bernard, *An Illustrated History of Destroyers of the World*, Southwater, London, UK, 2010.

Ireland, Bernard & Eric Grove, *Jane's War at Sea, 1897-1997: 100 Years of Jane's Fighting Ships*, Harper Collins, New York, NY, 1997.

Johnson, David Alan, *Betrayal: The True Story of J. Edgar Hoover and the Nazi Saboteurs Captured During WW II*, Hippocrene Brooks, New York, 2007.

Jones, Ken, *Destroyer Squadron 23: Combat Exploits of Arleigh Burke's Gallant Force*, Naval Institute Press, Annapolis, Md., 1997.

Jourdan, David W., *USS Nautilus and the Battle of Midway: The Search for the Japanese Fleet*, Potomac Books, Omaha, Ne., 2015.

Kehn, Jr., Donald M., *A Blue Sea of Blood: Deciphering the Mysterious Fate of the USS Edsall*, Zenith Press, Minneapolis, MN, 2008.

Kehn, Jr., Donald M., *In the Highest Degree Tragic: The Sacrifice of the U.S. Asiatic Fleet in the East Indies during World War II*, Potomac Books, Omaha, NE., 2017.

Klobuchar, Richard P., *The USS Ward: An Operational History of the Ship That Fired the First American Shot of World War II.*, McFarland, Jefferson, N.C. 2006.

Lavery, Brian, *Churchill's Navy: The Ships, Men and Organisation 1939-1945,* Conway Maritime, London, UK, 2006.

Leeke, Jim, *Manila and Santiago: The New Steel Navy in the Spanish-American War,* Naval Institute Press, Annapolis, Md., 2009.

Lockwood, Charles, and Adamson, Hans Christian, *Tragedy at Honda,* Chilton Company, Philadelphia, Penn., 1960.

Love, Jr., Robert W., *History of the U.S. Navy Vol. 1 and 2,* Stackpole Books, Harrisburg, Penn., 1992.

Lyon, David, T. *The First Destroyers,* Caxton Editions, London, UK, 2001.

Lundstrom, John B., *The First South Pacific Campaign: Pacific Fleet Strategy December 1941-June 1942,* Naval Institute Press, Annapolis, Md., 1976.

Marriott, Leo, *Catapult Aircraft: The Story of Seaplanes Flown from Battleships, Cruisers and Other Warships of the World's Navies, 1912-1950,* Pen & Sword, 2006.

McComb, Dave, *U.S. Destroyers 1942-45,* Osprey Publishing, 2010, Oxford, UK.

McComb, Dave, *U.S. Destroyers 1934-45,* Osprey Publishing, 2010, Oxford, UK.

McDonald, Kevin, *Tin Can Sailors Save The Day: The USS Johnston and the Battle off Samar,* Paloma Books, Ashland, OR, 2015.

Miller, Edward S., *War Plan Orange: The U.S. Strategy to Defeat Japan, 1897-1945,* Naval Institute Press, Annapolis, Md., 1991.

Miller, Nathan, *War at Sea: A Naval History of World War II,* Scribner, New York, NY, 1995.

Milton Giles, *Churchhill's Ministry of Ungentlemanly Warfare: The Mavericks Who Plotted Hitler's Defeat,* Pocador, New York, NY, 2016.

Morgan, Daniel & Taylor, Bruce, *U-Boat Attack Logs: A Complete Record of Warship Sinkings from Original Sources 1939-1945,* Seaforth Publishing, 2001 South Yorkshire, UK.

Morison, Samuel Eliot, *History of United States Naval Operations of World War II, 14 volumes*, Little Brown, New York City, NY, 1955-1960.

Mullin, J. Daniel, *Another Six Hundred*, Self-Published, M. Pleasant, S.C., 1984.

Nelson, Craig, *Pearl Harbor: From Infamy to Greatness*, Scribner, New York City, NY, 2016.

Newcomb, Richard F. Savo: *The Incredible Naval Debacle off Guadalcanal*, Holt, Rhinehart & Winston, New York, NY. 1961.

Nolan, Liam & John E., *Secret Victory: Ireland and the War at Sea 1914-1918*, Mercier Press, Dublin, Ireland, 2009.

Offley, Ed, *The Burning Shore: How Hitler's U-Boats Brought World War II to America*, Basic Books, New York, 2014.

Offley, Ed, *Turning the Tide: How A Small Band of Allied Sailors Defeated The U-Boats and Won The Battle of The Atlantic*, Basic Books, New York, NY, 2011.

O'Hara, Vincent P., *The U.S. Navy Against the Axis: Surface Combat 1941-1945*, Navy Institute Press, Annapolis, Md., 2007.

Orita, Zenji with Joseph Harrington, *I-Boat Captain: How Japan's Submarines Almost Defeated the U.S. Navy in the Pacific*, Major Books, Canoga Park, Calif., 1976.

O'Tolle, G.J., *The Spanish War: An American Epic 1898*, W.W. Norton, New York, 1984.

Paine, Ralph D., *The Fighting Fleets: Five Months of Active Service with the American Destroyers and Their Allies in the War Zone*, Houghton Mifflin Company, Boston, 1918.

Parkin, Robert Sinclair, *Blood on the Sea: American Destroyers Lost in World War II*, DeCapo Press, Cambridge, Mass., 1995.

Parrish, Thomas, Editor, *The Simon and Schuster Encyclopedia of World War II*, Simon and Schuster, New York, NY, 1978.

Parshall, Jonathan and Anthony Tully, *Shattered Sword: The Untold Story of The Battle of Midway*, Potomac Books, Washington, D.C., 2007.

Phillips, C.E. Lucas, *The Greatest Raid of All*, Pan Books, London, UK, 1958.

Pleshakov, Constantine, *The Tsar's Last Armada: The Epic Voyage of the Battle of Tsushima*, Basic Books, New York, NY., 2002.

Polomar, Norman and Whitman, Edward, *Hunters and Killers: Anti-Submarine Warfare from 1776 to 1943 (Vol. 1), and (Vol. 2) Anti-submarine Warfare from 1943*, Naval Institute Press, Annapolis, Md., 2015.

Potter, E.B., *Admiral Arleigh Burke: A Biography*, Naval Institute Press, Annapolis, Md., 1990.

Potter, E.B., *Nimitz*, Naval Institute Press, Annapolis, Md., 1976.

Prokop, Robert, *Goalpost: The Battle for Port Lyautey-November 1942*, Self-published, 2011.

Prange, Gordon W., with Donald Goldstein and Katherine V. Dillon, *Dec. 7, 1941: The Day the Japanese Attacked Pearl Harbor*, Wings Books, New York City, NY., 1991.

Prange, Gordon W., with Donald M. Goldstein and Katherine V. Dillon, *Miracle at Midway*, MJF Books, New York, NY, 1982.

Puleo, Stephen, *Due to Enemy Action: The True World War II Story of the USS Eagle 56*, The Lyons Press, Guilford, Conn., 2005.

Rielly, Robin L., *Kamikaze Attacks of World War II – A Complete History of Japanese Suicide Strikes on American Ships, by Aircraft and Other Means*, McFarland, West Jefferson, N.C., 2010.

Rohwer, J., and G. Hummelchen, *Chronology of the War at Sea 1939-1945*, Naval Institute Press, Annapolis, Md., 1972.

Roscoe, Theodore, *United States Destroyer Operations in World War II*, United States Naval Institute, Annapolis, Md., 1953.

Rose, Lisle A., *America's Sailors in The Great War: Seas, Skies and Submarines*, University of Missouri Press, Columbia, Mo., 2017.

Sandler, Stanley, *World War II in the Pacific: An Enclyclopedia*, Garland Publishing, New York, NY, 2001.

Sauer, Howard, *The Last Big-Gun Battle: The Battle of Surigao Strait*, Glencannon Press, Palo Alto, Calif. 1999.

Savas, Theodore P., editor, *Silent Killers: German U-Boat Commanders of World War II,* Savas Publishing, Campbell, Calif., 1997.

Savas, Theodore, editor, *Hunt and Kill: U-505 and the U-Boat War in the Atlantic,* Savas Beatie, El Dorado Hills, Calif., 2004.

Schoenfeld, Max, *Stalking the U-Boat: USAAF Offensive Antisubmarine Operations in World War II,* Smithsonian Books, Washington, D.C., 1995.

Sears, David, *At War with the Wind: The Epic Struggle with Japan's World War II Suicide Bombers,* Citadel Press, New York, NY., 2008.

Sears, David, *The Last Epic Naval Battle: Voices from Leyte Gulf,* Prager, Westport Conn., 2005.

Shogan, Robert, Hard Bargain: *How FDR Twisted Churchill's Arm, Evaded the Law, and Changed the Role of the American Presidency,* Scribner, New York, NY, 1995.

Silverstone, Paul H., *The Navy of World War II, 1922-1947,* Routledge, New York, NY, 2008.

Sims, William Sowden, *The Victory at Sea,* Naval Institute Press, Annapolis, Md., reprinted 1984.

Smith, S.E., *The United States Navy in World War II,* William Morrow, New York City, NY, 1966.

Snow, Richard, *A Measureless Peril: American in the Fight for the Atlantic, the Longest Battle of World War II,* Scribner, New York, NY, 2010.

Sondhaus, Lawrence, *The Great War at Sea: A Naval History of The First World War,* Cambridge University Press, Cambridge, UK, 2014.

Spector, Ronald, *Eagle Against the Sun,* McMillian, New York, NY, 1985

Spencer, Patrick, *Capturing the Enigma: The Unsung Heroes of HMS Bulldog,* Mouseworks Publishing, Denton, Texas, 2016.

Staton, Michael, *The Fighting Bob: A Wartime History of the USS Robley D. Evans, DD-552,* Merriam Press, Bennington, Vt., 2001.

Stern, Robert C., *Fire from The Sky: Surviving the Kamikaze Threat,* Naval Institute Press, Annapolis, Md., 2010.

Stille, Mark, *USN Destroyer vs IJN Destroyer: The Pacific* 1943, Osprey Publishing, Oxford, UK, 2012

Stille, Mark, *US Navy Ships vs Kamikazes 1944-45*, Osprey Publishing, Oxford, UK, 2016

Symonds, Craig L., *The Battle of Midway*, Oxford University Press, Oxford, UK, 2011.

Taussig, Joseph, *The Queenstown Patrol, 1917: The Diary of Commander Joseph Knefler Taussig, U.S. Navy*. Edited by William N. Still, Jr., Naval War College Press, Newport R.I., 1996.

Tully, Anthony P., *Battle of Surigao Strait*, Indiana University Press, Bloomington, IN, 2009.

Vause Jordan, *Wolf: U-Boat Commanders in World War II*, Naval Institute Press, Annapolis, Md., 1997

Veesenmeyer, Jeffrey R., *Kamikaze Destroyer: USS Hugh W. Hadley (DD-774)*, Merriam Press, Bennington, Vt., 2014.

Walling, Michael G., *Bloodstained Sea: The U.S. Coast Guard in the Battle of the Atlantic, 1941-1944*, McGraw-Hill, New York City, NY, 2004.

Wheeler, Gerald E., *Prelude to Pearl Harbor: The United States Navy and the Far East 1921-1931*, University of Missouri Press, Columbia, Mo., 1968.

Whitley, M.J., *Destroyers of World War II: An International Encyclopedia*, Naval Institute Press, Annapolis, Md., 1988.

Wildenberg, Thomas, and Polmar, Norman, *Ship Killers: A History of the American Torpedo*, Naval Institute Press, Annapolis, Md., 2010.

Williamson, Gordon, *U-Boats vs Destroyer Escorts: The Battle of the Atlantic*, Osprey, Oxford, UK, 2007.

Williamson, John A., *Antisubmarine Warrior in the Pacific: Six Subs Sunk in Twelve Days*, University of Alabama Press, Tuscaloosa, Ala., 2005.

Willoughby, Malcolm F., *The U.S. Coast Guard in World War II*, Naval Institute Press, Annapolis, Md., 1957.

Winslow, W.G., *The Fleet the Gods Forgot: The U.S. Asiatic Fleet in World War II*, Naval Institute Prss, Annapolis, Md., 1982.

Wukovits, John, *For Crew and Country: The Inspirational True Story of Bravery and Sacrifice Aboard the USS Samuel B. Roberts,* St Martin's Press, New York, NY., 2013.

Wukovits, John, *Hell from the Heavens: The Epic Story of the USS Laffey and World War II's Greatest Kamikaze Attack,* 2015.

Wukovits, John, *Tin Can Titans: The Heroic Men and Ships of World War II's Most Decorated Navy Destroyer Squadron,* DeCapo Press, New York, NY., 2017.

Y'Blood, William T., *Hunter-Killer: U.S. Escort Carriers in the Battle of the Atlantic,* Naval Institute Press, Annapolis, Md., 1983.

Internet Sources:

www.DestroyerHistory.org is a website dedicated to the history of American naval destroyers.

www.CombinedFleet.com is a website detailing the Imperial Japanese Navy.

www.History.navy.mil is a website maintained by the Navy History and Heritage Command, including the Dictionary of American Navy Fighting Ships, a history of each commissioned vessel that has served in the U.S. Navy. It has thousands of high definition photographs online, including a searchable list of American destroyers by name or hull number.

https://uboat.net/ is a website detailing the history of German submarines from both World War I and World War II. This is a great resource for finding details on the patrols of individual U-boats.

http://www.navy.mil/ah_online/department_arch.html has all the back issues of "All Hands," a navy magazine dating back to 1922.

https://www.usni.org/ is the United States Naval Institute, which publishes many detailed and valuable books on naval history. USNI members can find online back issues of "Proceedings," a magazine dating back to 1874 and Naval History magazine dating back to 1987. This is a wonderful resource for just a few dollars per year. Just reading back issues of Proceedings is a joy.

http://www.destroyers.org/ is The National Association of Destroyer
   Veterans, better known as Tin Can Sailors, is dedicated to Destroyer
   Men of all wars.

www.navsource.org is a website keeping photographs of U.S. Navy
   ships.

http://www.hazegray.org/danfs/ is a website detailing the known history
   of every American ship.

Acknowledgments

J oseph Vallely of Swagger Literary Agency had been my literary agent since 2006. He was a tough taskmaster when it came to writing proposals, but they worked. Joe passed away while I was still making the final edits on *Tin Cans & Greyhounds* on August 15, 2018, so he did not live to see this book in print.

Joe passed one day before the forty-first anniversary of the death of his rock and roll hero, Elvis Presley, and the day before the death of Aretha Franklin, Joe's soul music hero. He would have loved to have gone out on August 16, but maybe he got the last of his big, boisterous laughs on all of his friends and writers anyway. His widow called me and told me that when she was closing out her Words with Friends games online to deal with Joe's sudden death, she noticed something unusual. Among the words left in one game was "Elvis." Joe may have been sending her a message that he was in rock and roll Heaven and was meeting all the men and women whose thousands of recordings he owned.

Thanks, Joe, for trusting my abilities as a writer.

Thanks to Alex Novak of Regnery History in Washington, D.C. for taking on this book, Jennifer Duplessie and the editors and designers at

Regnery for turning the manuscript and photo selections into a book, and Gary Neid, a freelance editor down in Texas, for doing the first pass of copyediting. Regnery Publishing published my book, *The Politically Incorrect Guide to the South*, in 2007. They are a fine organization.

I never met David McComb, founder of www.DestroyerHistory.org, but the world owes him a great debt for this wonderful source of information on United States destroyers. If a destroyer was constructed, Mr. McComb found out what he could about it, and that information rests on this website. His widow, Meredith, is keeping the website up. This is also a great source for personal stories from some Destroyer Men who posted their experiences on the site.

Steve Bragdon and Randy Price helped me sort through hundreds of entries from the Dictionary of American Fighting Ships to find destroyers that were "historic" in some fashion. Steve was my chief researcher. He made several trips with me to the National Archives in College Park, Maryland, for the painstaking process of reading through the after action reports of those destroyers. He and I shared the thrill of holding in our hands the original typed reports—not copies—of battles. We stared at the signatures of famous men like William F. Halsey, Chester Nimitz, and Arleigh Burke on some of those reports. Steve says his National Archives researcher card is one of his most prized possessions.

Raymond Robinson, a U.S. Navy veteran, read the manuscript with an old salt's eye for naval errors. He once almost started World War III with a Shop-Vac aboard a nuclear submarine, but that is a story that won't make this book.

Mike Wenger, a fellow history writer who is more experienced at naval research than I, walked me through the process of how to find World War II records at the National Archives in College Park, Maryland.

Robert Henshew is a curator at the National Museum of the United States Navy in Washington, D.C. He pointed me to a lot of photos that appear in this book.

Tambrie Johnson, a fine destroyer researcher, encouraged me to look into the accounts of the USS *Strong* (DD-467), on which her great-uncle served during World War II.

Dick Bonheim, an old Army guy, encouraged me to further research the USS *Robinson* (DD-562). He even compiled all of the reports he could find on it and sent me a CD copy.

Ken Dunn helped me sort out the numerous and mostly false stories about the mission and sinking of the *U-85*, sunk by the USS *Roper* (DD-147) off of the North Carolina Outer Banks.

Michael Lowrey of Uboat.net helped sort out some U-Boat accounts, particularly those of the *U-53*, the U-Boat that cruised into Newport, Rhode Island harbor in October 1916.

Stephen Harding, editor of *Military History Magazine*, was able to answer some questions about why the Americans did not see the Japanese on radar when they torpedoed the USS *Strong* (DD-467).

Thanks to Chris Hauff and David Clark of the USS *Laffey* (DD-724) ship museum at Patriot's Point, opposite Charleston, South Carolina, for giving me a great orientation and tour of this most famous of the surviving World War II era destroyers.

Gerhard Kalmus sat down with me and translated the *U-53's* logs from German to English. That proved challenging as we were working from photocopies of microfilm. The other members of the German Club of Ashe County, North Carolina also helped with the translations.

Laura McPherson, adult services librarian of the Ashe County Public Library in West Jefferson, North Carolina, was able to find research books through Interlibrary Loan that were too expensive to buy.

The staff of the National Archives at College Park, Maryland, was always friendly, helpful, and understanding to researchers who had never tried to find any records in their vast holdings. They are a great asset to the nation's historians.

Billy Gene Conatser with the help of Larri Littlefield in Henryetta, Oklahoma, wrote me a letter about his wartime experiences on the USS *Murray* (DD-576).

The members of the Facebook page "Destroyers: Greyhounds of the Sea" were able to answer some technical destroyer questions for me.

My wife, Barb, read the final draft and helped catch some of those nagging little typos before the manuscript made it into print. At least I hope we caught all the typos and errors.

Notes

Chapter 1

1. David Lyon, *The First Destroyers*, (London: Caxton Editions, 1996), 17.

2. Admiral Togo's report on the battle, http://russojapanesewar.com/togo-aar3.html.

3. Ibid.

4. Ibid.

5. E.B. Potter, Nimitz (Annapolis, Maryland: Naval Institute Press, 1976), 61.

6. Ibid, 61.

7. Thomas B. Buell, *The Quiet Warrior* (Annapolis, Maryland: Naval Institute Press, 1987), 29.

Chapter 2

1. https://wwi.lib.byu.edu/index.php/. President_Wilson's_Declaration_of_Neutrality.

2. Fraser M. McKee, "An Explosive Story-The Rise and Fall of the Common Depth Charge," *The Northern Mariner, Vol. 3. No. 1* (January, 1993), 51.

3. Arthur, Link, *The Papers of Woodrow Wilson, Vol. 3,* (Princeton, New Jersey: Princeton University Press, 1966), 5.

4. Hans Rose, "With The U-53 to America-Part I" (*The Living Age,* Nov. 15, 1926), 328.

5. Ibid, 332.

6. Ibid, 333.

7. Hans Rose, "With the U-53 To America II," (*The Living Age,* Dec. 1, 1926), 423.

8. Ibid, 424.

9. Washington Post, 1 Oct. 10, 1916.

10. Washington Post, 6 Oct. 9, 1916.

11. Nashville Tennessean, 1 Oct. 10, 1916.

12. Hans Rose, "With the U-53 to America-Part II", (*The Living Age,* Dec. 1, 1926), 423.

Chapter 3

1. William S. Sims, *Victory at Sea,* (Annapolis, Maryland: republished by Naval Institute Press, 1984), 8-9.

2. Joseph Taussig, *The Queenstown Patrol (*Newport, R.I.: Naval War College Press, 1917), 19.

3. Sims, *The Victory at Sea,* 58.

4. Taussig, *The Queenstown Patrol,* 25.

5. Paine, Ralph D., *The Fighting Fleets: Five Months of Active Service with the American Destroyers and their Allies in the War Zone* (Boston: Houghton & Mifflin, 1918), 66-67.

6. Taprell Dorling, *Endless Story-Destroyer Operations in the Great War* (reprinted from 1931 edition by Seaforth Publishing: Barnsley, UK, 2016), 337.

Chapter 4

1. Robert W. Love, Jr. *History of the U.S. Navy—Vol. 1*, (Harrisburg, Pennsylvania: Stackpole Books, 1992), 519.

2. Ibid, 526.

3. Norman Friedman, *US. Destroyers* (Annapolis, Maryland: Naval Institute Press, 2004), 40.

4. Love, *History of the U.S. Navy-Vol. 1*, 530.

5. Charles Lockwood, *Tragedy at Honda* (Philadelphia, Pennsylvania: Chilton & Company, 1960), 140.

Chapter 5

1. Love, Jr. *History of the U.S. Navy, Vol. 1*, (Harrisburg, Pennsylvania: Stackpole Books, 1992), 560.

2. Ibid, 565.

3. Friedman, *US. Destroyers* (Annapolis, Maryland: Naval Institute Press, 2004), 87.

4. Ibid, 87.

Chapter 6

1. Patrick Abbazia, *Mr. Roosevelt's Navy* (Annapolis, Maryland: Naval Institute Press, 1975), 5.

2. Ibid, 30.

3. Peter Dickens, *Narvik*, (Annapolis,Maryland: Naval Institute Press, 1974), 61.

4. Abbazia, *Mr. Roosevelt's Navy*, 94.

5. Ibid, 142.

6. Ibid, 149.

7. Deck Log of Niblack, National Archives, Record Group 38.

8. Ian Hawkins, *Destroyer* (London: Conway Books, 2003), 165.

9. Ibid, 166.

10. Ibid, 166.

11. Abbazia, *Mr. Roosevelt's Navy*, 205.

12. Fireside Chat 100 (http://www.presidency.ucsb.edu/ ws/?pid=16012).

13. Fireside chat on USS Kearny (http://www.usmm.org/fdr/kearny. html).

14. Abbazia, *Mr. Roosevelt's Navy*, 306-307.

15. Lyric to The Sinking of the Reuben James, words and music by Woody Guthrie, 1942.

Chapter 7

1. USS Ward War After Action Report, Dec. 7, 1941, National Archives, Record Group 38, 1.

2. Ibid.

3. USS Helm After Action Report, U.S. Archives, RG 38, 2.

4. USS Breese After Action Report Dec. 9, 1941, National Archives, RG 38.

5. Gordon Prange, *Dec. 7, 1941* (New York: Wings Books, 1991), 270.

6. Samuel Eliot Morison, *History of the United States Naval Operations in World War II- Vol. III,* (Boston, Massachusetts: Little, Brown and Company, 1954), 220.

7. L.A. Abercrombie and Fletcher Pratt, "Scratch One!"-*The United States Navy in World War II* (New York: William Morrow & Co., 1966), 57.

8. Ibid, 58.

9. www.destroyersonline.com/usndd/dd366.

Chapter 8

1. Diary of Erich Degenkolb, Uboatarchive.net/U-85.

2. Ibid.

3. USS Dallas After Action Report, National Archives, Record Group 32.

Chapter 9

1. Destroyer Squadron 29, www.Destroyerhistory.org.
2. USS Peary, www.Destroyerhistory.org.
3. Andrew Wilde, Jr., History of the USS Peary, www. DestroyerHistory.org.
4. Theodore Roscoe, *United States Destroyer Operations in World War II*, (Annapolis, Maryland: Naval Institute Press, 1953), 91.
5. Ibid, 93.
6. USS Alden After Action Report, National Archives, Record Group 38.
7. APD Conversions, www.Destroyerhistory.org.
8. USS Patterson, Destroyerhistory.org.
9. William Halsey letter, Destroyer Squadron 12, www.Destroyerhistory.org.

Chapter 10

1. USS Rowan After Action Report, National Archives, Record Group 32.
2. Norman Polmar and Edward Whitman, *Hunters and Killers Vol. 1* (Annapolis, Maryland: Naval Institute Press , 2015), 147.
3. William T. Y'Blood, *Hunter-Killer* (Annapolis, Maryland: Naval Institute Press, , 1983), 79.
4. USS Borie After Action Report, National Archives, RG 38.
5. Ibid.
6. Ibid.
7. Ibid.
8. Ibid.

Chapter 11

1. Robert Cressman, *The Official Chronology of the U.S. Navy in World War II*, (Annapolis, Maryland: Naval Institute Press, 2000), 145.

2. Richard B. Frank, *Guadalcanal* (New York: Penguin Books, 1990), 588.

3. Eric Bergerud, *Fire In The Sky: The Air War in the South Pacific* (New York: Basic Books, 2001), 592.

4. John Wukovits, *Tin Can Titans*, (Philadelphia, Pennsylvania: DeCapo Press, 2017), 133.

5. Theodore Roscoe, *United States Destroyer Operations in World War II*, (Annapolis, Maryland: Naval Institute Press, 1953), 235.

6. Samuel E. Morison, *History of the United States Naval Operations in World War II Vol. VI- Breaking The Bismarks Barrier*, (Boston: Little, Brown and Company, 1955), 321.

7. Roscoe, *United States Destroyer Operations in World War II*, 246.

8. Decatur Daily News, June 25, 1945.

Chapter 12

1. Robert F. Cross, *Shepherds of the Sea* (Annapolis, Maryland: Naval Institute Press, 2010), 102.

2. USS Buckley After Action Report, National Archives ,Record Group 38.

3. Ibid.

4. Theodore Roscoe, *United States Destroyer Operations in World War II*, (Annapolis, Maryland: Naval Institute Press, 1953), 351.

5. USS Nelson After Action Report, National Archives, RG 38.

6. Roscoe, *United States Destroyer Operations in World War II*, 503.

11

Chapter 13

1. USS Burns After Action Report, National Archives, Record Group 38.

2. Ibid.

3. John Williamson, *Antisubmarine Warrior in the Pacific*, (Tuscaloosa, Alabama: University of Alabama Press, 2005), 127.

4. Ibid, 140.

5. After Action Narrative, Vice Admiral Jesse Oldendorf, National Archives, RG 38.

6. James Hornfischer, *Last Stand of the Tin Can Sailors* (New York: Bantam Books 2004), 150.

7. Ibid, 49.

8. Ibid, 48.

9. Ibid, 264.

Chapter 14

1. John S. Keating, "Mission to Mecca: The Cruise of the Murphy," (Proceedings magazine, Annapolis, Maryland: U.S. Naval Institute, Jan. 1976).

2. Letter from Roosevelt to King Saud, http://articles.baltimoresun.com/2002-09-01/topic/0208310033_1_saudi-arabia-ibn-saud-king-of-saudi.

3. Samuel Eliot Morison, *History of United States Naval Operations, Vol. X -The Atlantic Battle Won*, (Boston: Little, Brown and Comapany, 1955), 348.

Chapter 15

1. George Fleming Davis Medal of Honor Citation, http://www.cmohs.org/recipient-detail/2706/davis-george-fleming.php.

2. Elmer Bigelow's Medal of Honor citation.

3. USS Franklin After Action Report, U.S. Archives, Record Group 38.

4. Theodore Roscoe, *United States Destroyer Operations in World War II*, (Annapolis, Maryland: Naval Institute Press, 1953), 467.

5. After Action Report of LSM-189, RG 38, National Archives.

6. Julian Becton, *The Ship That Would Not Die*, (Missoula, Montana: Pictorial Histories Publishing 1980), 229.

7. Ibid, 255.

8. USS Morrison commendation, http://destroyerhistory.org/ fletcherclass/index.asp?r=56000&pid=56006.

9. USS Hugh Hadley after Action Report, National Archives, RG 38.

10. Hugh Hadley After Action Report, National Archives, RG 38.

11. Ibid.

12. Roscoe, *United States Destroyer Operations in World War II*, (Annapolis, Maryland: Naval Institute Press, 1953), 496-497.

13. Interview of 5 members of Charles S. Ausburne, Nov. 1, 1945, National Archives, RG 38.

14. Billy Gene Conatser letter to Clint Johnson March 2017.

15. William F. Halsey order, www.destroyerhistory.org.

Index

1930 London Treaty, 57-8, 63, 106

1936 London Treaty, 65

1st Marine Raider Battalion, 138

A

Abner Read, 225

Admiral Austin Knight, 23

Admiral Daniel Callaghan, 145

Admiral Erich Raeder, 122

Admiral Ernest King, 90

Admiral Frank Friday Fletcher, 34, 84

Admiral Hipper, 120-21

Admiral Husband Kimmel, 95

Admiral Jesse Oldendorf, 218

Admiral John Jellicoe, 31

Admiral Karl Donitz, 122

Admiral Kurita, 224

Admiral Norman Scott, 40, 141

Admiral Togo Heihachiro, 9

Admiral W.L. Ainsworth, 183

Admiral William Pratt, 66

Admiral Yamamoto, 104, 149, 171

Alban L. Gwynne, 18

Almirante Condell, 4

Almirante Lynch, 4

American British Dutch Australian Command (ABDA), 127

American Civil War, 1, 162

Andrew Jackson Higgins, 67

Anglo-Japanese Alliance, 42

Arleigh Burke's Little Beavers, 209

Arundel Island, 176, 179

Asiatic Fleet, 105, 125-26, 128, 130, 134, 159, 165, 196, 265, 268, 270, 275

Atlantic Squadron, 72, 80

Azores Islands, 48, 235

B

Batangas Harbor, 129

Battle of Balikpapan, 130, 173

Battle of Bandung Strait, 130

Battle of Cape Esperamce, 140

Battle of Cape St. George, 190-91

Battle of Coral Sea, 34, 134, 136, 171

Battle of Guadalcanal, 145, 147, 168, 175, 252, 259,

Battle of Jutland, 19, 28, 42, 77-78

Battle of Kula Gulf, 100, 180-83

Battle of Leyte Gulf, 100, 215, 224, 241, 274

Battle of Midway, 34, 135-36, 142, 148, 174

Battle of Narvik, 76, 78, 106

Battle of Palawan Passage, 216

Battle of Santiago, 6-7

Battle of Sibuyan Sea, 216

Battle of Surigao Strait, 217-18

Battle of the Coral Sea, 134, 136, 171

Battle of the Java Sea, 132, 134

Battle of Vella Gulf, 136, 184-86

Battle off Samar, 218, 220, 226

Bay of Biscay, 110

Bethlehem Hingham Shipyard, 200

Bethlehem Steel, 58

Bismarck, 73

C

Cape May, 108-10, 239

Captain A.B. Coxe, Jr., 96

Captain Albert Gleaves, 23

Captain Arleigh Burke, 188

Captain Bernard Warburton-Lee, 75

Captain D.T. Eller, 208

Captain D.V. Gallery, 200

Captain Edwin W. Watson, 51

Captain Frank R. Walker, 187

Captain Frederick Julian Becton, 176, 182, 252-53

Captain John Paul Jones, 129, 133

Captain John Williamson, 213

Captain Robert Copeland, 221

Center Force, 215-16, 218-20

Charles J. Moore, 14

Chester Nimitz, 13, 126, 139, 280

Chief Frank S. Wright, Jr., 261

Chief Henry Clyde Daniels, 103

Chilean Civil War, 4

Colonel William A. Eddy, 230

Commander B.J. Mullaney, 257

Commander Bernard A. Smith, 230

Commander C.J. Van Arsdall, Jr., 259

Commander David W. Bagley, 26, 36

Commander Donald MacDonald, 174

Commander Ernest E. Evans, 221, 225

Commander Frederick Moosbrugger, 184

Commander George Fleming Davis, 242

Commander George Rees Wilson, 250

Commander George W. Johnson, 86

Commander J.H. Wesson, 247

Commander James E. Kyes, 163

Commander Joseph Knefler Taussig, 30-32, 34-36

Commander W.W. Outerbridge, 226

Commander Watanabe Yusumasa, 136

Commodore John S. Keating, 232

Corregidor Island, 245-46

Czar Nicholas II, 8

D

Destroyer Design Office, 182

Dinagat Island, 217

Dover Barrage, 29

E

Eastern Sea Frontier commander, 109

Elmer Charles Bigelow, 245

F

Fighting Freddie, 237

First Battle of Dover Strait, 28-29

First Happy Time, 152

Ford Motor Company, 238

Franklin D. Roosevelt, 35, 49, 155

Fuhrer Adolf Hitler, 73

G

General Douglas McArthur, 215

Gilbert Islands, 190, 207

Glenn Curtiss, 48

Goldplaters, 60, 72, 80

Great White Fleet, 11

H

Hans Rose, 22, 36, 39

Henderson Field, 144-45, 170, 269

Henschel Hx293, 194

Herbert Taylor, 18

Herman Wouk, 228

High-Frequency Direction Finder (HF/DF OR "Huff Duff"), 154

I

Imperial Japanese Navy, 93, 149, 168, 171, 215, 241

J

Jesse Whitfield Covington, 41

Josephus Daniels, 36, 46

K

Kolombangara Island, 166, 171-72, 176, 180, 184, 186

Komandorski Islands, 174

Korean War, xi, 162

Kriegsmarine, 73

Kula Gulf, 100, 177, 180-83

L

Landing Craft Transports (LCTs), 170

League of Nations, 45

Leyte Gulf, 11, 215, 224, 241, 247, 274

Leyte Island, 215, 217, 241

Lietuenant Raymond Spruance, 13, 14

Lieutenant A.L. David, 201

Lieutenant Commander H.W. Howe, 114

Lieutenant Commander Herald F. Stout, 98

Lieutenant Commander Robert Brodie, Jr., 119

Lieutenant Commander Wade McClusky, Jr., 135

Lieutenant Commander Wayne A. Parker, 190

Lieutenant Frank Jack Fletcher, 34

Lieutenant G.R. Heppel, 74

Lieutenant Hugh Barr Miller, 179

Lieutenant James M. Stewart, 250

Lieutenant Norman Scott, 37, 40

Lieutenant Stanton F. Kalk, 39

Lingayen Gulf, 241-42

Lutzow, 120

M

Mare Island Shipyard, 47

Mare Island, 47, 97, 174

Marshall Islands, 43, 207

Medals of Honor, 6, 41, 146

N

Narragansett Bay, 238

Naval Act of 1916, 20

Neafie and Levy Ship, 7

Neutrality Patrols, 72, 80, 159, 205

Noma Reef, 167

O

Old World Europeans, 9

Operation Teardrop, 235, 237

P

Philippines Islands, 8, 42, 215, 241, 245-46, 252

Port Lyautey, 119

President Herbert Hoover, 57

President Theodore Roosevelt, 11

President Woodrow Wilson, 17, 30

Q

Quartermaster Frank Monroe Upton, 41

R

Rene Maavernge, 119

Rip Van Winkle, 179

Roanoke River, 1

Robert Whitehead, 2

Russo-Japanese War, 11, 19, 48

S

Saint-Nazaire, 11, 113

Seventh Fleet, 216, 218-19, 226

Solomon Islands, 136, 143, 151, 165, 190

Sub-Lieutenant David Balme, 82

Sulu Sea, 242

T

Task Force 64, 140

Task Force TG77.4.3, 219

Tenanbo River, 167

The Battle of Empress Augusta Bay, 189

The Battle of Santa Cruz Islands, 144

The Battle of the Bulge, 229

The Battle of Vella Lavella, 186-87, 250

The Caine Mutiny, 228

The First Battle of Savo Island, 139-40

The Fourth Battle of Savo Island, 148, 176

The Fritz X, 194

The Great Depression, 72

The New Georgia Sound, 143

The Second Battle of Savo Island, 140

The Second Happy Time, 115, 152

The Spanish-American War, 4, 8, 130

Town class, 79, 88, 111

Tripartite Pact of 1940, 80

Tsushima Strait, 10

Two-Ocean Navy Act of July
    1940, 79, 84

U

U.S. Admiral William Sowden
    Sims, 28

U.S. Naval Academy, 12, 36, 221

Union Jack, 193

V

Vice Admiral Sir Lewis Bayly, 31

W

Warren G. Harding, 46

William B. Cushing, 1

Winston Churchill, 79, 162

Winston Churchill, 79, 162

Woody Guthrie, 91

Worth Bagley, 5

Y

Yangtze River, 71

Yugumo, 85, 166, 183, 187, 191,
    250

Ships/Destroyers Index

A

Acasta-class destroyer, 19

Admiralty M, 15

Admiralty R class, 21

Akatsuki class, 64, 124

Allen M. Sumner class, 181, 182, 202, 203, 252, 254, 256, 264

Almirante Condell, 4

Almirante Lynch, 4

American Navy's Task Force 18, 184

Anton Schmitt (Z-22), 75

Arashio, 131, 172

Asahio, 123, 172, 173, 176, 217

Asashio class, 62, 69, 70, 124, 131

Attack Transports (APDs), 84, 102

Audacity, 156, 157

B

B-25s, 49, 172

B class, 81

Bagley class, 95, 96

Benson class, 66, 88, 146, 166, 174, 183, 229

Bernd von Arnim (Z11), 77

Blanco Encalada, 4, 8

Bogue, 157, 158, 162, 237

Bristol class, 66

C

Caldwell class, 20, 21, 40, 46, 47, 68, 79, 105, 137

Cavite, 126, 127

Chikuma, 223

Contessa, 120

Convoy HG76, 157

Convoy HX 150, 87

Convoy JW 51B, 120

Convoy KR8, 209

Convoy ONS 5, 154

Convoy SC 118, 154

Convoy TM 1, 153

Convoy UGS 32, 234

Convoy UGS 38, 234

CSS *Albemarle*, 1

D

Destroyer Division 12, 184

Destroyer Squadron 11, 50

Destroyer Squadron 23, 188, 191, 243, 270

Destroyer Squadron 29, 126, 127, 286

Destroyer Squadron 54, 217

Drayton, 26, 37, 103, 128

E

Eagle 56, 110, 238, 273

Enoki class, 22

Enterprise, 99, 100, 101, 144, 247

Eureka, 67

Evans, 256, 257, 258, 274

F

F4F Wildcats, 249

F4U Corsairs, 249

F6F Hellcats, 249

Faulknor class, 29

Fletcher class, 34, 106, 142, 190, 224, 263

Friedrich Eckoldt (Z-16), 120, 121

Fubuki class, 62, 124, 126

Fubuki, 61, 62, 63, 124, 125, 126, 141, 172, 190

Furor, 6, 7

G

G42 torpedo boat, 29

G85 torpedo boat, 29

George Thiele (Z-2), 76, 77

German U-9, 17

Grenville class, 74

Gridleys USS Craven (DD-382), 184

H

H-class destroyer, 74

Hamakaze, 180

Harusame, 10

Hatsuharu class, 62, 183

Hayate, 101

Herman Kunne (Z19), 75

Hiei, 146

Hinoki, 244

HMCS Annapolis, 87

HMCS Athabaskan (G-07), 195

HMNZS Leander, 183

HMRS Canberra, 140

HMS Achates (H-12), 121

HMS Ark Royal (91), 156

HMS Audacity (D-10), 156, 157

HMS Beverly (H-64), 154

HMS Broadway (H-90), 82

HMS Broke, 29

HMS Bulldog (H-91), 81, 82, 274

HMS *Campbeltown*, 110, 111

HMS *Cockatrice*, 19

HMS *Courageous* (50), 156

HMS *Daring*, 3

HMS *Decoy*, 3

HMS *Flirt*, 29

HMS *Furious*, 77

HMS *Hardy* (H-87), 74, 75

HMS *Havock* (H-43), 75, 77

HMS *Hostile* (H-55), 75

HMS *Hotspur* (H-01), 75, 77

HMS *Hunter* (H-35), 75, 77

HMS *Janus* (F-53), 195

HMS *Lightning*, 2

HMS *Nubian*, 29

HMS *Obdurate* (G-39), 121

HMS *Obedient* (G-48), 121

HMS *Onslow* (G-17), 121

HMS *Orbi* (G-66), 121

HMS *Orwell* (G-98), 121

HMS *Petard*, xi, 117, 209, 266, 269

HMS *Prince of Wales* (53), 86

HMS *Rattlesnake*, 3

HMS *Stanley* (I-73), 157

HMS *Swift*, 29

HMS *Vesuvius*, 2

HMS *Vimy* (D-33), 154

HMS *Warspite* (03), 77

HNLMS *Piet Hen*, 131

HNLMS *Tromp*, 131

I

I-15, 144

I-168, 136

I-70, 101

J

Jintsu, 183

K

Kaba, 16, 21, 22

Kamikaze Special Attack Corps 3rd Ryuko Squadron, 260

Kisaragi, 102

Kiyonami, 183

L

Landing Ship Medium-Rocket (LSM-R), 249

Landing Ship Tanks (LSTs), 170, 176, 212, 242

Lexington carrier, 99, 100, 134, 136

Lutzow, 120

M

Mahan class, 94, 97, 103,

Makinami, 168

Marine F4U Wildcat, 102

Mark 14, 129, 141, 142

Michishio, 131, 176, 217

Minegumo, 173

Minelayers, 69, 105, 124, 176

Minesweepers (DMS), 68, 100, 101, 105, 124, 202, 242

Mitsubishi GM-4, 251

Momi class, 139

Momi, 139, 244

Momo class, 21, 22

Murasame, 173

Mutsuki class, 54, 102, 124, 139, 177, 183, 190

Mutsuki class, 54, 102, 139, 177, 183, 190

N

Nakajima B5Ns, 257

NC-1, 48

NC-3, 48

NC-4, 48, 49

Niizuki, 177, 178, 180, 181

O

O'Brien class, 25, 31, 35, 190, 226, 248

Oerlikon cannons, 85, 112, 143, 181, 210, 221, 244

Ohkas, 251

ONS *5*, 154, 155

Oshio, 131

Osmond Ingram, 33, 158, 162

P

P-40, 120

Pacific Fleet, 13, 93, 94, 99, 106, 124, 126, 271

Patriot's Point Museum, 264

Paulding class, 14, 25, 35, 42

PBY Catalinas, 68

Porters, 63, 64, 143

R

Richard Beitzen (Z-4), 120

RMS *Lusitania*, 19, 27, 30

RMS *Titanic*, 30

RO-106, 212

RO-116, 213

S

Sampson class, 14, 15, 31, 41, 95, 101

Seaplane tenders (AVDs), 68, 100, 101, 105, 124, 126

Sendai, 189

Shiratsuyu class, 62, 124, 173, 180, 184

Shirayuki, 172

SM *U-53*, 22, 23, 38

Smith class, 14, 25, 42

SS *Aquitania*, 41

SS *Khedive Ismail*, 209

SS *Tuscania*, 40

T

Task Force 34, 118

The Sullivans (DD-537), 263

Theodor Riedel (Z-6), 120

Tirpitz, 111, 112

Toku Daihatsu, 139

Tribal class, 29, 69, 195

Tucker class, 25, 31, 34, 36, 108

Tulagi, 137, 138, 184, 185

Type 23, 111, 112

Type 34, 74

Type 36, 74

Type IXC/40, 154, 235

Type VIIC, 153, 159, 233

Typhoon Cobra, 227

U

U-110, 82, 83, 200

U-1235, 235

U-156, 117

U-172, 162, 163

U-187, 154

U-248, 233

U-256, 159

U-30, 83

U-371, 234

U-39, 156

U-405, 159, 161

U-505, 201, 268, 269, 274

U-518, 236

U-549, 200

U-559, 117, 209

U-613, 158

U-652, 86, 87

U-801, 202

U-85, 114, 115, 116

U-853, 238

U-866, 234

U-870, 204

U-880, 235, 237

U.S. Navy's Destroyer Division 8, 30, 36

Unconverted destroyers (DD), 124

USS *Aaron Ward* (DD-483), 175, 176, 252, 254, 255

USS *Ahrens* (DE-575), 200

USS *Albert Grant* (DD-649), 218

USS *Alden* (DD-211), 133, 196, 286

USS *Allen* (DD-66), 95, 101, 182

USS *Alywin*, 25

USS *Amick* (DE-168), 238

USS *Anderson* (DD-411), 207, 208

USS *Antares* (AG-10), 94

USS *Anthony* (DD-515), 259, 288

USS *Arizona*, 99

USS *Atherton* (DE169), 238

USS *Atlanta* (CL-51), 146

USS *Bagley* (DD-386), 140

USS *Bailey* (DD-492), 174

USS *Barr* (DE-576), 200

USS *Barry* (DD-248), 33, 161

USS *Barton* (DD-599), 146

USS *Belknap* (DD-251), 158

USS *Benham* (DD-397), 65, 146, 155, 184

USS *Bennion* (DD-662), 217

USS *Bernadou* (DD-153), 118

USS *Birmingham*, 216

USS *Blakeley* (DD-150), 117

USS *Block Island* (CVE-21), 198, 200, 202

USS *Blue* (DD-387), 139

USS *Bogue* (CVE-9), 157, 158, 162, 237

USS *Borie* (DD-215), 158, 159, 160, 161, 286

USS *Braine* (DD-630), 244

USS *Branch* (DD-197), 154

USS *Breese* (DD-122/DM-18), 96, 176, 285

USS *Buchanan* (DD-484), 110, 111, 141

USS *Buck* (DD-420), 66

USS *Buckley* (DE-51), 197, 198, 199, 200, 201, 236, 287

USS *Burns* (DD-588), 208, 287

USS *Bush* (DD-529), 249

USS *Callaghan* (DD-792), 259, 260

USS *Card* (CVE-11), 157, 158, 159, 161

USS *Carter* (DE-112), 236

USS *Cassin*, 14, 25, 33, 34, 35, 97, 260, 263

USS *Charles Ausburne* (DD-570), 188, 244

USS *Chatelain* (DE-149), 200, 201

USS *Chauncey*, 33, 34, 52, 53

USS *Chevalier* (DD-451), 179, 186, 250

USS *Chew* (DD-106), 94

USS *Claxton* (DD-571), 188

USS *Clemson*, xi, 45, 47, 158,

USS *Cole* (DD-155), 118

USS *Colhoun* (DD-801), 249

USS *Colhoun* (DD-85/APD-2), 138, 250

USS *Condor* (AMc-14), 94

USS *Converse* (DD-509), 188, 246

USS *Conyngham* (DD-58), 31

USS *Corry* (DD-463), 201, 202

USS *Cummings* (DD-365), 94

USS *Cushing*, 3, 4, 7, 146

USS *Dale* (DD-353), 96

USS *Dale* (DD-4), 33

USS *Dallas* (DD-199), 87, 119, 120, 286

USS *Dashiell* (DD-659), 190

USS *Decatur*, 12, 13, 33

USS *DeHaven* (DD-469), 169, 170

USS *Delphy* (DD-261), 51, 52, 53

USS *Dennis* (DE-406), 220

USS *Donnel* (De-56), 197

USS *Downes* (DD-375), 97

USS *Drayton* (DD-23), 26, 37

USS *Drayton* (DD-366), 103

USS *Du Pont* (DD-152), 157, 158, 162

USS *Duncan* (DD-485), 141

USS *Dunlap* (DD-384), 64, 184

USS *Dyson* (DD-572), 188

USS *Edsall* (DD-219), 128, 132, 270

USS *England* (DE-635), 210, 212, 214

USS *Enterprise* (CV-6), 144

USS *Enterprise*, 99, 100, 101, 103, 247

USS *Ericsson*, 4, 6, 87

USS *Farragut* (DD-348), 58, 59, 63, 95, 96, 227

USS *Fiske* (DE-143), 204

USS *Fitch* (DD-462), 202

USS *Fletcher* (DD-445), 106, 147, 245, 246

USS *Fogg* (DE-57), 204

USS *Foote*, 188, 189

USS *Franklin* (CV-13), 247, 288

USS *Frederick C. Davis* (DE-136), 195, 236

USS *Frost* (DE-144), 235

USS *Gambier Bay* (CVE-73), 223

USS *Gamble* (DD-123/DM-15), 176

USS *George E. Badger* (DD-196), 157, 158, 162

USS *Gleaves* (DD-423), 166

USS *Glennon* (DD-620), 203

USS *Gloucester*, 6

USS *Goff* (DD-247), 161

USS *Greene* (DD-266), 158

USS *Greer* (DD-145), 86

USS *Gregory* (DD-82/APD-3), 137-38

USS *Gridley* (DD-380), 64

USS *Guadalcanal* (CVE-60), 200 U-110, 82-83, 200

USS *Gwin* (DD-433), 183

USS *Hamman* (DD-412), 136

USS *Hayter* (DE-212), 233

USS *Heermann* (DD-532), 220

USS *Helena* (CL-50), 100, 180

USS *Helm* (DD-388), 95, 242

USS *Henley* (DD-391), 96

USS *Herbert C. Jones* (DE-137), 195

USS *Heywood L. Edwards* (DD-663), 214

USS *Hickox* (DD-673), 247

USS *Hoel* (DD-533), 220

USS *Honolulu* (CL-48), 183

USS *Hornet*, 49, 144

USS *Hovey* (DD-208/DMS-11), 243

USS *Howard D. Crow* (DE-252), 234

USS *Hubbard* (DE-211), 233

USS *Hugh Hadley* (DD-774), 256

USS *Hull* (DD-350), 227

USS *Hunt* (DD-194), 82

USS *Hutchins* (DD-476), 245

USS *Hyades* (AF-28), 205

USS *Iowa* (BB-61), 162, 261

USS *Irwin* (DD-794), 216

USS *Jacob Jones* (DD-130), 108

USS *Jacob Jones* (DD-61), ix, 26, 31, 36, 140

USS *Jenks* (DE-665), 201

USS *John D. Edwards* (DD-216), 133, 196

USS *John D. Ford* (DD-228), 129, 133

USS *John E. Butler* (DE-439), 220

USS *Johnston* (DD-557), 220-21

USS *Jouett* (DD-396), 194

USS *Kalinin Bay* (CVE-68), 224

USS *Kidd* (DD-661), 263

USS *Killen* (DD-593), 217

USS *Kimberly* (DD-521), 248

USS *La Vallette*, 186

USS *Laffey* (DD-459), 146, 254

USS *Laffey* (DD-724), 182, 252, 264, 281

USS *Langley* (AV-3), 132

USS *Lea* (DD-118), 157

USS *Leary* (DD-158), 67, 163

USS *Leopold* (DE-319), 196

USS *Lexington* (CV-2), 99, 134

USS *Little* (DD-79/APD-4), 138, 255

USS *Little* (DD-803), 254

USS *Long* (DD-209/DMS-12), 243

USS *Lowe* (DE-325), 234

USS *Mahan* (DD-364), 63-63, 166, 184, 244

USS *Manley* (DD-74/APD-1), 137

USS *Mannert L. Abele* (DD-733), 250

USS *Maury* (DD-401), 184

USS *Lang* (DD-399), 184

USS *Mayrant* (DD-402), 155

USS *McCalla* (DD-253), 157

USS *McDougal* (DD-358), 86

USS *McKean* (DD-90/APD-5), 138

USS *Melvin* (DD-680), 217

USS *McDermut* (DD-677), 217

USS *Menges* (DE-320), 234

USS *Meredith* (DD-726), 202, 203, 268

USS *Missouri* (BB-63), 261

USS *Moberly* (PF-63), 238

USS *Monaghan* (DD-354), 96, 227

USS *Monitor*, 4

USS *Monssen* (DD-436), 146

USS *Montgomery* (DD-121/ DM-17), 167

USS *Morrison* (DD-560), 216, 255

USS *Mosley* (DE-321), 234

USS *Murphy* (DD-603), 229, 231

USS *Murray* (DD-576), 248, 261, 281

USS *Nautilus*, 135

USS *Neal Scott* (DE-769), 236

USS *Nelson* (DD-623), 203

USS *New York* (BB-34), 67

USS *Newcomb* (DD-586), 217

USS *Niblack* (DD-424), 80, 90

USS *Nicholas* (DD-311), 54

USS *Nicholas* (DD-449), 142, 165, 169-70

USS *North Carolina* (BB-55), 190

USS *O'Bannon* (DD-450), xi, 146, 165, 174, 186, 261

USS *O'Brien* (DD-415), 190

USS *Oklahoma*, 99, 281

USS *Ommaney Bay* (CVE-79), 242

USS *Osmond Ingram* (DD-255), 158

USS *Otter* (DE-210), 233

USS *Panay*, 71

USS *Parrott* (DD-218), 128-29

USS *Patterson* (DD-392), 140

USS *Paul Jones* (DD-230), 128-29, 133

USS *Peary* (DD-226), 127

USS *Pennsylvania* (BB-38), 97, 245

USS *Percival* (DD-298), 52

USS *Perry* (D-11), 11

USS *Phillip* (DD-498), 244

USS *Pillsbury* (DD-227), 127

USS *Pope* (DD-225), 128-29

USS *Porter* (DD-356), 144

USS *Preble* (DD-345/DM-20), 167, 176

USS *President Lincoln*, 41-42

USS *Prichett* (DD-561), 260

USS *Pride* (DE-323), 234

USS *Princeton* (CVL 23), 216, 255

USS *Pruitt* (DD-347), 65

USS *Quincy* (CA-71), 230

USS *Radford* (DD-446), 190

USS *Radford* (DD-486), 167

USS *Ralph Talbot* (DD-390), 177, 186

USS *Ranger* (CV-4), 156

USS *Raymond* (DE-341), 220

USS *Reuben James* (DD-245), 89, 236

USS *Rich* (DE-695), 203

USS *Ringgold* (DD-500), 190

USS *Robinson* (DD-562), 214-15, 244, 281

USS *Robley D. Evans* (DD-552)

USS *Roper* (DD-147), 113-14

USS *Roper* (DD-467), 281

USS *Rowan* (DD-405), 155

USS *Russell* (DD-414), 244

USS *Samuel B. Roberts* (DE-413), 220

USS *San Francisco* (CA-38), 146

USS *Saratoga* (CV-3), 99

USS *Schley* (DD-103/APD-14), 139

USS *Selfridge* (DD-357), 186

USS *Shaw* (DD-373), 97, 244

USS *Shaw* (DD-68). 14, 41,

USS *Sims* (DD-409), 65, 134

USS *Slater* (DE-766), 264

USS *Smith* (DD-17), 42

USS *Smith* (DD-378), 144

USS *Somers* (DD-301), 52

USS *Somers* (DD-381), 64, 193, 204

USS *South Dakota* (BB-57), 100, 144

USS *Southard* (DD-207/DMS-10), 144

USS *Spence* (DD-512), 188, 227

USS *St. Lo* (CVE-63), 224

USS *St. Louis* (CL-49), 183

USS *Stack* (DD-406), 184

USS *Stanly* (DD-478), 188, 251

USS *Stanton* (DE-247), 235

USS *Sterett* (DD-407), 146, 184

USS *Stewart* (DE-238), 264

USS *Stringham* (DD-83/APD-6), 138

USS *Strong* (DD-467), 177, 281

USS *Strong*, 177, 178, 179, 180, 186, 281

USS *Tabberer* (DE-418), 227

USS *Taylor* (DD-468), 186, 261

USS *Thatcher* (DD-514), 188

USS *Tracy* (DD-214/DM-19), 167

USS *Truxtun* (DD-229), 87, 106

USS *Turner* (DD-648), 194

USS *Varian* (DE-798), 233

USS *Wadsworth*, 31, 34

USS *Wainwright*, 31

USS *Walke* (DD-723), 242

USS *Waller* (DD-466), 173

USS *Ward* (DD-139/APD-6), 226, 248

USS *Ward* (DD-483), 252

USS *Ward*, 47, 93-95

USS *Warrington* (DD-30), 42

USS *Warrington* (DD-383), 205

USS *Wasp* (CV-7), 141, 190

USS *Whipple* (DD-217), 132, 196

USS *William D. Porter* (DD-579), 162

USS *Yorktown* (CV-5), 136

USS *Young* (DD-312), 53

UUS *Winslow*, 5-7, 24, 36

V

V-1 buzz bombs, 194, 235

V-2 rockets, x, 235

V class, 154

Vizcaya, 6

W

Wickes APD, 68, 102, 118, 137, 139, 158, 165, 226, 250, 255

Wickes class, 45-48, 54, 58, 68-69, 86, 94-96, 100, 105, 158, 226, 250, 255

Wilhelm Heidkamp (Z-21), 75

Y

Yugumo class,

Yukikaze, xi

Z

Z-29, 120

Z-30, 120

Z-31, 120